Civil Servants and Military Officers, 2000–2010

2005	2006	2007	2008	2009	2010	2011	2012	2013

nvasion of Iraq | **Apr–May 2006—Deployment to Helmand**

Rt Hon Dr Gordon Brown MP

Rt Hon David Cameron MP

Rt Hon Dr John Reid | Rt Hon Des Brown May 2006–Oct 2008 | Rt Hon John Hutton | Rt Hon Ains

D1437287

Sir Bill Jeffrey   Nov 2005–Oct 2010 | Ms Ursula Brennan

Michael Walker
–28 Apr 2006 | Air Chief Marshal Sir Jock Stirrup 28 Apr 2006–29 Oct 2010 | General Sir David Richards 29 Oct 2010–Jul 2013

n West
 2006 | Admiral Sir Jonathon Band Feb 2006–July 2009 | Admiral Sir Mark Standhope Jul 2009–April 2013

Sir Mike Jackson
003–Aug 2006 | General Sir Richard Dannatt Aug 2006–29 Aug 2009 | General Sir David Richards | General Sir Peter Wall 15 Sept 2010–

hal Sir Jock Stirrup
03–13 Apr 2006 | Air Chief Marshal Sir Glenn Torpy 13 Apr 2006–31 July 2009 | Air Chief Marshal Sir Stephen Dalton 31 July 2009–Jul 2013

Air Marshal Glenn Torpy | Lt General Sir Nicholas Houghton | Air Marshal Sir Stuart Peach

l Rob Fry | Vice Admiral Charles Style | Lt General Peter Wall | Lt General Simon Mayall | Lt General Richard Barrons

HIGH COMMAND

High Command

*British Military Leadership in the Iraq
and Afghanistan Wars*

CHRISTOPHER L. ELLIOTT

HURST & COMPANY, LONDON

First published in the United Kingdom in 2015 by
C. Hurst & Co. (Publishers) Ltd.,
41 Great Russell Street, London, WC1B 3PL
© Christopher L. Elliott, 2015
All rights reserved.
Printed in India

355.309

A Cataloguing-in-Publication data record for this book
is available from the British Library.

ISBN: 9781849044608

This book is printed using paper from registered sustainable
and managed sources.

www.hurstpublishers.com

For Naomi,
and for those who did not return

Christopher L. Elliott, CB, MBE, retired from the British Army as a Major General in 2002 and is currently a visiting professor of Cranfield University. This book was written over two years whilst he was a research fellow at the universities of Oxford and Reading.

*　*　*

From 2001 Britain supported the United States in wars in Iraq and Afghanistan. 'Victory' in such conflicts is always hard to gauge and domestic political backing for them was never robust. For this, the governments of Tony Blair and Gordon Brown were held responsible, and paid the price, but the role played by the High Command in the Ministry of Defence also bears examination. Critics have noted that the armed services were riven by internal rivalry and their leadership was dysfunctional, but the truth is more complicated.

In his book Elliott explores the circumstances that led to these wars and how the Ministry of Defence coped with the challenges presented. He reveals how the Service Chiefs were set at odds by the system, almost as rivals in the making, with responsibility diffuse and authority ambiguous. The MoD concentrated on making things work, rather than questioning whether what they were being asked to do was practicable. Often the opinion of a junior tactical commander led the entire strategy of the MoD, not the other way around, as it should have been. While Britain's senior officers, defence ministers and civil servants were undeniably competent and well-intentioned, the conundrum remains why success on the battlefield proved so elusive.

CONTENTS

CONTENTS

CONTENTS

CONTENTS

FOREWORD

Christopher Elliott has written a perceptive and influential book which should be widely studied by those senior politicians, officials and servicemen who have that profound responsibility for committing a country to war. He describes how Britain was confronted by formidable enemies in both Iraq and Afghanistan and concludes that our own young officers and soldier were every bit as heroic and competent as we might have expected. However, what they were up against day after day was often misunderstood in London, including by some senior servicemen. *High Command* does not shrink, like so many military campaign books, from criticising those in Whitehall who failed to understand the nature of the war they were now fighting.

Of course no nation wants to spend more on a war than it has to, but once committed to conflict it is no good adopting the attitude that it could be done on the cheap. If we are not prepared to provide the resources to win, then it is the responsibility of those in the MoD to say so before the commitment is entered into. Once we do go to war, though, the MoD must play its part in ensuring the political will is sustained to see it through. To those on the ground in Iraq and Afghanistan, just too often it felt as though both those wars were being run by accountants. Elliott explains how Whitehall fell into the trap of doing just enough to satisfy the demands of the hour, but never enough to give a chance for strategic success, and he explores why the structure and personalities of the MoD helped to frustrate a better outcome.

This book will be controversial and if it leads to debate, as it should, it will do much for those who will be responsible for our defence in the future and for their understanding of the friction war creates.

Field Marshal the Lord Guthrie of Craigiebank, GCB LVO OBE DL,
Chief of the Defence Staff, 1997–2001

Map 1: Iraq

Map 2: Helmand

1

PROLOGUE

'The problem with comprehension is that … it often comes too late.'

Rasmenia Massoud, 'Human Detritus'

The British High Command made a number of judgements with poor outcomes in the decade from 2000 to 2010 when fighting in Iraq and Afghanistan. Not least, that there were never enough troops for the tasks that they set out to achieve and, as a result, the UK armed forces were deployed into two theatres of war with very slim chances of being successful in either. The outcome in some eyes has been humiliation, accusation of defeat in Basra, an unexpected high level of conflict in Helmand and significant loss of life for our servicemen and women as well as local civilians—so far, without the compensation of it all being worthwhile.

Evidence presented to the inquiry into the UK's involvement in Iraq—the 'Chilcot' Inquiry, after its chairman Sir John Chilcot—has already indicated as much.[1] But what the witnesses at the Chilcot Inquiry have not revealed is why good, principled, capable public servants took the actions that they did. Trivial reasons have instead appeared in the press: unhelpful or detached politicians; conniving civil servants; military officers driven by inter-service rivalry; and gung-ho field commanders too concerned with their own reputations. None of this was generally true and the reasons were much more complex, as this book will try to unravel.

Things did go wrong, so inevitably criticism occurs and some of it is pretty harsh. One senior officer of the time described the Ministry of Defence as being 'like a nuclear reactor running out of cooling water, with no experts in the control room'.[2] However, it should become clear that these were responsible public servants acting with integrity and high moral purpose. Making this point is not clearing the decks with faint praise so as to side-swipe later, for the author himself was complicit in similar events as part of the same system during the previous decade, although never at the level to carry the singular burden of deciding issues of life and death, as they had to. It raises the conundrum that, if the people at the top of the UK Ministry of Defence were as good as has been described, why didn't things go better? Why couldn't a guiding point to aim for be expressed more accurately? Why did they concentrate on the day-to-day, whilst overlooking the strategic hazards? Why didn't they reform the system so that it could cope better with the challenges that arose?

This can be taken a little further. From experience gained on both sides, it became clear that people in the armed services were head and shoulders above their industry equivalents in certain aspects of character, for the military ethos encourages dedication, selflessness, moral courage, collegiate behaviour and breadth of view. Yet, with honourable exceptions, many at the top of industry were motivated by self-interest, narcissism, a narrow focus on the financial bottom line, they were more ruthless when dealing with people and they had a poorer understanding of team work. Bear with me before dismissing this as the view of institution man, for an argument will emerge that the military High Command in Whitehall were ill-equipped to manage the challenges that soon enough presented themselves in the decade 2000–10. That being well-intentioned and public-spirited was just not enough. You will see how those individuals were battling against an entrenched MoD 'system', whose default settings were set to strangle enterprise, discourage initiative and work to the lowest common denominator of all the parties involved. Worse still, the system was perfectly capable of generating complexity out of simplicity and muddling-up motives, where responsibility was concealed and accountability buried. Inevitably, you ask how it was that the system was allowed to run the individuals, rather than the other way around if the individuals were, indeed, so capable. You may conclude that a bigger dose of those animal spirits found in industry—with that intense focus on the essentials and a ruthless determination to succeed—would have served the UK's senior military leaders better when mastering the entrenched structure of the Ministry of Defence and in the jungle that is statecraft and politics.

Inevitably many aspects of this book reflect much of my own experience and I start by recounting my first days working in the Ministry of Defence, which occurred in middle life. It illustrates the MoD's Byzantine processes, how extraordinarily unprepared some officers can be for working in it and the way that the MoD organisation propagates and defends itself.

It was certainly a daunting experience as I entered that imposing building in Whitehall for the first time, discarding my uniform in exchange for a suit. I reflected that I had had only scant previous contact with civil servants and none with politicians. Nervous on first arrival, surely it was just a case of applying common sense? As I settled into my hallowed office on the fifth floor of the MoD's 'Main Building'—with one wall completely covered in formal photographs of my predecessors dating back well over a century—my new secretary Sandra came tut-tutting in with a handful of files and put them into my in tray. I was her fifth Director of Military Operations and clearly wet behind the ears.

Sandra said, 'These are for you, and how do you take your tea?' With that, she tut-tutted out again.

I reached for the first file and cautiously opened it as though it might explode. Inside were a dozen or so sheets of impeccably typed text, tied neatly at the margins by a cotton string India tag. The first sheet was headed with the formal royal cipher used by the MoD and the words 'Chiefs of Staff Committee: Paper for Circulation'. The text itself was elegant and taut; three options were offered and a recommendation made for the obviously preferable course. I read it in detail, marvelled at the balance shown by such a young author and then signed it off as ready for submission to the Chiefs of Staff. I reached for a second file and went through the same process. Then, the third, fourth, fifth and sixth. After an absorbing two hours, I had got to the bottom of the pile. Feeling hugely satisfied, I leaned back in my chair. All the files had been very interesting and they were wonderfully put together. This could be fun.

Sandra entered quietly again and scooped them all up. A moment later the Head of 'Military Operations One', Colonel Peter Currie (later to be promoted to Major General), came in. He looked rather ashen-faced. He made a brief welcome and then said:

'Brigadier, you signed off those files!'

'Yes…?' I replied, looking a bit cagey but thinking that this question was either idiotic or impertinent. After all, what was I meant to do—correct the English?

'Brigadier, you signed off the files,' Peter repeated, '… without socialising them.'

'Well, Peter, they were brilliantly written and I agreed with all the recommendations.' I then became rather short. 'What did you expect me to do, disagree with them?'

Peter clearly thought that life was getting dangerous for him and he made a retreat, mumbling something that I failed to pick up.

The rest of the morning progressed uneventfully and I was feeling increasingly pleased with myself. I had time to look out of the window at my privileged view of the River Thames through the tree-lined Embankment. Perhaps I could crack this after all. Pride before the fall.

Just before lunch Bill Reeves, the ever-genial Assistant Under Secretary for Commitments and the senior civil servant responsible for oversight of military operations, breezed in. Bill would become a very good friend and excellent mentor as time went by and he was of the very best that the Civil Service could produce, leaving later to become company secretary of the Price Waterhouse Coopers accountancy practice. Bill opened by saying that he had always got on extremely well with all the Directors of Military Operations and it was a considerable pleasure to meet the latest one. We chatted pleasantly for fifteen minutes, during which time he was able to assess that I was a complete idiot as far as the Ministry of Defence was concerned. As he was leaving, he turned and said:

'Christopher … oh, by the way … you signed off all those files this morning?'

I began to feel that I had made some frightful mistake, but still couldn't work out quite why. I went on the offensive:

'Bill, did I make the wrong decisions? I am new here, and you must tell me.'

'Oh no, you made absolutely the right decisions.'

PROLOGUE

'Bill, then I have lost the plot completely. For goodness sake tell me what I have done wrong.'

'Well, Christopher, we usually discuss things, you and I, before you make any decision. And it is useful to discuss it with the Head of Secretariat. And with Finance. And with the other two services. And occasionally the Foreign Office likes to know. No surprises, you see.'

'But Bill, we both agree that the right decisions have been made. I can't see that anyone else will come to a different decision either? And I know that our desk officers have already walked the files around the other branches, because they have included some of their comments.'

I was becoming a bit short. What on earth was this world I had entered?

He sighed. 'Ah well, but that was at their level. It is always useful to socialise these things.' At that, he left.

I sat and stared at the desk. To call the files back to absolutely no purpose as far as I could see would result in humiliation. Everyone agreed that they were the right decisions. All I had done was to follow the recommendations made in each case. Let them go.

Over the next couple of weeks the other MoD staff branches prepared their comments on the files as they wound their way up through the labyrinthine decision layers of the MoD, before finally being discussed by the Chiefs of Staff in committee. One of the decisions was rejected outright and another one fatally wounded on a technicality brought up by one of the other services. Clearly, this 'socialising' had some value. I was incandescent. And damaged.

Worse was to happen. Two days later, I came into the MoD at about 7 a.m. to find my office wound up with blue and white MoD police tape, like a Christmas present. There were two MoD policemen on duty in the corridor. People hurrying past to their offices could not conceal their disapproval.

'I'm sorry sir, you cannot go in there. There has been a security breach.'

'But I work in there …!'

Somehow, an unthreatening file about the size of guardsmen's boots or the future scale of battlefield rations had been left out overnight on my window-sill. Somehow, somebody had known to look out for it. I could have left it there, but I had no recollection of doing so and hadn't seen the offending file before. However irrelevant to the security of the nation, it was of course still graded 'Restricted' in the necessarily security-conscious MoD head office.

Later that morning possession of my office was returned to me after I had completed the paper-trail of forms explaining what had happened.

I entered the MoD Operations Room deep underground some twenty minutes later for the morning operations briefing—red-faced, embarrassed and trying to be cool. My misfortunes had spread rapidly and widely in the rumour service of the building and the Chairman paused as I sat down, looked in my direction and raised an eyebrow in a kindly way:

'Having a difficult week, DMO …?'

You may be surprised that such an innocent could be released into the heart of a complex, national politico-military headquarters, but it was by no means a unique experience. The education of British Army officers had looked inwards to producing competent field commanders, worldly enough to be a safe pair of hands on a foreign detachment, and staff officers who were masters of the complicated ballet of moving and launching armies. Experience of Whitehall, the programming of defence projects, finance and budgets, political issues and public policy were largely learned on the job.

And, as always, there were good reasons for this endless paper-chase of file-sharing—'socialisation'—in such a large and complex bureaucracy; I was to learn later of that awful feeling of knowing something was going on without being aware of what it was.

Most importantly, it was a scarring introduction. After I had put myself back together, I decided to learn the 'system' and to master it. Better to work within it than to be outside it. Better to get things done than prove a point. However, by adopting the 'system' of course I became part of it and its ways, and I deployed its procedures and propagated its vices. As did everyone else. It is from that Ministry of Defence 'system' that the second thread of an argument is found, about how good people and capable public servants could find themselves making perverse decisions—despite their talents. A third thread will be to explore whether the politicians, military officers and the civil servants in the Ministry of Defence had sufficient training, education or, even, aptitude to deal with the challenge of successfully conducting a war. And finally, I aim to discover whether the Ministry of Defence had the capacity to reform itself and its procedures in the face of new circumstances.

I hope that I have done this with sufficient humility to make fair judgements on men and women who were facing challenges of a special sort. I am acutely aware that neither I, nor probably the reader, have borne the exquisite human pressures that such high command demands. Neither has this been an easy book to write, for someone shaped and nurtured over long years within the military tradition, leaving as it does strong imprints of loyalty and, perhaps, an instinct to conform. I explain at length later how people's experiences in life affect their judgements and I readily accept that, although I have struggled mightily to remain objective, inevitably I must fail on that count to some extent. After 35 years Army service I will have inevitably what is known in the UK Armed Services as a 'khaki' brain. All I can ask is that, aware of my grounding, you filter the arguments in this book and make conclusions as you see fit.

I am hugely indebted to all the people who helped me with my research. I had expected to be pushed back and told to stop interfering in an area where emotions are still pretty raw, but everyone that I approached was objective, helpful and encouraging. Although much of this book is about institutional relationships, inevitably when examining the years 2000–10 it was necessary to look at the personalities involved; I have taken the precaution of discussing my conclusions with many of them individually, as a result of which many new insights arose and necessary corrections were made. Of course, this is a highly contentious subject and responsibility for the conclusions drawn remains with me; and, indeed, there will be many other interpretations.

I must especially thank the people who allowed me to interview them: Lord Browne of Ladyton, Admiral Lord Boyce, General Lord Walker, Marshal of the Royal Air Force Lord Stirrup, General Lord Richards, Admiral Lord West, General Lord Dannatt, Admiral Sir Jonathon Band, General Sir Roger Wheeler, Air Marshal Sir Glenn Torpy, Air Marshal Sir Brian Burridge, Vice Admiral Sir Jeremy Blackham, Lieutenant General Sir John Kiszley, Sir David Omand, Sir Sherrard Cowper-Coles, Lieutenant General Gerry Berragan, Lieutenant General Andrew Graham, Major General James Cowan, Major General Andrew Sharpe, Major General Patrick Marriott, Major General Mungo Melvin, Brigadier Ben Barry, Colonel Rob Rider, Professor Ian Wallace, Professor Matt Uttley, Professor Michael Clark, Desmond Bowen and Mark Philips. A special few allowed themselves to be both interviewed and then spent many, many hours discussing aspects and reviewing texts. Here I am extraordinarily grateful to Field Marshal Lord Guthrie, General Sir Mike

Jackson, Lieutenant General Sir Rob Fry and Sir Ian Andrews for their time freely given and their advice. I was especially struck by the complete readiness of this group to assess the actions that they were a part of in an objective way. Various drafts were reviewed by General Sir Rupert Smith, Major General Bill Robins, Commodore Toby Williamson, Colonel Christopher Davies, Colonel Adrian Brett, Major Richard Clifford, Professor Anthony King, Nicholas and Elizabeth Heaven, Beverley Helps, Tom Bower, Hilde Rapp, Edward Bourne, Bruce Mauleverer QC, Hamish Thompson, Matt Kavanagh, Allan Collinson, Sarah Gleadhill, Brigadier David Ross; as a result, many new ideas were included and much rubbish was removed. The syntax has much improved under the eagle eye of my wife, Maggie. Lieutenant Colonel Paddy Clarke let me look through the records held at the Defence Concepts and Doctrine Centre (they are well worth looking at) and Air Vice Marshal Ray Lock and Rear Admiral James Morse, Commandants of the Joint Services Command and Staff College of the UK Defence Academy at Shrivenham, and their staffs gave me free access to all the student lectures and the superb library at the college. These were special gifts. Christopher Lightfoot at the Dulverton Trust very kindly lent me their boardroom for some of the interviews. My former PA, Louise Roderick, has been outstanding in providing the administrative back-up that I had all too easily taken for granted before I retired; Louise knows that I could not have coped without her support. I must thank my publisher Michael Dwyer and all at Hurst, who had the courage to take me on in the first place.

After a life largely outside academic circles, I needed considerable guidance and this was readily and generously given by my supervisor at Oxford University, Professor Sir Hew Strachan, the Chichele Professor of the History of War at All Souls College. I sometimes thought that he could have written the whole piece himself in a day, but he gently escorted me through the mine-fields and across the rapids in the most patient way. This is his subject and his own footprints are all over this book in consequence. I worked at Oxford within the Changing Character of Warfare Programme in the Faculty of History and I am grateful for the considerable help given by the Directors, Dr Rob Johnson and Dr Jan Lemnitzer, and the programme coordinator Ruth Murray as I unravelled what the University had to offer. Pembroke College kindly gave me a congenial daytime roost for two years. Kit Power introduced me to the works of Professor Robert Massie, from whom many useful ideas arose. I was also generously taken in by Professor Alan Cromatie at the University of Reading and discussed strategy for long hours with Professor Colin Gray and Professor Beatrice Heuser. It is difficult to express how grateful I am to all these individuals.

Finally I should thank retired United States General Jack Keane, an old comrade from army years and a great supporter of the British, who bluntly and honestly told a very senior audience at Sandhurst on 8 May 2011 just how bad the British Army's actions in Iraq and Afghanistan had looked from the outside. By doing so, he planted a seed.

PART 1

WHAT HAPPENED

2

A CASE TO ANSWER?

'… one of the follies of our current age has been an unmatched ambition to change the world without bothering to understand it first.'

General Sir Nicholas Houghton, Annual CDS Lecture 2013

Sarajevo looked magnificent in the early afternoon sunshine from the old Turkish fort high up at the eastern end of the city, at the point where the main road up the Miljacke valley disappeared into the Serb enclave. A jewel of a city, a bustling human arena enclosed by a ring of green, wild, forested mountains rising up all around to 1,500 metres.

Of course that was an illusion. It was October 1993. The Hercules dived down at an extremely steep angle into the airport approach to avoid stray fire; known as a 'Khe San' descent following the manner used to resupply a cut-off garrison in the Vietnam War. After landing, we offloaded ourselves into the wrecked airport terminal building, passed through the very vigilant French legionnaires manning the checkpoint and on out past the smashed-up buildings into the suburbs; then, at very high speed, down the broad central boulevard of the city. A few artillery shells thumped into the multi-storey flats high above us as we passed, the buildings seeming strangely to swallow up the outrage with little more than a puff. Later, we were told that there had been nineteen dead and wounded amongst the civilian occupants; this was all part of an obscene demonstration put on for the benefit of a VIP convoy.

We soon arrived at the UN forward headquarters, later to be commanded by British generals, located in an old government residency. Here we were in the ludicrous position of being observers to the occasional shells whizzing directly overhead, but neither in danger ourselves nor able to intervene. Yet the UN staff and soldiers were wearing uniforms and carrying guns, and the UN ran military operations rooms deploying detachments of UN soldiers— all as though there was some martial intent.

Looking down from the crumbling castle walls of the Turkish fort, I could hear the occasional rattle of machine-gun fire or crump of a mortar echoing across the bowl of Sarajevo city. Each detonation meant that some finger had deliberately just pressed a button, sending high explosive racing through the sky to land amongst the homes, gardens and markets of unarmed civilians. I remember saying to myself, as the mind raced to take it all in: 'We're playing games at this. We have given ourselves medals for being present in a conflict, without being part of it. Somebody with murderous motives and strong convictions will call this bluff. It will end in tears; somewhere, sometime, unthinkably, we are going to suffer a defeat.' But I confess that the moment soon passed and we busied ourselves with getting on with the matters of the moment and making the chosen arrangements work.

It was that strange juxtaposition of dressing the part and carrying the outward signs of military force, with no intention of actually using it, which grated the most. Nemesis came soon enough two years later, when the Serbs over-ran the Muslim enclave of Srebrenica (a UN 'safe area'), killing up to 7,000 Muslim men and taking the local UN battalion hostage.

Our hubris had developed over the previous decade as we had tried to work out a role for the UK, following the collapse of the Soviet Union. We were not alone and other nations were as guilty, but Foreign Minister Douglas Hurd formalised ideas for the UK by championing the leverage that a smaller armed force might make for greater military tasks: that is to say, 'punching above our weight'. Not a real force, but a token one purportedly carrying the menace of greater retribution. It was inevitable that this fatal over-confidence would be tested at some stage and found wanting.

We had been conditioned, of course, by our experience. The Falklands War in 1982 had been conducted professionally by those at the sharp end, but quite enormous strategic and operational risks had been taken overall in

London. The UK had got away with that, but it lent weight to the lie that all we had to do for success was to be bold enough. Risk became underwritten by hope, echoing Oscar Wilde's comment that 'good resolutions are simply cheques that men draw on a bank where they have no account'.

In parallel, the British Army was going through a period of significant intellectual change. For good reasons—not least that the Germans were loath to cede one metre of their domestic territory—we had become too static in our Cold War plans for the defence of the Central Front against the Soviet Union. This mindset was broken by Lieutenant General Sir Nigel Bagnall, commander of the 1st British Corps in 1980, who demonstrated that a better defence was to manoeuvre the defending army divisions, breaking up and harrying the massive Soviet assaulting formations into clarifying their intentions so that they could be annihilated with nuclear weapons, rather than taking their hammer blows head on.[1] From this, a cult of 'manoeuvre' emerged, both in deployments and in attitude of mind. Bagnall was right, but the Army's brain became infected with 'manoeuvre warfare' to the exclusion of all else and it soon became a god, its imprint emerging most often as parroted templates of the original idea. 'Manoeuvre' became evangelised as though it was the only approach: that manoeuvre would always be possible to accomplish, and that the alternative of attritional destruction of the enemy was for the stupid. Arguments were made that agility and adaptability could be substitutes for a lack of combat power. Gradually over time 'manoeuvrism' became the policy, not something that might be adopted if circumstances allowed. The facts of history were ignored in all of this—that an unavoidable attritional slog was much more the usual condition in war. Worse, Bagnall's ideas began to be applied completely inappropriately, with recklessness being substituted for sensible risk-taking.

So the government was leaning forwards to use military force, and the armed forces were fully prepared to provide it.

I had the chance to see, first hand, the whole Whitehall decision-making machinery at work. In many ways it was admirable. There was a culture of resolving disputes between the different UK departments of state before leaving for discussions in another capital, giving the UK a united front. This was in sharp contrast to Washington, which seemed to have, in the vernacular of the time, at least three warring factions: the State Department, the Pentagon

15

and the White House; or to Paris, where there was always a marked difference of opinion between the Elysée, the Quai d'Orsay[2] and the Defence Ministry.

But it also seemed that policy was often made on the hoof and the available intellectual engines poorly used. I experienced one example of this first hand and it will be useful to recount it here.

It happened in May 1995. The Bosnian imbroglio had droned on in an indecisive way and we seemed forever to be reacting to events, of which this was the latest and most serious, causing consternation in London: the Bosnian Serbs cut off a British battalion in Gorazde and effectively made it hostage.

A Cabinet meeting was convened to discuss what to do about it. After three hours with little progress, Michael Heseltine reminded Prime Minister John Major that both the world and his predecessor Lady Thatcher were waiting to see what sort of decisive action he would take to meet the Bosnian Serb challenge. The Prime Minster turned to the Chief of the Defence Staff (CDS) for advice. Field Marshal Sir Peter Inge, much admired for his directness and firm leadership, said that he would consult the British commander on the ground in Sarajevo, Lieutenant General Rupert Smith. General Smith agreed that some sort of reinforcement would be needed, but felt that an airmobile brigade would be the least appropriate option, for the Lynx attack helicopters of the period might have good anti-tank missiles, but were soft-skinned and vulnerable to sniper fire.

The Chief of the Defence Staff returned to the Cabinet Room and declared that General Smith had requested the UK Airmobile Brigade.[3] There was some logic in this misunderstanding, because such a brigade could deploy into theatre very quickly. Also, the discussion had taken place between the two officers over a secure telephone line and these devices were often difficult to use, with the speech compared to speaking with a bucket on your head and a clip on your nose. But it settled the matter in Cabinet quickly and the Prime Minister was able to announce that deployment of the UK's 24th Airmobile Brigade would happen in a number of days. On the CDS's return to the MoD, the pitfalls inherent in the decision began to emerge and the vulnerability of helicopters moving over enemy-infested terrain was hotly argued. The Commander-in-Chief of Land Forces at Wilton, General Sir John Wilsey, rang me up in considerable anger to say that it was a completely stupid decision.

Overnight, the same argument must have been put to the Prime Minster by the military grandees of his party. Next morning, John Major called a meeting at 10 Downing Street to run over the decision of the night before with his Secretary of State for Defence, Malcolm Rifkind. Field Marshal Inge was required in Brussels, so as Director of Military Operations I was assigned to support Mr Rifkind. We sat opposite each other around the Cabinet table and John Major opened the conversation calmly by saying that '… he was going to play devil's advocate, if he might, to flush out the background to the decision'. He turned to Malcolm Rifkind and asked: 'So … why *are* we sending an airmobile brigade?'

Without pausing, Rifkind replied: 'Well, this is a military matter … and the Director of Military Operations will now explain.'

I only found out later how the decision had been made, so I replied rather weakly: 'Prime Minster, because you decided to send them.'

An hour of fractious debate followed, with unhelpful thoughts emerging about how inappropriate an airmobile force alone was for this operation (not least because the MoD already had a worked-up and practised plan involving other specialist forces to reinforce and extract the British battalion, if it became endangered). The Prime Minster became increasingly short with everyone, as he realised that he had been boxed in with no obvious exit.

Eventually, Roderic Lyne, the Prime Minister's private secretary, lifted his eyes wearily from his notepad and said: 'Prime Minister, you're giving a press conference in an hour's time and you're going to have to decide to say something …'.

He might have added that the Conservative Party would be waiting for his decisive answer in the House of Commons an hour after that. We seemed to reach an impasse and no further progress was being made.

Looking at it from a narrow military perspective, rather cautiously I offered a suggestion: 'Prime Minister, what you might say is that Britain had deployed a force to Bosnia with humanitarian intentions. That the force has been taken hostage in an outrageous manner by one of the parties that we had gone there to help. That your government sent those troops there with good intention and that your government would do *whatever it takes* to get them back.'

The mood in the room seemed to lighten. The type of troops to be sent became a side issue; instead, the UK's overall military resolve could be signalled. The Prime Minister, the consummate politician, conducted a masterly press conference an hour later (which for one ghastly moment an hour before they were going to ask me to give, for reasons I could not help feeling were to do with achieving the maximum separation between military judgement and political responsibility).

At that press conference, Prime Minister John Major looked steadily ahead towards the ranks of journalists in the elegant No. 10 ballroom and said, in a confident, inclusive way: 'Ladies and Gentlemen … of course I shall answer your questions … but I should just like to start by saying something important. My government sent our soldiers out there to help these people … and my government will do whatever it takes to get them back.'

The rest of the press conference was a walk-over and the statement in the House of Commons later was equally well received. Over a drink afterwards in the flat upstairs in No. 10, to which I was kindly invited, there was much approval for how it had turned out.

But I wasn't so sure. Of course, I returned to the MoD with what, almost by accident, the serving soldiers that I represented had wanted most—an unequivocal and binding public statement from the government that they would do whatever it took to get them out of the mess, and confirmation that they wouldn't be traded in some long-running hostage crisis (as had happened to the US in Tehran when the Shah was overthrown). But what an odd way to do business. We had a very large bureaucracy full of talented and trained officers and the original decision had completely passed them by.

The first helicopters from the UK Airmobile Brigade began arriving in theatre within a week. Its commander, Brigadier Robin Brims, flew into Zagreb and presented himself to the UN military commander to sign on his force. General Bernard Janvier, a man with few words of English, looked up from behind his desk as Brigadier Brims entered and asked, 'Why are you here?'

Disavowed any aid from the UN but helped by a very good UK Ambassador in Zagreb, the Airmobile Brigade found itself a big enough patch of ground to bivouac on the flood plain at Ploce, at the mouth of the River Neretva in Croatia. It was as good a location as any to strike forward into the Sarajevo area and had an adequate port close by, but it was still a flood plain and it duly flooded. Some months later a pilot from the Airmobile Brigade told me, with a half-smile, that he had just been treated for Weil's disease, transmitted by rats, and he had had to wade to his helicopter through putrid knee-high water that morning. As ever for British servicemen, he took it as just part of the game.

The UK Airmobile Brigade certainly contributed to the overall force level—helicopters of that generation were invaluable for operating across close terrain, if kept out of contact with the enemy—but they did not play a significant part. Lieutenant General Rupert Smith, the UN commander in Sarajevo, recalls that he was hardly aware that they were there.[4] By gaining acceptance from General Mladic and by duping the local Bosnian Serb commander, the British battalion taken hostage at Gorazde escaped one night across the River Drina into more neutral Serbia.[5] The departure of the UN force from Gorazde left the fragmentary ABiH, the Bosnian Muslim army, alone to protect the Muslim population in Gorazde. Overall, the Bosnian Serbs only began to yield when the Croats successfully occupied the Krajina region and France and Britain sent artillery regiments to the old Sarajevo ski resort, high up on Mount Igman, to direct accurate counter-fire onto the Serb battery positions every time they fired artillery shells onto the city below. Further pressure came as Lieutenant General Smith used NATO aircraft to bring down progressively the infrastructure of Republika Srpska, the Serbian entity in Bosnia. The decision to deploy the UK Airmobile Brigade had been taken during a tense Cabinet meeting and was based on military instinct—not itself a bad thing—but without a serious consideration of its role, suitability and longer-term consequences. In the event, it was little used and side-lined.

It seemed that decisions were taken too much on a whim. The Foreign Office would see advantage in the UK deploying military force here or there and would start lobbying around Whitehall. Or there would be a discussion at a Heads of State meeting about an emerging problem, with an unrecorded commitment made to 'see if we could do something'. It might come onto No. 10's radar, if it hadn't started there, and the Prime Minster would fall into conversation with somebody from the MoD, usually the Chief of the Defence Staff, about whether 'something could be done'. As the genocide in Rwanda was unfolding in 1994, General Sir Rupert Smith recalls a conversation he had with the UK's Foreign and Commonwealth Office (FCO) about whether to deploy a UK military force and what it might do when it got there:

FCO: What can we do in the face of events in Rwanda?

MoD: What do you want us to do?

FCO: We ought to act. Something must be done. We can't have people being massacred. As a permanent member of the UN Security Council, we cannot be seen to be doing nothing.

MoD: So you want us to use military force?

FCO: Yes.

MoD: To do what? To stop the killing?

FCO: Yes. Exactly.

MoD: Who do you want us to fight? We are not clear who is doing the killing: is it tribe on tribe, or is it force from a tribe? And Rwanda is a big country. Where do we start? Kigali, presumably, it's the capital and we would want an air-head?

FCO: Well, there must be an international force, of course.

MoD: And what would be the British aim in joining the international force?

FCO: To play our part as a permanent member of the UN Security Council.

MoD: Is Britain to lead the force?

FCO: No, it should be led by the UN.

MoD: That will take some time to assemble, so it will probably be too late to stop the killing.

FCO: Then the mission should be aimed at bringing post-conflict order.[6]

So the MoD would find itself astride a very nasty fence. The MoD would get derided if it asked for too specific a mission statement, or an 'end state'. Whilst the MoD could see the advantage of being involved (support the Prime Minster and you get support for your funding: 'use it or lose it'), it also knew that the UK armed forces were stretched and, as a medium-sized power, the UK military structure was very thin if out on a limb. The MoD would know clearly enough what was required to do the job properly, but it was crucified by its own downward assessment 'of what the market would bear' and so too many times it made do with just too small a force.

I finished my military service just before the coalition invaded Iraq in 2003. I watched the events that unfolded in the next decade through the prism of my own understanding. From what I read, I fully supported the decision to invade Iraq by the US-led coalition and I joined many others in a visceral rejection of arbitrary rulers, thinking, in an echo of the FCO conversation above, that something *should* be done. The rest of my family disagreed with that and went on the million-person protest march against the invasion through London.

I loved my life in the armed services. It had delivered huge satisfaction and I stood taller in my own estimation because of its hard-won reputation for competence and for being on the side of the angels. So it was very painful indeed to hear of the suggestion that we had been 'defeated' in Basra. To see casualties in Iraq and then Afghanistan mount, month by month. To watch the story of a Royal Navy patrol meekly taken captive by the Iranians beamed around the world. To read the criticism of our operational commanders as being somehow unthinking in their design for battle and vainglorious in pursuit of their own brigade's reputation. To listen to the UK Ambassador from Kabul declaring that the British Army had gone to Helmand 'not to defeat the Taliban, but to defeat the British Treasury, the Royal Navy and the Royal Air Force [in battles for funding]' and that British generals 'were keen to deploy there because they enjoyed the challenge'.[7] To learn of the number of civilians who were killed as a result of our military operations, considered as unavoidable victims of 'collateral damage'. To see the damage to our pre-eminent foreign policy objective—the 'special relationship' with the United States—caused by our precipitate drawdown in Iraq, at exactly the moment the US as coalition leader was surging a much bigger force back into Baghdad. To believe that we were not succeeding, despite the evident cost in blood and treasure.

I came to the conclusion that our service personnel had done everything asked of them, indeed they had consistently fought like lions and cheerfully endured great privation. They had also waged an unpopular war without complaint. I began to be reassured that the field commanders were as imaginative in their plans and had done at least as well (and sometimes much better) as my own generation might have. But somewhere above them their instructions were too full of contradictions.

To take one powerful example, the British Army knew in its very DNA that an insurgency in Belfast less than ten years previously had only been contained by the permanent deployment of thirteen battalions of infantry, yet after the initial benign period the UK attempted to meet an even more violent challenge in Basra, a city three times the size, with only three. We were bound to fail, so who allowed that to happen?

This book sets out to explore why that occurred: why good people at the top of the MoD could allow poor policies, with bad outcomes, to emerge. If it has any purpose, it is to illustrate the traps and hazards that challenge the military High Command and how short-term judgements invariably contain the asp of longer-term consequences within them, so that they may become more wary of them in future conflicts.

3

JUMPING TO THE CONCLUSION

'The scale of the military ambition was always greater than the military instrument could provide.'[1]

Lieutenant General Sir Rob Fry

At one level, it is easy to say why things did not go well for the UK armed forces in the decade 2000–10. They never had a chance of doing otherwise. The UK consistently failed to match its policy aspirations with sufficient military resources to deliver them. Moreover, the UK's grand strategy was to support the USA whatever, since America had been underwriting the security of the UK for at least half a century. This required the UK to be the junior partner of US-led coalitions—a follower, rather than an initiator—and thereby largely losing control over the rhythm of events as they happened. It is a debate for a separate place about the extent to which the US, in turn, delivered on its responsibility to help address the problems faced by its principal coalition subordinate.

If coalition was a fact of life for a middle-sized power, the reasons why the mismatch of policy and resources was allowed to happen were much more complex. This is the subject of the book. A starting point will be to examine how the Ministry of Defence works. I then review the events of the preceding decades, especially the military adventures of the 1990s, noting how recent history had powerfully shaped decision-makers' perspectives. The UK's operations in Iraq and Afghanistan will be described, examining the part that Britain played in the wars and telling the story from the British point of view. It will emerge that events followed tortuous twisting paths that were very often difficult to predict. The UK met each task with just enough armed force to match what was expected, leaving her poorly placed if things turned out to be more demanding. Which they often did. Furthermore, we will see how a whole-of-government approach and sustained direction from the top political leadership, both essential for success in such expeditions, were absent. We will unravel the contradictions in the orders given out from Whitehall to the field commanders. Many of them contained inconsistencies—'do this, but also do that at the same time'—which made the orders impossible to achieve concurrently, or even consecutively. It is a complex web and you may be as surprised as I was by how events in the two different theatres ricocheted back and forth and constantly tripped over each other; how events were never as they had first appeared.

I shall attempt to decipher why all this happened, leaning on a description of the interplay between the politicians, military commanders and civil servants and of how the Ministry of Defence decision-making machinery operates. Finally, I draw the arguments together by looking at the part played by the senior leaders, principally the military chiefs. Was it the architecture of the MoD that caused the problems, or was it that people failed to be the master of it?

Deciphering the Code

The structures and arrangements for UK defence can be very confusing, so this chapter will conclude with a description of how it all fits together. These are essential building blocks to gaining an understanding of what makes the armed forces tick and why they act as they do, although if this is your subject you could easily skip ahead. Soldiers, seamen and airmen are different.

One of the defining influences on the way the UK's armed forces are structured occurred during the closing stages of the English Civil War (1642–51), when Oliver Cromwell as Lord Protector dominated the elected Parliament through menace with his New Model Army. To counter this, the UK armed forces now take their instructions from the elected government but swear their loyalty to the sovereign. Likewise, funding for defence is granted annually by Parliament, so as to keep the tightest control over defence activities (through the annual Bill for the Defence Estimates), however inefficient this might be in commercial terms. Parliament sits in oversight of a current government's handling of defence issues by means of its powerful cross-party committee, the House of Commons Defence Committee. This was led during the decade in question by two astute and able back-benchers:[2] Bruce George (Labour Party) and James Arburthnot (Conservative Party). They consistently held the MoD to account and their proceedings form one very valuable record of how things developed and of attitudes at the time.

Most of the UK's governmental departments are clustered around the broad central avenue of Whitehall, off which leads Downing Street and the Prime Minister's office, and at the end of which sits Parliament. Since most government business is conducted around this cluster, 'Whitehall' is used as a term to describe the offices, politicians, civil servants and specialists who make up the machinery of government in Britain. Likewise, 'London' is used to refer to what is happening collectively in the political heartland of the United Kingdom. 'Defence' is used to describe the whole apparatus that maintains the nation's defence, from trained fighting personnel, through equipment, scientists, logistics, education, industries and all the people who have a hand in directing the armed forces, or have influence upon them.

The UK armed forces are arranged into three distinct 'tribes': the Royal Navy, the British Army and the Royal Air Force. The heads of these services are respectively known as the First Sea Lord, the Chief of the General Staff and the Chief of the Air Staff. Sitting above them is the Chief of the Defence Staff, with a deputy to assist him, the Vice Chief of the Defence Staff. The latter pair could be drawn from any of the three services and are chosen on merit. All these officers are of the highest military rank, i.e. 'four star': Admiral/General/Air Chief Marshal. A table showing the allocation of 'stars' given to ranks is included at Annex 5.

Each service includes one or more combat groups whose skills would more properly lie with a sister service; they are included because they give vital support to that service's primary task. For instance, the Royal Navy sustains and commands a light-infantry marine commando brigade, whilst the Army has a considerable fleet of its own helicopters and the Royal Air Force deploys its own specialist infantry companies to defend its airfields.

No combat unit of whatever type can operate completely independently, except in extremely limited circumstances, and there is a need to bring them together into joint groups for action and mutual support. These were known as 'all arms' groupings (if the elements come from a single service) and 'combined arms' groupings (if two or more services are contributing). Grouping them together has a multiplying effect on the base capability, making the whole very much more powerful and resilient than the parts alone. This is what being 'joint' is about—multiplying the effect by being together. In any 'joint' operation, a lead element is nominated as the 'supported force', with all other combat elements designated as the 'subordinate supporting forces', and the individual services readily accept their role—lead or subordinate—in any particular drama without difficulty. The need to be 'joint' has been there throughout history—the Royal Navy delivered General Sir John Moore's force to the Iberian Peninsula during the Napoleonic Wars and then rescued the remnants from it—but it has taken on increasing importance in recent years in the face of the rise of precision attack, and also because it became practical to command larger groupings through hugely improved secure communication systems. The trend to 'jointness' ratcheted up a step with the appointment of Marshal of the Royal Air Force Sir William Dickson as the first 'joint' Chief of the Defence Staff in 1959.

The armed forces are large and disparate organisations that are located throughout the UK and overseas operational theatres, but their nervous system has its cortex back at the Ministry of Defence in the Main Building in Whitehall, London. This is both a department of state and a military supreme headquarters. Governed by politicians, it makes the arrangements for, and commands, the combat and support units of the UK armed forces. Under the appointed political Secretary of State for Defence, the department of state aspects are run by the Permanent Under Secretary (PUS—a top civil servant), whilst the military headquarters element is commanded by the UK's senior military officer, the Chief of the Defence Staff (CDS). In the decade 2000–10 a hierarchy of committees existed to direct the work of the MoD, with the Defence Council (chaired by the Secretary of State for Defence) at the top, supported by the Defence Board (chaired by the PUS) and the Chiefs of Staff Committee (chaired by the CDS). The structure of defence in the UK is re-examined every so often, so as to adjust to changing circumstances and, indeed, it has been changed already from the period studied here.

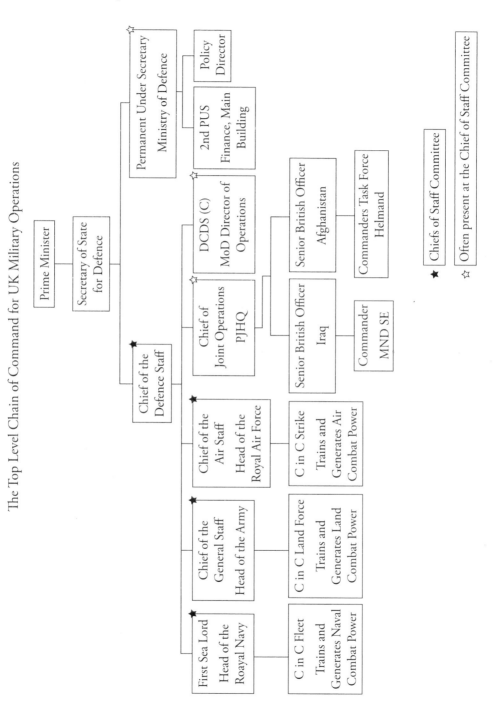

The Top Level Chain of Command for UK Military Operations

The incoming Labour government in 1998 conducted the most widely applauded root-and-branch review of recent times, which set the conditions for the armed forces into the decade 2000–10. The overall conclusion was that the UK armed forces should be 'expeditionary'—capable of projecting military combat power at a distance—and 'contingency based', i.e. structured to meet a range of threats, rather than a specific one. It was directed that the UK would be able to project a divisional-sized force abroad (with all the enablers needed to support it) for a short duration to help to solve an international crisis. This is what happened when 40,000 troops were deployed to support the invasion of Iraq in 2003. Simultaneously, the UK was to be able to meet a longer-term task—an 'enduring commitment'—requiring a lesser force of about a combat brigade and appropriate naval and air forces. These large and smaller operations could be concurrent for no more than six months. The different services were then structured, sized and funded so as to be able to deliver the directed military capability, with the human contribution based on the concept of tolerable 'harmony guidelines'.

The 'harmony' scheme has its roots in the Royal Navy and was designed to ensure that all the demands on service personnel remain roughly in balance—individual training, unit/ship training, deployments to operations, sufficient leave and family life, etc. As it turned out, the commitment of a force into Helmand in 2006, well before troops were released from Iraq in 2009, caused these guidelines to be broken. There were far too few combat elements available to meet the requirements of Iraq and Afghanistan simultaneously. So both operations went under-resourced, combat tours came around too frequently for an individual's wellbeing, and training for major combat operations (that is, preparation for the defence of the nation's really vital national interests) was deficient.

Armed Forces are Different

The Ministry of Defence is unlike any other government department in Whitehall, not least because it combines a supreme military headquarters with the department of state responsible for defence, functions that did not always mesh well together. Moreover, defence is like a form of insurance policy, consuming resources but without providing an economic benefit or providing a regulatory framework for the nation, as the other departments of state achieve.

Defence is about dealing with the unexpected, so it is difficult to judge just how much 'defence' is needed. Furthermore, in most other activities there is a place for an honourable second or third, but in mortal combat only first place is of any worth. In the race to retain that edge, everything by definition must be either a prototype or untested, or both. So maintaining the correct equipment in type, quantity and quality is both subjective and speculative, with only a few worthwhile comparators against which to make a judgement (and they are usually the best and most expensive available globally). This makes the financing of defence a very uncertain art, but always expensive.

There is also uncertainty about when 'defence' might need to be triggered—an uncertainty deepened by some of the conundrums that appeared as a result of the ending of the Cold War, which will be explored later. In theory, a government should decide its long-term policy intentions and then consider how much armed force was necessary to meet them, with a bit more added in as a reserve. But this never happens, not least because the arguments are so varied and the circumstances are always changing. It is also very difficult to predict *when* armed force might be needed, and whether it will be at a moment's notice in the short term, or longer, and for how long it will last.

So, armed forces are an expensive, complicated coiled spring which have to be kept alert and tested, ever prepared to face fear, danger and the unexpected. Strong internal cohesion is required to overcome such challenges, as well as from the increasingly restrictive legal considerations of lethal force.

Some Wars are Different

The types of combat that armed forces engage in will vary enormously. Some combat operations are discretional—'limited wars' or 'wars of choice'—where the UK will use its military power in a constrained way to further its economic, political or humanitarian aims. It might involve peacekeeping, peace enforcement, counter-piracy, counter-drugs, counter-insurgency, counter-terrorism, stabilisation of failed states and humanitarian relief. These are optional tasks and the military will be withdrawn if the cost of using them becomes too high for the gains being accrued. Limited operations are usually against less well equipped forces that, typically, use asymmetric means—roadside bombs, snipers, terror attacks against civilians, etc.—to overcome the better equipment and resources of the UK's armed services. In the last hundred years, despite two World Wars, eighty per cent of warfare has been of this type.

There are also wars that the UK simply could not consider losing. These are 'wars of vital national interest', where the nation will continue to fight on until it has either won or been defeated, for its very existence and freedoms would be challenged, as in WWII. In the past these were termed 'total' wars, or alternatively Clausewitz referred to them as 'absolute', denoting the seriousness of the consequences and the necessity for the complete commitment of a nation's strength. The enemies who could pose this threat will have first-league armed forces themselves and these wars involve what are called large-scale major combat operations or high-end warfare. These demand equality or overmatch in firepower and protection, with resilient command and control systems balanced across land, sea and air. At the moment, major combat operations need missiles, protected launch platforms on the sea, land and air, a robust surveillance apparatus, secure and resilient command systems, resistance to cyber assault, etc. Just occasionally a limited war might require some of these capabilities too, as happened in the Korean and Falklands Wars.

This disparity between the types of warfare presents an eternal conundrum for defence policy-makers. Should the armed forces be configured for their most likely use—wars of choice—or structured to safeguard the UK's interests in a war of survival? Since a war of survival would inevitably involve the defensive alliance of NATO, could the UK specialise its role within the alliance and optimise in certain defined areas, such as maritime? And where does the proper balance for the UK's armed forces lie, if they are to be prepared at any one time for both major combat operations and limited wars? There is also a challenge of attitude, in that major wars are unrestrained and about literally beating the enemy to death, painting a picture of defeat as early as possible in the latter's mind. This is not an approach that has much utility in peacekeeping or counter-insurgency.

Warfare in a State of Evolution

Land warfare down the centuries has traditionally been dominated by the side which had the better weapons and by any advantage conferred by the territory it was fought over. Muskets replaced longbows, and were themselves replaced by rifles; the rapid firing machine gun was devastating against troops armed only with single-shot rifles. Terrain remained more of a constant, with the difficulty of crossing it and the distance you could see (hills, trees, cities foreshorten the view, elevation of view lengthens it) dominating tactics. The skill of the general was to choose where to fight his battle. Attackers would attempt to find a weak spot in the opponent's defence and then crush it with a locally overwhelming superiority, gained by thinning out forces elsewhere. In reverse, the defender would attempt to lure the attacker onto terrain that hindered his movement and view. Key to success in both attack and defence was in knowing where the enemy's forces were, whilst keeping the position of your own troops and the 'going' of the terrain hidden. As Napoleon advanced towards Brussels, Wellington fell back behind the ridge at Waterloo, where he could conceal the position of his reserves and hide his intentions until the last minute. He protected his numerically inferior forces from view and cannon, and forced Napoleon to attack up a long slope. Before engaging in battle on 18 June 1815, both sides waited until well after dawn and the clearing of early morning mist, and then until the overnight rain had drained away, allowing for easier movement for their massed battalions of infantry, cavalry and field guns. Likewise, Nelson attacked the French fleet at anchor in Aboukir Bay in 1801, with the horns of the land on either side severely restricting the ability of the French ships to manoeuvre so leading to their defeat.

Orders had to be brief, and changing them was difficult because the carrying of orders forwards was by runner or someone on horseback. Similarly, once a naval fleet had left its base, it was up to the admiral to deliver the intention as best he could, with news of an engagement or the issue of new orders sometimes taking months to arrive. Much of this was still true until after the second world war, although the development of radio allowed much improved and speedier command and control, and radar began to detect combat platforms at greater distances.

Since then, astonishing changes have taken place as new technologies have overturned those earlier constants. Image intensifiers now allow people to see clearly at night, so battle may be engaged by day and night. Radio conversation is secure and reliable, giving a dependable and instantaneous link (if needed) from the most senior commanders to the individual soldier, and thus close control over far larger forces. This both increases the span of command and allows much more rapid redirection of forces, with closer coordination between them. Streaming video pictures back from the front line permits a commander to assess the progress of a battle as it is happening from much further away. The Global Positioning System (GPS) gives a precise location to everything that can access it; if internet protocol addresses are added, the positions of people, platforms, even individual warheads, can be displayed on a single screen, leading to 'situational awareness' and authentic 'ground truth', so that commanders have a much greater chance of knowing what is actually going on. Combining secure radio links with GPS gives warheads pin-point accuracy—a missile can be directed through a president's office window or a shell down through the ventilation shaft of a bunker. Furthermore, it is no longer possible to gather sizeable combat forces together without being detected; for instance, a Doppler radar in an aircraft looking forwards over the battle zone will detect absolutely everything that moves within its range. So the old trick of massing forces unnoticed to produce a sudden devastating attack on a weak point is denied. Since soldiers can cue firepower from weapons located much further away, there is no longer any purpose in giving away their own position by firing weapons themselves and a traditional front line of battalions and regiments is unwise, because they would simply be destroyed.

This massive change in the way wars between modern nations are fought—described here largely in terms of land warfare, but equally applicable to air and sea—has been called variously a 'revolution in military affairs', or 'networked warfare' using 'net enabled capability'. The changes have been unevenly embraced. Some instinctively understand the scale of what is happening, whilst others see it as more of the same—just better provided for. Whatever, the wars of national survival between first-league nations—now networked and using precision attack—will remain very different from how nations will continue to counter armed insurgencies and piracy (e.g. using 'boots on the ground', helicopters and patrol vessels), all the while teasing defence planners about how to construct armed forces that can do both.

Soldiers Will Die and They Will Cause Death

The armed forces are a disciplined, uniformed body with an obvious and visible command hierarchy. In this, they resemble the police and fire services but, in the matter of taking and sacrificing life, they differ from those other organisations in two distinctive ways.

First, members of the armed forces are deliberately trained to kill, whereas only a tiny proportion of the police are. Second, a policeman or a fireman will not expect to be killed in the course of his normal duty, but death and wounding awaits a measurable proportion of all those who join the armed forces, a risk which is both understood and accepted.

Young servicemen and women hardly think about this and they certainly don't dwell on it; if they do, they leave. They like to be challenged, deliberately seeking out the tests that soldiering brings—for as Samuel Johnson said, 'Every man thinks meanly of himself for not having been a soldier.'[3] The prospect of death or maiming injury is seen in terms of an ultimate challenge, without thinking too much about the grisly and heartbreaking consequences that inevitably follow.

Older soldiers and more senior officers know better than that and have a more realistic view of the inherent dangers of soldiering. This gives them a duty to make the calculation that adventurous and hot-headed youth is unable to formulate. That is, whether the outcomes sought by sending armed forces can justify the deaths and maiming that could result, to the soldiers, their opponents and to the civilians caught up in the violence. For the issues of vital national interest—protection of the homeland from a direct threat—such death and loss can easily be justified and will be readily accepted. For 'wars of choice', however, the calculation is more troubling. In deciding to go to Iraq and Afghanistan, it is doubtful if this judgement was made with the seriousness it deserved when the military options were being considered; rather than calculating and weighing the risk of death, armed forces with inherently high internal cohesion accept it as a fact of life.

The issue of casualties never goes away. In limited wars, especially, it creates tensions and ambiguities between purpose and result, and casualties are seen as a crude indicator of success or failure by the public. The patrol or platoon in Iraq and Afghanistan suffering a loss had the immediate task of dealing with the casualty, but almost always the dead or wounded were whisked away within minutes in an efficient, airborne evacuation system. This was different in previous wars, where casualties would have remained close to the fighting echelons for very much longer and initial recuperation might have taken place in field hospitals close enough for the wounded to be visited. Today, after a violent engagement with the enemy or an explosion, the casualties rapidly disappear in a whirl of helicopter blades, and it might explain how the field units have coped with such high injury rates without becoming more overtly distressed by them.

Casualties, though, were very much the litmus of the success or failure of those campaigns in domestic terms; and the drumbeat of repatriation ceremonies bringing the dead back to the UK for burial, with elaborate and mournful parades through Wootton Bassett, both tested and stiffened the nation's resolve to continue. In the past, British soldiers had always been buried overseas where they had fallen, their graves in elegantly maintained Commonwealth cemeteries, but now the return of a body to the UK requires a Coroner's Court to be convened to examine the situation at time of death—a process strangely dislocated in location and time from its circumstances. Inside the MoD, a stern conviction emerged not to be overly distracted by the issue, with one general suggesting that the repatriation ceremonies were being overplayed and that the British had become 'mawkish' about them. One senior naval officer confided that he was 'jealous of the Army's casualties [in Afghanistan] because of the public profile it gave to the Army', whilst Desmond Bowen (Ministry of Defence Policy Director 2004–8) was very disturbed to hear another very senior Army officer declare 'we need to be shedding more blood to show that we are in there with the Americans'.[4] A one-time UK Deputy Coalition Commander in Kabul, General Sir Nick Parker, gave a much more sober view after his retirement: 'Military interventions are bloody … and I feel deeply now about the human cost of what we do. An enthusiastic military desire to intervene must be tempered by an understanding that … you are doing things that have pain attached.'[5]

What is certain is that the issue of unintended *civilian* casualties caused in military operations—which were numerous in both Iraq and Afghanistan— was never given the profile it deserved, neither did it influence policy-makers to the degree that the civilian victims involved would have hoped it might.

4

INSIDE THE MINISTRY OF DEFENCE

A Walk through the MoD

The headquarters of the Ministry of Defence is a handsome, clean-faced, neoclassical building in Whitehall designed by Vincent Harris in 1912, but eventually built between 1938 and 1959. The northern entrance is flanked by two monumental statues by Charles Wheeler entitled 'Earth and Water'. There are gardens to east and west, with pleasant views across the broad, tree-lined Whitehall thoroughfare towards Downing Street or out over the River Thames. All around the building there are statues commemorating military individuals or events. The whole complex is known as the 'Main Building' of the Ministry of Defence.

The Main Building sits on the site of the old Palace of Westminster and, below ground level, part of Henry VIII's original wine cellar has been preserved intact in a brick-arched labyrinth, still used today for entertaining. Inside the building are five large 'historic rooms' for general meetings, which are exact replicas (complete with high ceilings, classical pillars, large paintings and awful acoustics) of the rooms in the Georgian houses that also once occupied the site. They make for a bizarre presence in a modern office block and their tradition and sense of gracious living must influence those who use them.

The building was initially occupied by the Air Ministry and the Board of Trade. When the three services were combined into a single defence staff in

1964, the Army and Naval staffs left the Old War Office and the Admiralty Building and joined the Royal Air Force in what became known as the Main Building, at which point the Board of Trade departed. At that time the building consisted of seven floors of offices, looking outwards onto the street or inwards into two large internal courtyards. As communication systems and security requirements burgeoned, the corridors became festooned with a latticework of cables suspended from the corridor ceilings, which were already low enough. (The idea had been to have the cable runs exposed so that they could be checked for interference, but even so some forty surveillance bugs were found in the building when the wires were eventually stripped out.) When I started my first job in the MoD, I commented to my opposite number in the Civil Service that I could not have existed for all the years that he had in the dark rat-hole that was then the MoD. He replied 'Ah, but Christopher, there is no aphrodisiac quite like running the country...'.

In those days, offices accrued significance in a number of ways: by the floor on which an office was located (the sixth floor had all the chiefs and ministers), the size of office, the view from the window, whether the office was shared, and the type of door the office had. On reaching 3-star rank, officers and civil servants were entitled to an *oak* door, so any internal rearrangement would result in doors shuffling down the corridors as well as individuals. The shadows of these habits live on.

In the 1990s a plan was put together to strip out the building completely. The idea was to replace all the building services and, most dramatically, change to open-plan working. This was bravely pushed through by the then civil servant Second Permanent Under Secretary, Sir Roger Jackling; controversially so, because a cash-strapped MoD was spending over £300 million on its own head office. But it needed doing and the result was regarded as a great success, not least because it promoted a much more open style of working. The MoD staffs hot-desked in offices around Whitehall whilst the building work was undertaken in 2000–4, a period covering both the 9/11 terrorist attacks and the subsequent invasion of Iraq, but it was generally agreed that it was efficiently done and the disruption caused had little effect on decision-making.

As you enter the Main Building by the grand entrances at the North or South, you first have to navigate the security process and airlock system. This is difficult enough for those working in the office, but can be a nightmare for visitors. But once inside, and with the right pass, you have freedom of movement. In such a huge building with so many different departments it can take people a long time to discover 'how the building works' and old hands are noticeable for their adeptness at doing so. 'Corridor-walking' in such a dispersed arrangement is more than just an idle activity; rather it is a useful way of finding out what is going on, picking up rumours and discovering where experts are hiding. Military officers on short tours of a couple of years might only master this skill as the time to leave approaches, whilst to the much longer serving civilian staff of course it is home.

The two large interior courtyards were glazed over in the refurbishment and then divided up in spectacular fashion to create very pleasant recreation and meeting areas. Close by, there is an excellent library and a cafe. You get around the building by knowing the floor and numbered location of clusters of working desks, known as a 'branch' or 'directorate'. There are wall maps to help you decide a route to get there and off you go.

Seeing One of the Chiefs

On arrival in the vicinity of your final destination in the building, you will see scores of individuals head down at computers across the multi-layers of low-walled desk partitions. Typically, there will be clusters of smartly dressed individuals talking in groups. Many modern banks or commercial enterprises would look similar.

At the centre of your intended target will be the office of the local chieftain (if he was important enough to have one), looking rather like a marooned portacabin amongst all the other open-plan desks. His elegant, articulate, confident and completely all-together military assistant will take your coat off to somewhere behind the photocopier, shoo out a junior officer from his seat for you to sit on and offer you a cup of coffee from the machine, usually because so-and-so 'is still tied up at the moment, but will see you very shortly'.

The staffs in the rebuilt head office say that it works very well and they like the informality, although it must be quite difficult to write a testing policy paper needing lack of distraction if the single meeting room in the area is already taken. One is struck by the relentless pace at which the chieftain is driven, only made possible by the efficiency and dedication of his or her staff.

Here the super-optimised machine is fitting as much as possible into the diary and the head man or woman ricochets from one meeting to another, all efficiently prepared for beforehand by the staff, but with precious little time for reflection in between. As the time for the end of any meeting approaches, the door opens softly and the military assistant gesticulates at his watch, whether the purpose of the meeting was resolved or not. It is time to go.

The Motivations of the Actors

'The man who never alters his opinion is like standing water … and breeds reptiles of the mind.'

William Blake

In a perfect world, the way in which an organisation takes decisions is decided by how to achieve the best outcome. But in our world there are, of course, other considerations. For instance, the risks involved will be calculated differently by different people. The spill-over effects will be scored according to where you sit in an organisation. Opportunity costs will be measured by how they affect an individual's own work. Underlying everything (and sometimes corrosively so) will be the personal motives and biases of the individual actors involved. The last of these is evident throughout everyday life, as people jostle or conspire to promote their own agendas, and is worth exploring in a little more depth.

Using this as a starting point helps to explain why the key actors in the Ministry of Defence—politicians, the military and civil servants—function in the way that they do, especially the influence of preconception, unrecognised by the individual but often held with surprisingly strong conviction. Cognitive factors control behaviour, for good and ill, and they influence good decision-making in demanding circumstances. To deal first with preconception, it is known that about 95 per cent of the human brain is engaged entirely in *subconscious* activity completely unseen to the individual, whilst only the remaining 5 per cent of the brain is what an individual is aware of—the *conscious* mind. The much larger subconscious part is where memories of previous activity are stored. These memories cannot be accessed directly but, paradoxically, their stored imprint is continually and automatically exerting its influence on current behaviour. Therefore a naval officer is a naval officer, by imprint of experience, and he or she will never think exactly like an army officer, a civil servant or a politician.

The memories become acquired knowledge and they are stored in the unconscious brain in two ways. They are either handed down over generations and hard-wired in from birth—a mayfly knows the physics of flight from the moment it emerges from the nymph—or stored cumulatively as a result of encounters in an individual's own life. Second by second fresh connections are created in brain material, as experience increases, and these linkages then predispose people towards acting in a certain way. Thus people acquire bias.

A bias can come from an ephemeral source. Alan Clark's book *The Donkeys*, first published in 1961, highlighted a myth that in 1915–18 senior British officers were incompetent and led a detached and comfortable existence behind the lines whilst their soldiers suffered at the front.[1] The truth was very different, not least because the highest percentage of casualty by rank was at the level of Brigadier General.[2] The majority of the survivors of the war had lauded not despised their generals, as Sir Max Hastings commented 'until the late 1920s, senior officers such as Haig, French, Plumer, Byng and Rawlinson received respect and even homage. The belated victors of the western front were loaded with titles......a million people turned out for Haig's funeral procession in 1928'.[3] Another historian wrote that 'the idea that [the generals of the First World War] were indifferent to the sufferings of their men is constantly refuted by the facts, and only endures because some commentators wish to perpetuate the myth that these generals, representing the upper classes, did not give a damn what happened to the lower orders'.[4] But the bias formed by Clark, amongst others, has endured and continues to be quoted today.

A second, very important discovery in human behaviour is that it takes time for a person's stored 'wisdom' (or accumulated patterns of solutions that they know will work) to be accessed by the conscious brain. This is often done whilst asleep, or when free from other distractions, and explains the value of calm reflection and the need for 'thinking things through'. Conversely, being pressured by too full a programme or distracted by endless trivia can be destructive. Given proper time for reflection and rest, 'a light bulb will go on' on waking, or a solution will be found while away from the hurly-burly of the office when out for a walk. The brain needs time to trawl its subconscious store of acquired experience and produce some new and useful connections between factors, some of which will emerge as solutions. The importance of this in higher-level policy-making cannot be overstated: individuals need to be presented with logically constructed papers that lay out the factors and options, and then be given time to digest the information *before* being required to come to a decision. The chief policy-deciders should have time to reflect on substantial issues, free from other distractions. As will be described later, the scope of activity of the Service Chiefs in particular made this essential breathing space and thinking time an almost unknown luxury for them.

So, everyone becomes hostage to their previous experience. As we grow older, we become wiser and more effective, despite a declining memory, because we can see more routes through problems to solutions. We also become more prejudiced and more predictable. We develop mental pictures of what works and what might fail; this conditions our responses when presented with new circumstances.[5] We view failure with increasing dread, especially if it leaves us highly exposed, so where we might once have been capricious, we become cautious. We need moments to reflect before coming to decisions but, if we are consumed with too much other activity, we never have the time to ponder issues to allow solutions to reveal themselves, and our decisions are very much the poorer for that.

Other Influences

'The opinions that are held with passion are always those for which no good ground exists.'

Bertrand Russell, 'Sceptical Essays'

There are also emotional pressures at work here too. Lieutenant General Sir Rob Fry, as Director of Operations in the Ministry of Defence, described the 'thrill of being in the bear pit of world events' that pervaded the top of the MoD in 2005, and which provided a strong incentive to get involved militarily. Sir Ian Andrews, as Second Permanent Under Secretary, recalled how his Secretary of State for Defence, Dr John Reid, had such enthusiasm for his job that he had to be dissuaded from 'turning his private office into a war room', not least because it risked the perception that he was interfering with detail that properly lay with the chain of command.[6] The Butler Review, in its report about the assessments regarding weapons of mass destruction in Iraq, concluded that the misperceptions were in part due to a strong element of emotional 'group think', where ideas loop back and forth between commentators and become reinforced and distorted in the process.[7] Jack Straw remembered the run-up to the decision to invade Iraq, as UK Foreign Secretary (2000–6), commenting on the emotional pressures to support a call to war:

'I became aware, in retrospect, how you could be sucked into a decision-making process ... at each stage the gate marked "war" became wider and wider, and sort of psychologically more enticing ... whilst the one marked "peace" became narrower and apparently more difficult...'[8]

These facts are important in trying to understand the behaviour of individuals in the complex MoD system. The previous experience of the people working in the MoD—their preconditioning—exerts strong influences on their behaviour and their emotions, inevitably carrying the group together in a given direction. The effect can be seen in politicians, military officers and senior civil servants alike.[9]

These cognitive factors go some way to explain why rational individuals do perverse things, why the trivial might gain ascendancy over the vital, and why service loyalties and civil service practices will distort decision-making. As Air Chief Marshal Sir Jock Stirrup pointedly said of his experience as CDS, 'in war ... analysis of any conflict shows how the human interplay becomes a major factor ... this will never change'.[10]

5

THE TRIBES AND THE SYSTEM

Defence Politicians

'I came to the job with no experience of military matters. Of course I would have been a much better S of S now—after 3 years' experience in the job.'[1]

Des Browne, Secretary of State for Defence 2006–8

The Ministry of Defence is populated by three very distinct groups: politicians, civil servants and military officers. Individual characteristics and differences between these groups give many clues to the struggle to achieve clarity and unity of purpose, or in getting the MoD to lift its eyes above the day-to-day problems to address the strategic challenges.

At the top of the tree of authority in the Ministry of Defence are the three or four ministers assigned by the government of the day to defence. None of these was a fool during the decade 2000–10 and most were extremely able. In my view, all but one made a really good effort to prosper the cause of the UK armed forces, trying to use the bureaucracy of the Ministry of Defence sensibly to achieve it. This might seem a surprising statement, given the blame that has been heaped on those politicians in the press for their military shortcomings, and the acrimony that has disfigured so many memoirs and anecdotes of the period, but I found no senior officer of the time who would challenge it.

Running through the list of Secretaries of State (the leading politician in the MoD) during 2000–10, the first, Geoff Hoon, brought a cautious, consistent, lawyer's mind to the job. Hoon was replaced in 2005 by John Reid, who had served previously as a junior defence minister, knew the MoD well and had prepared himself over many years for the top job. Reid clearly regarded the post as a deep and personal honour and was 'very cautious and thorough when taking decisions'.[2] By 2006, Des Browne had arrived from the Treasury with the purpose of halving the size of the MoD, but soon found it was more complicated than it had appeared from the outside and did his best to support his Chiefs. One senior official commented on Des Browne's 'enormous heart and patent humanity'.[3] John Hutton, a noted military historian with a serious reforming bent, assumed the appointment in October 2008 but had resigned from it within nine months. The reasons for which are still opaque, but he was Blair's man and uncomfortable with his successor Gordon Brown's manner.[4] Hutton was replaced by Bob Ainsworth, originally a trade unionist in a Coventry car plant, who was wise, balanced and caring.

It is really very significant that all the military chiefs who worked with the Secretaries of State of the decade had nothing but admiration for them. But it did not follow that they were effective as Secretaries of State. For a start, Prime Minister Blair turned over his Defence Ministers with bewildering frequency. During the period 2000–10 there were five holders of the office, whilst in the US there were only two. For most of them the job was an impossible task, because they carried all of the responsibility for the work of the armed forces with few of the specialised intellectual tools or the experience to discharge it. No politician could completely master the labyrinthine process of controlling the military budget, even though he or she might be an accountant by training. So for financial decisions, for instance, they relied on their civil servants to guide them.

Likewise, on military issues: service-speak has its own peculiar staccato of shorthands and acronyms, with complex and nuanced issues being compressed into short references and presentations. Thus comprehension is hard work and often leaves the non-experts bewildered, realising that they have only achieved a half-understanding. Add to that the outward confidence and certainty that characterises senior uniformed officers, talking about issues about which they are expert (and the failure of which might result in death, but about which the politician has absolutely no first-hand experience), and the politician can find himself diminished to the role of an approving cipher.

Some Defence politicians would be bemused by military issues in the face of contradictory and conflicting advice. Sir Sherard Cowper-Coles thought that 'the Generals bullied their ministers and, because they lacked military experience, ministers did not know military bullshit when they heard it'.[5] Whilst he was UK Ambassador in Kabul, Cowper-Coles remembers telling a Defence minister not to succumb to military requests to send UK Tornado aircraft to Afghanistan (where there were already adequate numbers of NATO aircraft available). The minister had replied: 'but I don't know a Tornado from a torpedo...'.

Brigadier Ed Butler, having been commander of the Helmand Task Force, reflected on this by saying to the House of Commons Defence Committee:

'I remember Des Browne [newly appointed Secretary of State for Defence] turning to me, about two years after, and saying, "Ed, I tried to give you all the support I could. I supported you when you wanted more helicopters ... but then I had Brigadier John Lorimer [Commander 12 Mechanised Brigade] asking for tanks ... and [then] so and so asking for something else." He said that he was only taking the best military advice ... [which] was confusing sometimes to our political masters.'[6]

You could add that, as Secretary of State, Browne was not blameless in this remark, for here was a person who did not completely understand what was going on, for in combat nothing stands still and circumstances constantly change and evolve, requiring a guiding hand at the top. It illustrates the disadvantage Defence politicians were at when dealing with complex matters involving the application of armed force, but also the pressure they feel themselves under, as Des Browne said later:

'I arrived on 5 May 2006. One day later a Lynx helicopter was downed and 5 servicemen killed. You have asked me about strategy, but death and the human cost of the wars often dominated my life.'[7]

Moreover, key military issues tend to be issues of national interest and they are often decided by the Prime Minister in person, not by his Secretary of State—further reducing the latter to a conduit between discussions in the MoD and the authority of the Prime Minister.

Faced with this, Defence ministers often find it easier to work around the uniformed services than to confront them head-on. Instead, they use their political Special Advisers and civil servant Private Secretaries to prepare policy options, with the service officers finding out that something is afoot quite late in the day and bypassing or collapsing the formal decision-making process of the MoD. Sometimes, Defence politicians have a keener ear to the way public opinion and events are moving than their military experts. One example occurred when the Army persisted in following a long-term programme to develop a new armoured vehicle for infantry units to use in major combat operations—the Future Rapid Effects System (FRES)—whilst allowing the war of the day in Iraq to continue to be fought in thin-skinned Land Rover Snatch vehicles, resulting in mounting casualties from rocket-propelled grenades and roadside bombs. Lord Paul Drayson, as the Defence Procurement Minister, was stark in his instructions, having to tell the Army 'he didn't care about FRES; just get on with obtaining a proper MRAP (Mine Resistant and Ambush Protected vehicle)'.[8] Furthermore, whatever their other interests, all politicians are concerned with getting re-elected and this inevitably distorts the logic of some of their decisions.

Surprisingly, this uneven relationship between the elected politicians and their military experts often worked very well, not least because all sides had a sense of common purpose in sustaining the armed services.

Civil Servants in the MoD

Supporting their politicians, civil servants are the longest-serving group in the MoD. Their role in translating a government's policy into practical programmes is essential. They are personally accountable to Parliament for the proper use of defence funds: overseeing the military to ensure that money is spent with propriety, regularity and 'value for money'. Civil servants are also policy advisers for politicians and are responsible to ministers for exposing the risks, the resources needed and the legality of any scheme. They gather facts, scope alternatives, cost the resources and then evaluate preferred options. Politically neutral, they are appointed by the Crown, but remain answerable to Parliament, especially over the use of public funds. They form the backbone of any government department, bringing continuity, implementation skills and a corporate memory.

On the recommendations of the Northcote–Trevelyan Report published in 1854, a clear division was established between staff responsible for routine 'mechanical' work and a higher 'administrative' class engaged in policy formulation and implementation.[9] It is from the latter that the ruling Permanent Secretaries of all the government ministries are found and much good is achieved across different departments because of the bonds established between them as they rise up through the Civil Service system together.

The elite Administrative Grade is traditionally drawn from the most talented students in the best universities, although the Civil Service always seeks to draw through candidates from within the wider organisation. They are exceptionally clever people but usually remain generalists, moving around many posts and disciplines during their careers. This produces people with a broad view but without any particular specialist skills. For instance, until very recently the top civil servant responsible for the budgeting of some £30 billion per annum in the MoD was never a qualified accountant and no reason was seen why he should be. Intellectual horsepower would suffice. The Administrative Grade cannot help feeling superior, because of course in many ways they are. They have either excelled at a top university, or are so gifted that they are welcomed into the group as though they had. They sometimes carry an air of superior purpose and struggle to find a bridge to the less able; instead of just saying 'that is rubbish', a response might be 'I have some intellectual difficulty with what you are proposing', a phrase calculated to annoy a military officer with an instinctively more open approach.

The MoD is one of the largest government departments in the UK, being both a department of state and military headquarters. The MoD runs lots of ships, tanks, and aircraft and organises and administers hundreds of thousands of people. By contrast, the Department for Environment, Food and Rural Affairs (DEFRA) does not run its own farms and the Department of Energy does not operate power stations. There are also much more complex policy requirements in Defence—nuclear deterrence, alliance policy, war-fighting doctrines, for example—quite apart from an exceptionally difficult budgetary structure to master. All this demands a very capable group of civil servants, and in the past some at the top have been spectacular. Examples who come to mind are Sir Frank Cooper for his administrative skills and political instinct, Sir Michael Quinlan as a high priest of deterrence theory yet having a humble approach in putting over complex arguments, Sir Richard Mottram and Sir David Omand for their sharp minds and open manner.

Under political pressure to adapt, the Civil Service began to change in the 1990s; outsiders were brought in and different skills were championed, usually more operational than cerebral. Admiral Sir Michael Boyce reflected that he had been used in the past to seeing Permanent Under Secretaries who would 'champion the best interests of UK defence', but found that when he was CDS the head of the MoD Civil Service saw his role as 'advising and looking after the best interests of the defence politicians, not necessarily the best interests of the defence of the UK'.[10] Anthony Sampson summed this up in his book *Who Runs Britain*, suggesting that Sir Kevin Tebbit (Permanent Under Secretary 1998–2005) was 'more the master bureaucrat … "Kevin Paperclip" … than the military authority', although this is somewhat surprising because Tebbit had started his Civil Service career in the Ministry of Defence and had gained extensive experience in military policy work dealing with deterrence issues in NATO and Washington.[11]

Tebbit's tenure was also the time when General Sir Mike Jackson was driven into an open collision as CGS (2003–6) with the MoD civil servants. General Jackson said:

'I was constantly battling the civil servants … I noticed a tendency for the civil servants to want to limit the [Army] Board's power … my determination to do the "right thing" did not endear me to the mandarins.'[12]

The Civil Service member of the Army Board during Jackson's time was the Second Permanent Under Secretary, Sir Ian Andrews, who had served as a young officer in the Army on a short service limited commission. That experience should have allowed a bridge to be built if the circumstances had not been driving the parties apart. When Vice Admiral Sir Jeremy Blackham was appointed as the first Deputy Chief of the Defence Staff Equipment Capability, a job that required him to write the specifications for what Defence should buy, he recalls his first conversation with Sir Roger Jackling, the Second Permanent Under Secretary. Jackling announced (only half in jest) 'you must write me a paper on how I can control you'. Admiral Lord West remembers as a junior officer answering a parliamentary question openly and in good faith, and being berated by the top civil servant in the Royal Navy (it was the job of the Civil Service to answer such parliamentary questions) with: 'you must never answer the question asked; we always reply by telling them things they already know'.[13]

Civil servants as a body are talented, invariably courteous, intelligent, and hard working. By nature they seek consensus, and success to them is when opposing pressures are elegantly brought together, when policy is correctly drafted and the books are balanced. Their instincts and training are to try to reconcile dissenting parties and they are very good at it, yet that might confuse a hot-blooded combat officer into thinking that issues were being dumbed down to the lowest, commonly acceptable solution. Failure for civil servants is when there is a policy train-crash, or if ministers contradict themselves in public, or when a budget comes in over or under the projection. They worry about propriety and have a well-tuned ear to constitutional niceties. In discharging their accountability to Parliament for the propriety, regularity and value-for-money of the funds voted for defence, they often come into head-on collision with military officers who want the fewest constraints; this is especially so when it involves subjective assessments, not absolutes. They get pilloried by House of Commons Select Committees if there is poor budgetary reconciliation, whereas often the truth is that they are being required to achieve over-exact results from an imperfect system. They end up getting blamed by all and loved by none.

But there is also mischief at work, as much true of civil servants as the rest of us, and their position in the Ministry of Defence between the revolving millstones of politicians and the military gives any shortcomings a distinctive hue. Because civil servants are alongside the chain of command but rarely having direct authority in it, they only exercise implied power not command. A civil servant's power is defined by the committees on which they sit, the papers they write, their access to top people's ears and their control of the financial instruments. They might subtly rearrange circumstances to improve that power—or tweak the levers to demonstrate it. They instinctively support the 'system', and are reluctant to make changes to it, even if it is not working. This can make them appear evasive and their motives opaque to others and, again, such obliqueness contrasts strongly with the more direct world-view of the military.

Driven by a desire to make the best use of the resources available, civil servants are centralisers and tidy-uppers by nature, eternally pressured to find economies within the budget. This puts them in contention with the Service Chiefs, who naturally do *not* want their fiefdoms centralised, tidied up or constrained. There is also a basic law of the military that he or she is there to support the soldier in harm's way *whatever* the cost, whereas the civil servant is attempting to do the same thing *within* costs. As General Sir Mike Jackson put it:

'Officers are taught with their mother's milk that soldiers come first; this is not the approach of the Civil Service.'[14]

At senior levels, military commanders on operations will have expert civil servants embedded in their headquarters, as the Civil Secretary (responsible for financial matters and propriety) and as a 'Polad' (policy adviser). These people invariably form the closest relationship with their commanders on operations: protecting and helping the commander, ensuring visibility back to the Ministry of Defence of what is going on, and pointing out when a scheme will not fly politically. The same officer who later found such difficulty with the approach of the civil servant caucus in the MoD, General Sir Mike Jackson, nevertheless described his Polad in 1999 in Kosovo, Mike Venables, as: 'first class; absolutely excellent; admirably questioning [of what I was up to]; [he] identified completely with the front line'.[15] There is an important clue here: it is not so much the character of the civil servants that is the problem as the circumstances of the MoD system that they are responsible for propagating in Whitehall.

In trying to do what they understand to be their task, civil servants give the impression that they form a 'concrete layer' in the bureaucracy, through which things only pass with difficulty. General Sir Michael Walker (in his evidence to the Chilcot Inquiry) said that he felt that Prime Minister Blair 'got it', but more than once when he had decided that things should happen this way or that, his executive instructions got lost:

'Trying to get things to happen at the far end was difficult. Somehow, from the order being given at the top to its arrival at the bottom, the mattress mice got at it to an extent that it didn't happen in the way that the lever puller at the top had anticipated ... we never seemed to be able to grip this rather slippery bar of soap that was Iraq properly.'[16]

Jonathan Powell, Chief of Staff at 10 Downing Street from 1997 to 2007, wrote similarly, believing that this effect was a characteristic of a Civil Service operating in a democracy:

'The purpose of government is to make things happen. However, actually making something happen is extremely difficult in a well-developed democratic system. Checks and balances are built in to prevent radical change, and amongst the most effective of the brakes is the Civil Service.'[17]

Some of this is unfair and the causes lie more properly in the overall arrangements of how UK governments operate in Whitehall. Money—the fuel required to make the engine turn—is divided up and allocated to individual Departments of State by a three-year Comprehensive Spending Review, thereafter held by individual ministers and not centrally by the Prime Minister. So, if the Prime Minister wants to achieve some cross-departmental outcome, he has to ask his ministers to give some money back. Furthermore, any excess or contingency money is not in the Prime Minister's gift, but in the hands of the Chancellor of the Exchequer. To the military, it seemed that under Gordon Brown as Chancellor those hands were most often kept in his pocket. Achieving a difficult outcome requires sustained heavy lifting and arm twisting by a Prime Minister, and too often his attention has moved elsewhere before an outcome is achieved. When reinforcements were required to follow up the early success of Operation Sinbad in Basra in 2008, for instance, Prime Minister Blair said 'OK guys, sort it out—the money must be found', but it never materialised.[18]

Admiral Blackham, an experienced MoD hand, had strong views about the way the Civil Service operated in the Defence head office. He thought that the central problem was that:

'Success for [MoD] Civil Servants was hard to come by, but failure was ever present. This led them to ticking boxes and keeping their head down, the "deification of process" as a way of avoiding blame, to dragging decision-making by Civil Servants up to the highest level, thus preventing those lower down in the civil service from taking responsibility.'

When a decision could not be avoided, Blackham felt that:

'... the Civil Servants would spin it out over a very long time, look for excessive quantities of proof, look for a process to shelter in, or just defer to the military.'[19]

From their side, civil servants believe that the military have an exaggerated view their own role and importance. Desmond Bowen (MoD Policy Director 2004–8) summed this up by saying:

'… the military are the servants of the state, not the other way around. They do what the politicians ask, not what they think is right, or what they want to do. Anyway, military strategy alone is always too simplistic. There is always a bigger strategic picture and real policy is always more multi-faceted [than the military allows]. During Iraq and Afghanistan the Government had to consider many other matters, not least: foreign policy and alliance needs, the emerging energy crisis for the UK, regional effects in the wider Middle East and the challenge of domestic terrorism. For any government, getting re-elected will always be the first priority and all that flows from achieving that. It is politics.'[20]

Bowen went on to say that:

'… the military are assertive by nature and have sharp elbows, so were often able to get their way in discussions in Whitehall. Organisationally, there was no equivalent to them and their ability to run complex operations [gave them a natural advantage compared with other departments].'

Here is a picture of civil servants who thought the military were constantly pushing at the boundaries of what they were supposed to do and, in their own minds, the civil servants saw themselves as an important bulwark against the military over-reaching within the democratic process. But that nannying view collided with where the military were coming from, as General Sir Mike Jackson observed:

'Civil servants refused to accept, indeed did not recognise, the absolute nature of war, which required us as individuals to subordinate ourselves to the team. Rather, Civil Servants imagined that they represented democratic civilian control of us the military, whereas that task lay more properly with our political masters.'[21]

In summary, civil servants are highly intelligent, hard-working, capable, dedicated, principled, deft and accommodating; but they can be over-territorial, uncertain, process-bound, opaque and too ready to prove a point for the sake of it. They, of course, have a small but destructive quota of the vain, insecure and worried amongst them. The top stream of civil servants are too often guilty of patronising the rest and, like everyone else in the MoD, they are not beyond playing games and scoring points. Although many good working friendships were formed and many civil servants were held in very high regard, they were not as closely integrated with their professional military colleagues as they should have been and they were in collision with their military partners in the MoD on too many issues. Whereas, when dealing with issues of national security, these matters deserved and should have been given the closest of relationships and an acceptance of common strategic interest; as Desmond Bowen, a civil servant and Policy Director in the MoD, observed: 'Unity at the top of the political and military command chain is vital to success.'[22]

The First and Second Permanent Secretaries

The top civil servant in the Ministry of Defence is the Permanent Under Secretary (or PUS). He or she is the head of the Department of State for Defence (which, combined with the UK's highest military headquarters, makes the UK Ministry of Defence).[23] He or she is appointed as the Accounting Officer by Parliament and so is literally the person who accounts for all the money, a task that dominated the PUS's life in the decade 2000–10.[24] No military manager was ever satisfied that he had enough resources and it was the PUS's unenviable task to rein that in to ensure that the government's funds were used in the most effective way, overriding or disappointing the military in almost every case. The PUS was supported by a Second Permanent Under Secretary (2nd PUS), who acted as his chief operating officer on finance and administration, and so was similarly tarred (although the post ceased in 2010).

Sir Kevin Tebbit, the PUS 1998–2005, had been appointed with the task of sorting out the MoD's finances, which were widely perceived in Whitehall as being too loosely controlled and too poorly forecast. He inherited a financial dog's breakfast that followed from a £600m shortfall in the funding allocated in the Government's next Comprehensive Spending Review after the 1998 Defence Review. This was compounded by a new drive for efficiencies, where a wrong assumption was made by the MoD Finance Director that savings from efficiencies could be used elsewhere in the Defence budget. Too late it was discovered that the Treasury intended the efficiencies to be used to reduce the MoD's total allocation of funds. Tebbit was saddled with the wounding task of being the bearer of such bad news and he would say later that budget issues dominated his existence throughout his time as PUS.

Of course, distracted by finance, Sir Kevin Tebbit would have less energy for the other important parts of his portfolio, such as giving advice on policy or being a wise head in chiefly discussions. Despite that, he certainly influenced events, for instance framing the questions for Dr John Reid to put to the CDS over the feasibility of plans to go to Helmand. One of his subordinates suggested that Tebbit played a strong hand as PUS in ensuring that a legal justification existed for the invasion of Iraq, although that is not how Admiral Lord Boyce, who wrote to the government, remembers it. For someone who had formerly been head of GCHQ (the Government's main electronic intelligence-gathering body) and thus very familiar with the whole apparatus of intelligence in the UK, Sir Kevin Tebbit should have been well placed to spot the intelligence gaps that so fatally occurred later on.

Sir Kevin Tebbit was followed by Sir Bill Jeffrey, who had played an important role in the Northern Ireland Office as the Good Friday Accord was being implemented; he moved from being Head of the Immigration and Nationality Directorate to the Cabinet Office Security and Intelligence Coordinator and then to the Ministry of Defence. He better fitted Anthony Sampson's description of 'more the master bureaucrat … than the military authority', and one senior Civil Service colleague observed that 'Jeffrey was never comfortable in defence'.[25] But, yet again, Jeffrey had important credentials with which to make a decisive contribution to avoiding some of the events that subsequently went awry.

The Military in the MoD

'The character of a soldier is high. They who stand forth the foremost in danger, for the community, have the respect of mankind. An officer is much more respected than any other man who has as little money.'[26]

Samuel Johnson

So, finally, what of the soldiers, sailors and airmen who served in the MoD?

Military officers are noticeably shaped by their previous experience, which shines through everything they do and the way they act in an elemental way. Officers are taught from early adulthood that the individual is less important than the team, that much is expected of them in terms of example and personal courage, that loyalty is highly prized, that doing something is better than doing nothing, that perseverance and determination are admired, that chaotic situations need to be tamed by structure and order—and never to give up.

So the military officers in the MoD are characteristically dedicated, straightforward, capable and experienced. Many are articulate and clear thinking. They have a high sense of responsibility and public service. Generally outgoing and sociable, they want to contribute, but they often come to the MoD with little previous experience of the building or aptitude for working there.

Usually, officers alternate between combat units and working on the staff in two-year rotations. This has a sensible purpose: it keeps the staff in touch with the front line and the front line realistic about what the staff can deliver. It produces officers of wide experience, but often little specialisation. The speed of rotation through the postings means that he or she might commence a piece of work but would not be there for its completion, and inevitably they become disconnected from the consequences of that work. Alternatively, they might find themselves finishing a project that someone else had started and then struggle to capture the balance of factors and conditions that framed the original concept. He or she might lack understanding of what had been attempted, or might even decide to start all over again.

Work in the MoD can come as a shock for a number of reasons, not least that there is little previous training for it. Officers in units or ships will live near the top of a local hierarchy; in the MoD they are just another pair of hands. This is acutely so for the Service Chiefs, who have almost invariably just finished service as the Commander-in-Chief of all their combat units, with all the status, authority, camaraderie and satisfaction that goes with it. In the MoD, they are diminished: they carry out a *function* within a *bureaucracy*. They possess a much smaller personal staff, they are only one amongst some half dozen equivalents and, crucially, they have to strive to be heard. As General Sir Mike Jackson said, 'The Chiefs bear a heavy responsibility, but without the power to match.'[27]

A proportion of staff officers arrive in the MoD with no experience of working alongside civil servants and they struggle to understand their role in the process. The newness of this experience creates distrust about the motives of their civilian colleagues, unfairly so about a civilian cadre who were often only the messenger of bad budget news.

Life in a combat unit or ship is brisk compared with the MoD, where officers are physically very active, things happen quickly and decisions don't linger. Deskbound in the MoD they feel like caged lions, and the stately process of decisions comes to be seen not as sensible reflection, but as madness. As one senior officer commentated, 'they enter the MoD from the front line with their hair on fire, throw everything up into the air and depart frustrated. No wonder the Civil Service is bewildered and cautious.'

Other influences are at work which are more subtle and hardly mentioned, yet are just as strong. Officers are required to rise above their own service needs and to be 'joint' and instinctively they are, realising that their own service could only succeed by being supported within a wider organisation. But, if taunted by events or words, the joint approach soon closes down as they gather around the cause of their own home team. Not always, but often enough. In particular, in the deadly serious annual battle for resources, actions that would look distasteful in other circumstances are legitimised by an officer's sense that he or she was doing right by their own tribe.

Individual ambition sits uneasily within a strong team but, as von Clausewitz recognised, ambition is a key driver in successful commanders:

'… no substitute for a thirst for fame and honour. … It is primarily this spirit of endeavour on the part of commanders at all levels, this inventiveness, energy, and competitive enthusiasm which vitalises an army and makes it victorious … we may well ask whether history has ever known a great general who was not ambitious; whether, indeed, such a figure is conceivable.'[28]

Exaggerated ambition for one's own advancement, however, is regarded as very distasteful and such officers will be held at arm's length by their colleagues. So 'concealed ambition' is practised, making some officers Janus-like: one face for smiling upwards and one for frowning downwards. Of course this is inherent in all human nature, but the nature of the MoD gives it a special character and is an insidious restraint on the whole command chain in telling the truth to power.

Ambition and promotion are linked and exert a significant influence on behaviour. Advancement in rank as an officer is very visible and is at least as competitive in the armed services as in any commercial or public organisation, and most possibly more so.

For some, this is a scarring process and there are several reasons for it. The initial pool of officer talent is super-sifted by a refined entry process, which takes pains to select men and women who have the necessary talents to succeed. This makes them all rather similar. The raw material is then honed and improved by common officer training, into which all services invest greatly. The result is that most officers have similar attributes and each could easily be successful in posts of greater responsibility than they currently hold, at least in their early years. This is sensible—the services need more talent in peacetime than they can use, so that they can cope with expansion in times of tension. But it is an exquisitely painful experience for those who do *not* get selected for advancement, especially so for command of a unit or a major ship, which only occurs 15 years or so after the individual had committed himself, his life and his family to the process. It then reoccurs every few years or so as selection is made for higher commands or top jobs. Some are content to move sideways at these points but, to most, the spectre of *non-selection* sits ever present, influencing their actions.

The services have to cull numbers across each age stratum, so as to maintain a narrowing pyramid of officers towards the top and to make sure that the officer corps remains physically able and young. They do it as fairly as possible, with an open system whose rules are public. The Royal Navy promotes all officers to Lieutenant Commander by age and length of service, but then operates a system of 'up or out', whereby if after a specified number of years in a rank they have not been promoted, they leave. Promotion to Captain in the Army is almost solely by length of service, after which officers are batched by year of birth, coming into a 'zone for promotion' on a conveyor belt. The best of each year group are competitively selected for promotion. Since most postings last only two years, officers have to face the prospect that they might suddenly stop ascending every other year. With the next age-batch pushing in from just behind them, the chances of getting back into the competition, once excluded, are slim and these officers are termed 'passed over' for promotion. As a Brigadier, Mike Jackson was not selected for Brigade command until his third and last year for consideration, seriously rattling his confidence in his chances of future advancement; nonetheless he went on to become the Chief of the General Staff.[29] Towards the top, the field of candidates becomes narrower and narrower and General Lord Walker, reflecting on his own career, commentated that after Brigade command 'he had got onto a sort of escalator, which propelled him inexorably to the very top'.[30] Professor Anthony King has called this 'the golden escalator', which favours the chosen few whose jobs and experience are arranged so that they will continue to present as the most suitable candidate for advancement.

The rewards for those who are promoted are great and public. They gain a higher military rank, conferring authority, respect, privilege and prestige. Bizarrely to civilians, it might mean that their comrades of yesterday now salute and address them as 'Sir', at least in public. These benefits transfer in part to an officer's family—the size of house is determined by rank—and to the spouse in particular, exercising a special anxiety on the individual to succeed. And the penalties of not being selected are public too. This pressure is sustained as the very senior officers enter the zone for the top job in their service and this inevitably influences their behaviour in the run-up to final selection—who wouldn't want to improve their chances to advance? Once they gain that position in their own service, they find themselves thrust in yet another competition, with an even more glittering prize, for selection as Chief of the Defence Staff. For those officers who know that they would have been perfectly capable of doing a job in a higher rank but were not given the chance, the worm of jealousy can grow, leading some to retaliate at being 'passed over' with a stubborn lack of cooperation or a pedantic approach.

There is no real equivalent of this treadmill of advancement in commercial life, where reward is much more linked to pay (about which open discussion is rare) and performance. Significant promotions have much greater gaps between them, the steps are fewer and less conspicuously differentiated and the pool of talent within a company is smaller (whilst the pool within a global industry is for everyday purposes infinite).

The results of these influences are a curious mix. Many military officers are driven to work long hours, either because of the obligation their developed sense of loyalty places upon them or because they fear failure. In working such long hours, they exhaust themselves of the ability to think clearly and creatively. Some officers believe that application can substitute for talent, if only they can work hard enough. Orderly by nature, some officers invent schemes to stop chaotic circumstances overwhelming their task—templates, operational states boards, etc., all to the good—but this tempts them to reach too readily for process and become process-driven. They then became nervous of uncertainty, because it challenges the structure that they have created. By contrast, an instinctively able general is seeking chaos, since he knows it gives him the opportunity to out-think his opponent in rapidly changing circumstances. This produces an interesting tug of viewpoint between such a general and his staff, the latter more in tune with process and consensus than with the general's appetite for disorder and confrontation.

Officers in the MoD often have a surprising reluctance to step away from a policy position handed down to them through the chain of command. There are several reasons for this: a developed sense of loyalty; being long-schooled in team effort; the recognition of the need to 'support the chief'. This moral tension means that dissent is too rare, too muted and unlikely to be prosecuted beyond a first challenge.

Finally, their immediate superior has the deciding influence on whether they advance or not. This makes for a very complicated relationship. For some, telling the truth to their superiors becomes difficult because they feel that bad news or harsh advice reflects poorly on the messenger. For others, that they must display the intellectual plumage of a kingfisher and dazzle their superior with their ability. The awful truth is that a competent superior easily spots these false motives and the effect is exactly the opposite of what is intended, but meanwhile that superior is not getting the complete truth from his subordinates.

It has been emphasised several times how early experience is deeply formative, and if you look at any middle-ranking or senior officer you can see clear brush marks of his or her first experience as an officer. The difference in character between submarine commanders and surface ship commanders in the Royal Navy, both highly competent groups, is stark even today, with the former especially characterised as 'silent and deep'. Some parts of the military are ground down even in peacetime by the relentless demands of their existence. I think here of logisticians, aircraft engineers, or the combat signallers who connect the generals in the unforgiving territory of mobile communications. Fun and social diversion are remote bedfellows for these workmanlike branches. Given the unrelenting nature of their task, their senior officers typically evolve as rather more serious about themselves and their job, but probably with a narrower perspective.

Other officers have rather less to do and are less challenged in peacetime, even though they might be called upon to do startlingly brave and complex acts in battle. An armoured regiment finds itself with much time on its hands once the squadron work-up and regimental annual camp is out of the way, whereas a logistic unit delivers stores day in day out. Fighter squadrons need other diversions when a monthly allocation of fuel limits the number of hours they can fly, whereas search and rescue helicopter pilots are consistently busy. Robert Massie tried to unravel the reasons for the underperformance of the Royal Navy against the Germans at Jutland in 1916 and traced the failure in gunnery back to attitudes in the Royal Navy's Mediterranean Fleet in the years before the war, where 'form' and 'appearance' equalled or exceeded military function in a naval commander's mental map of the world.[31] Fun and/or society had become the important activity and diverted away from war-fighting purpose. Officers from this world can make expansive, confident but sometimes superficial leaders, not really serious about their jobs.

I shall not dwell on this because much of it is of course a huge generalisation. Any one of the units in the 'fun' end of the armed services can find themselves in a relentless grind of operational deployments, where fun is a distant cousin and hard-won experience is gained aplenty.

There are other influences on a flourishing career. It is extraordinary how, in certain ships, regiments and squadrons, a comet's tail of successful officers can rise from living within a culture of inspiring leadership, or through patronage. Many officers on ships commanded by Admiral Sir Sandy Woodward progressed to higher rank, crafted and moulded by the experience of serving under him.[32] One small battalion of infantry from Yorkshire with never more than 40 officers at any one time, the Green Howards, produced in thirty years Field Marshal Sir Nigel Bagnall (CGS and intellectual master of the UK's operational theory), Field Marshal Lord Inge (CGS, CDS), General Lord Dannatt (CGS) and General Sir Nicholas Houghton (Vice Chief of the Defence Staff and now CDS). This really is an exceptional clutch of developed talent and military success, far beyond happenstance. Likewise, for example, the Army's infantry regiment 'The Rifles' (with their decidedly academic outlook and strong tradition of professional competence back to 1803 with the creation of the first light infantry regiments by Sir John Moore) have produced a disproportionate number of successful military leaders.

At an early age these people have had their ambition set, their soldierly skills engrained, their minds opened and/or a pathway upwards opened. By contrast, very many regiments and units have never produced *any* successful senior officers, no doubt because there was none present to light the spark in a young mind or to act as a senior sponsor.

Different World Views

The public think of all officers as broadly similar, but the truth is that they are often poles apart, reflecting the differences in the environments in which they work and fight and the biases that have been created in an individual's mind over time. These differences expand to fill more of their creative space as they grow older and as they become more senior.

I shall attempt to show how different the founding experiences of these individuals are and how the services differ from each other, and here I am grateful for insights of a retired US Admiral J. C. Wylie.[33] Inevitably, as a long-serving army officer myself, I must struggle somewhat to achieve an even balance between the different services but, knowing that, you will be able to interpret the facts as you see them yourself.

The Royal Navy

In past centuries, warfare for the Royal Navy had combined the physical discomfort of years of ocean living, months of tedious blockade duties, long voyages away from home with very brutal close combat once it was joined. Naval officers had to be tough, inspiring and personally very courageous, as Admiral Lord Nelson amply demonstrated losing his arm leading a raid ashore against the Spanish at Santa Cruz in Tenerife and an eye from a shell splinter besieging the fortress of Calvi in Corsica. Later the Navy became much more technical, with new sciences of telegraphy, breech-loaded gunnery and turbine propulsion to be mastered, which combined together to produce, for instance, the Dreadnoughts. It is worth comparison that, by the start of the First World War, the Navy had developed the technologies to submerge a floating hull, fire a torpedo, and motor and breathe underwater, yet the Army took until 1917 to field a technically less challenging innovation, the tank, and much of the technology used to develop 'land ships' was provided by the Royal Navy (although the Navy itself was initially unsure about what it had conceived with submarines, with Admiral of the Fleet Sir Arthur Wilson VC summing up the opinion of the Admiralty Board in 1901 as 'underhand, unfair, and damned un-English ... treat all submarines as pirates in wartime ... and hang all crews').[34]

Neither was the form of naval warfare static. As signalling means developed and gunnery ranges increased, naval battles began to disperse over many miles and naval warfare itself emerged as a complicated ballet directed from central war rooms or command ships. Close combat was joined using battleships, submarines and aircraft, but by the end of the Second World War submarines and aircraft carriers (with their embarked fighters and bombers) had replaced battleships as the dominant naval platform. There was an echo to this more recently when the UK dispatched and sustained a naval taskforce in 1982 to do battle to recover the Falkland Islands, some 8,000 miles away from the UK. The ensuing campaign exposed both naval strengths and weaknesses— for instance, the supreme threat posed by hunter–killer submarines, the vulnerability of surface fleets lacking effective air defence and the deadly impact of anti-ship missiles. For the Navy, this was a brutal war and their leadership was not found wanting, but it begged the question of whether the Royal Navy should continue to be configured so as to be able to repeat it.

One part of the Royal Navy in the last two decades found itself continuously at the threshold of combat in a way not experienced elsewhere in the UK armed forces. The nuclear hunter–killer submarine fleet was tasked to shadow, plot and observe the Soviet Navy from very close quarters. One UK submarine positioned itself ten feet under the Russian aircraft carrier *Kiev* and tracked it for several days.[35] These operations required nerve, cunning, skill and resolve to a high order and their commanders were conditioned by the experience. It is little wonder that a disproportionate number of submariners subsequently reached high ranks.

Nowadays, the Royal Navy has twin purposes which are quite distinct. They must maintain the 'wooden walls' for the defence of the homeland of Britain, yet also secure global sea lanes for the nation's economic wellbeing. They think of the latter in terms of 'power projection', the ability to deliver armed force at a distance from the homeland in support of policy aims, so they need to equip themselves with carrier-borne aircraft and amphibious landing forces to deliver combat power at a distance. It evolved further into a broader concept of 'Maritime Strike', attacking land targets from the sea, a politically attractive way of influencing events from within neutral international waters. Since 1968, the Royal Navy has also provided the UK's nuclear deterrent from a fleet of ballistic missile, nuclear-powered submarines.

The Royal Navy knows about three-dimensional warfare, for instance deploying submarines below the surface and maritime aviation above it, but its view is unhindered by mountain ranges or deserts—navies go around them. In this, the Navy has a global, flat-sea world view. The ship-borne Navy has little contact with the messy circumstances of civilian populations in a conflict zone and little visual contact with the enemy, but warfare is as dangerous for the Navy as for any once battle is joined.[36] Modern naval warfare demands that the Royal Navy is ever-prepared and rehearsed, but that its ships fight infrequently, meaning that the onset of war is always a shock and time is needed to settle down to its realities. The Royal Navy was institutionally surprised at the onset of the Falklands campaign to discover that the aluminium superstructure of some of its frigates burned uncontrollably when struck by anti-ship missiles.

Naval officers specialise early: surface, undersea, maritime aviation and marine commando. These are very different tasks and produce senior officers with varying perspectives. In particular, command of a warship is a special and formative experience. Traditionally it is a very isolated life, as the ship's commander strives to keep a necessary separation between him or herself and the crew within a military structure. Given that a Royal Navy officer does many other things and only spends a third of their life at sea, ship-handling of iconic naval platforms in the public gaze is a challenge and more difficult than for his/her commercial equivalents. This act requires inner certainty and a containment of concerns not suffered by commanders in the other services, leaving a strong mark on personality thereafter. In a few cases, the enduring imprint is a reluctance to engage in open discussion.

The UK's First Sea Lord's existence for the last fifteen years has been completely dominated by safeguarding the future of the new Maritime Strike capability, to be finally delivered 2018–22, comprising two 65,000 ton aircraft carriers and embarked modern aircraft. This has subordinated the endless struggle of keeping the existing active fleet up to date, for that has declined seriously during the carrier development years. Capital ships such as aircraft carriers if undefended are potentially a single point of failure and subject to catastrophic loss if they are sunk or disabled—the whole capability is suddenly lost—so they must have very substantial protection across the piece. They require a layered defence of other vessels and aircraft around them. The capital cost of all this dwarfs many other items in a nation's defence inventory and can only be created as part of a measured long-term programme. Each year, the First Sea Lord has to win the argument about the utility of a capability which is not linked directly to the defence of the UK homeland, where there are more than enough land-based airfields available already. And every time it is presented, he has to defend the right for his service to fly the carrier aircraft from a predatory RAF, who naturally sees flying airframes as being their business. He has to galvanise the serving Navy behind the project, who are much more concerned with the challenges and excitement of day-to-day naval activity.

This must continue to be a lonely struggle, requiring an all-consuming and single-minded approach and creating a substantial bias in all his other dealings in top MoD committees. As Jonathan Powell, Prime Minister Blair's Chief of Staff, noted after listening to a brief from the Chief of the Defence Staff, Admiral Sir Michael Boyce, about a possible invasion of Afghanistan in 2002:

'We asked our military for a plan for an invasion, and Mike Boyce, the Chief of the Defence Staff, told us that it would take 250,000 men to mount. We were taken aback. He suggested, instead, deploying aircraft carriers, submarine-launched missiles and Royal Marines, which puzzled me given that Afghanistan was landlocked. Then I remembered he was an admiral.'[37]

In summary, for several centuries the Royal Navy was the most powerful navy in the world and proved itself to be amongst the most professional of all the armed services in the last World War. This inheritance lives on today with a strong feeling of being special, honed by a demanding life on the restless sea at the mercy of nature. Naval officers believe fiercely in the efficacy of sea power and, suspecting that Britain has lost its sea-mindedness, will fight relentlessly for the Naval budget, all the while delighting privately in their sobriquet as the 'Senior Service'.

The British Army

Being at war for the Army is rather different. During the period of imperial expansion from around 1700 until 1914, Britain saw her Army as less important than her Royal Navy, which had always been nurtured as the principal strategic fighting arm of the British Isles. Certainly Marlborough and Wellington won decisive land victories in Europe, but they were at the head of coalition, rather than national, armies. Wellington only took 30,000 troops to the Peninsular War in 1809, almost half the total British Army strength of only 80,000 men, at a time when the Royal Navy had 142,098 men and 755 ships in service and the French Grande Armée was 600,000 strong.[38] Later in the nineteenth century, a small British Army formed the core of a colonial security force, enhanced by much larger local levies. There were peaks in Army strength around the Battle of Waterloo (250,000), the Crimean War (250,000) and the Second Boer War 1901 (430,000), but overall it was still given proportionately less investment than the Royal Navy.

This changed somewhat in the run-up to the First World War with the creation of the first coherent, all-arms army formation: the British Expeditionary Force. Originally also intended for imperial defence, it was dispatched to the Low Countries at the outbreak of hostilities. A similar Mediterranean Expeditionary Force was created and took part in the landings at Gallipoli, and the model was followed for other theatres and for the forces raised in India. As the war progressed, the professional expeditionary forces were virtually destroyed and replaced by huge volunteer and then conscripted forces. The experience of the Second World War twenty years later was similar, with the small professional Army cadre soon either killed or diluted and reinforced by a very large expansion of volunteers and conscripts.

From the end of the Second World War, the British Army has been an army of three parts. An armoured army corps was garrisoned in Germany, known as the British Army of the Rhine (BAOR), until well after the end of the Cold War in 1989. Supporting NATO, this formed part of the front line against the Warsaw Pact on what was known as the Central Front (roughly modern Germany). BAOR exercises were tough and demanding but there was predictability about them, leading to the description of a 'Cold War warrior'—someone who was the master of process but would be unsettled by the unknown.

The second part of the Army was lighter, more mobile and with a global interest, known variously as the UK Strategic Reserve or 'out of area' force and the light infantry Royal Marine Commandos were de facto a part of it. These forces were mainly used to police the winding down of the British Empire and for civil emergencies. They formed the bulk of the troops used to counter the insurgency in Northern Ireland during the Troubles 1969–97. The final part of the Army was the Reserves, often ignored until the late 1990s. However, as regular manpower strengths were reduced year by year, the use made of the Reserves has expanded to become an essential 10 per cent of the forces sent on each Brigade rotation to Iraq and Afghanistan.

On operations, the Army frequently sees its enemy and comes into bloody, local contact with it. Casualties are expected and endured day in, day out, although the Army is unlikely to suffer catastrophic loss as when, for example, a ship is sunk. Even simple activities become difficult, codified by Clausewitz as the inherent 'friction' of land warfare. Mountains, rivers, and open spaces are hugely important; they decide the ease or difficulty of movement and they mask or reveal operations by either side. Human terrain—the local population—cannot be ignored and is often the dominating factor. Civilians get enmeshed in battles and their presence restricts the use of firepower. Civilians offer camouflage to the enemy, but looking after their safety could well be the reason that the Army was dispatched in the first place. What the terrain will look like once the war has passed limits the means employed to fight on it.[39]

Land warfare is a distinctly team activity, for it has many moving parts and strong team cohesion inspires soldiers to overcome the fears and stress of close contact with other people trying to kill them. Officers bond into their sub-tribe of a regiment or corps early in their careers and stay within that single unit for much longer than the other two services, giving a link so strong it seldom leaves them.[40] These bonds are vital in combat, but they result in an atomised force that struggles to find a common view about how it should fight or equip itself, and officers who are noticeably clannish.

The British Army is organised into field units of 400–700 men—battalions—and these are broken down into companies, squadrons and batteries of 100–200 men. They are arranged for different purposes: fighting units, supporting units and logistic units, but all come together into combat teams, often commonly facing danger. Some of the units are structured around individual fighters (the rifleman), whilst others organise around a weapon system (a tank and its crew). These are supported by combat aviation, indirect fire units (artillery), those who help others to live and move (engineers) or stay in communication (signals). Behind the front line, a fabric of logistic units provides supplies to the fighting echelons. Whilst a lot of high-tech equipment is present, platforms and technology do not dominate the Army to the same degree that they do in the other two services. There is truth in the homily that 'the Army equips the man, whilst the other two services man their equipment'.

War on the land is dominated by the terrain in all respects. It is a complicated, invariably chaotic, environment where there are typically lots of people—soldiers, prisoners, civilians, NGOs, media. The Army rapidly focuses down on to its given theatre of operations, which becomes its complete 'world'. This world is a bounded, relatively limited space dominated by the vagaries of the terrain, unlike the wider perspectives of the other two services. In this local world the Army regards itself as pre-eminent and supported by others. The trained strength of the British Army is more than twice the number found in each of the other two services, and it relies utterly on maintaining an intricate interdependent web of activity involving large numbers of people; it is a much messier, more manpower-intensive and less ordered environment than the other two services.

An Army officer's early career is largely spent within combat units, with progression to higher ranks at the age of 40, or over halfway through their career. This is an abrupt change in an Army officer's life, not mirrored so sharply in the other two services. Whilst they will stay in touch with their regiment or corps, they will now find themselves used for a wide variety of other tasks and commands, and contact with soldiers will be much more transient.

In contrast to the Royal Navy and RAF, the Army's equipment is noticeably less expensive and less technical, being lower value or using less technology. It is manpower numbers that drive the Army in the annual budgeting competition, making the Army vulnerable to short-term savings measures—for manpower numbers can be easily shaved and sliced to provide much quicker savings than large equipment programmes running over decades. The Army is a diverse organisation and it does not easily arrive at a settled view about its equipment priorities, so the Army's pitch for resources invariably lacks coherence and the commitment to a common line, and the supporting arguments are usually poorer. During the decade 2000–10 a confused debate emerged in Army circles around notions of a 'medium weight' fighting capability, thought necessary to fill in between heavy armour and lighter more quickly deployable infantry. The reality was that the Army needed to replace its infantry battlefield vehicle and had invented a concept for a new way of fighting around that new 'need', calling the vehicle the Future Rapid Effects System. Despite the name it was still only a vehicle, and its description had derived from the eagerly adopted but ridiculous notion of 'go first, go fast, go home' (a core theme of the 1998 Defence Review), as though the enemy had no influence over the rhythm of events and wars could be contained by arrangement. The glaring inconsistencies in these arguments were quickly unpicked by the rest of the MoD and were very wounding to the Army's credibility; people just laughed. As a result, the Army did less well in the annual budget competitions and became instinctively antagonistic towards the grand equipment programmes of the other services, which seemed to be hoovering up resources unfairly.

As if the annual budget rounds were not fractious enough for the Army, its Chiefs suffered even greater additional pressures during this period. Two confusing land wars—both under-resourced and lacking in public approval, and neither with a strategy to deliver victory—were being prosecuted. All the tribal loyalty that gave so much cohesion and fighting strength to the Army—bred and developed in an officer from their first day at Sandhurst—was piled onto the Chief of the General Staff as the casualties mounted and the banality of the current operational schemes became apparent. His was the burden of countering public scepticism around the wisdom of those adventures, as well as the ever-present worry of failure.

The Royal Air Force

Warfare for the Royal Air Force, or RAF, involves a mixture of technical competence for the many and stunning bravery for the few who fly and fight. Aerial combat—dogfights—dominated the birth of air power in the First World War, as solitary aircraft (usually) spotted for their artillery, dropped single bombs and fought off attackers, whilst enduring a very high casualty rate.

There was a tension between whether aircraft were just another weapon delivery system, like artillery, or a discrete armed force independently capable of achieving decisive effect against an enemy. Early ideas of the latter were framed by an Italian General, Giulio Douhet (1869–1930), who proposed that it should be possible to smash an enemy very quickly and decisively by assault from the air with overwhelming force. His hypothesis was strengthened following the bombing of the Spanish market town of Guernica by the Nazi Condor Legion in 1937, which gave a dramatic example of the destructive potential of air power. This led Britain's Prime Minster Stanley Baldwin to declare in Parliament 'I think that it is well for the man in the street to realise that there is no power on earth that can prevent him from being bombed. Whatever people may tell him, the bomber always gets through'. He went on 'the only defence is offence, which means that you will have to kill more women and children more quickly than the enemy if you want to save yourselves'.[41]

During World War II three important themes emerged to define air power for the UK. First, the fighter squadrons of the RAF were the immediate line of defence for the UK homeland during the crucial Battle of Britain, when invasion seemed inevitable. Indeed, the UK's fighter commander, Air Chief Marshal Sir Hugh Dowding, prevented any more fighters being sent to support the British Army retreating to Dunkirk in May 1940, so that they could be husbanded for homeland defence in the coming battle later that summer.[42] The fights of the Battle of Britain were often a meeting between two opposing aerial knights, alone, flying very powerful fighter aircraft. Second, in the desperate days of 1941 and 1942, the RAF's bombers were the only way left for Britain to continue to strike directly against the homeland of Nazi Germany, all at an appalling cost to the lives of bomber crews, with 55,573 killed, or 44 per cent of their strength. As Patrick Bishop observed 'flying in a bomber [in WWII] was a very dangerous business and it would become the most hazardous wartime activity open to British Servicemen'.[43] Third, the RAF also became very skilled at supporting the other services, cooperating with the Army in the Western Desert, Italy and across France, and with the Royal Navy as Coastal Command hunting submarines during the Battle of the Atlantic, for instance.

After WWII, enthusiasm for bombing waned as the Vietnam War demonstrated its limitations, but the advent of precision attack weapons fired from aircraft gave it a new purpose, with considerable success in the liberation of Kuwait and the no-fly zone over Iraq. Bombing was crucial in delivering the 'shock and awe' that led to the collapse of Saddam Hussein's regime in Iraq in 2003.

By the 1960s, air combat had developed into a precise calculation of numbers of aircraft and their rate of attrition relative to the enemy. As long as your losses were less than those of the enemy, you were winning. The efficient use of air resources demanded an unusually mathematical approach to combat planning which emerged in the form of an 'Air Tasking Order' covering each 24 hour period and generating numbers of sorties, delivering a tonnage of explosives to the battlefield according to a timed schedule. Conditioned by such arithmetic, air forces promoted an initiative known as the 'Effects Based Approach'. They proposed that, using information technology, all the components of an enemy's strength and will to resist could be listed and matched into a targeted attack plan. It soon became apparent that war situations were too complex to be orchestrated in such a mechanistic way, but precision attack by single warheads allowed air forces to move away from the simple delivery of gross tonnages, and air combat became increasingly a stand-off engagement, with crews shielded by distance from contact with the consequences of their actions.

That drumbeat of numbers is a connecting logic in the way that air forces organise themselves and is very different from the messy circumstances of land warfare or the element of chance inherent in naval operations. Administration, engineering, defence and piloting are all done by specialists and there is no career crossover between them. Aircraft are expensive, complicated, fragile and liable to catastrophic loss if just one link in the technological chain that keeps them aloft is broken—ships and tanks simply grind to a halt—and no other service is focused so acutely on a machine's vulnerability to sloppy practice. An irrefutable argument is made that each link of the chain has to perform: airfields, hangars, weapon systems, fuel etc., and the RAF has always been better organised and provided for in terms of equipment, accommodation and support than the other two services. The first aircrews flying into the airfield at Port Stanley after the cessation of hostilities in the Falklands rightly slept in an hotel, whilst their opposite numbers in the other services continued to survive in tents. Because the aircrews are the ones who do battle in an air force, they are regarded as the warrior caste and are privileged as such.

Military flying needs very particular human skills: spatial orientation, the ability to prioritise quickly between conflicting inputs, to work within processes, to focus on an output and, where required, to face danger.[44] Military flyers were initially a raffish, adventurous lot, who often as not had fitted uneasily into conventional military structures. As one early pilot in the Royal Flying Corps (the precursor to the RAF) said 'the RFC attracted the adventurous spirits, the devil-may-care young bloods of England, the fast-livers, the furious drivers, men who were not happy unless they were taking risks. This invested the RFC with a certain style. We had a sense of being the last word in warfare, the advance guard of wars to come'.[45] Today's pilots could not be more different, selected as they are for their ability to think linearly, using the 'logical' left side of the human brain, and that aptitude is honed by use of standard practices and checklists. The requirement to be creative—using the right side of the brain—inevitably scores less highly. Air Chief Marshal Sir Brian Burridge said that he saw this very clearly when Commandant of the UK's Joint Services Command and Staff College at Shrivenham. He noticed that, when compared to the Navy and Army, students from his own service had been bought up on detail (and were very good at it) but struggled when asked to do strategy.[46] He described how they came from an intensely technical world and 'had to work hard to lift their eyes above the tactical'. As young officers get promoted on the basis of their flying skills, there is inevitably a concentration of those with 'flying' skills at the top of the RAF.

The Royal Air Force is a young service, well used to rapid evolution and technical complexity. Like the Royal Navy, the RAF has a global, strategic vision and has husbanded the resources to enable it to reach worldwide. It only became a separate service after World War I and it still fears for that independence, so that preserving its size and demonstrating its utility have become part of an RAF officer's DNA. It is divided into fighter, bomber, reconnaissance and transport arms and contributes a significant number of helicopters to the UK's Joint Helicopter Command.

Maintaining the size and efficacy of their equipment fleet is—as in the Royal Navy—a dominant concern for senior officers in the RAF. This comes in two parts: continuing to purchase modern airframes with their weapon systems, and sustaining a pool of sufficiently qualified pilots. Key to this is an ordered flow of funds year in, year out, with surge expenditures for new aircraft types, whose costs are so large that they completely overwhelm all the other elements of the UK Defence budget. Paradoxically, it can be an easier task than that faced by the other big spender on capital projects, the Navy, because new aircraft are usually purchased within complicated multi-national procurement and industrial arrangements, with high penalties for withdrawal. But the total numbers are always under pressure, as cuts overall are demanded.

Like the First Sea Lord, the Chief of the Air Staff's life is dominated by keeping his air equipment programme 'sold' in the annual Defence budgeting bazaar. The special nature of flying exerts an additional distinct pressure: that aircraft fall out of the sky in incompetent hands or when poorly maintained. The Chief of the Air Staff is ever concerned about the safety of his airframes and the morale, quality, numbers and state of training of his pilots, and so is wary of the insidious effects of cutting fuel for training, spare parts, etc., or of over-runs by other projects in the Defence budget causing pressure on his own expenditure. These two demands make him a determined combatant in the annual Defence spending round.

Officers are Similar but Different

It should have become clear that whilst service officers are similar, they are by no means the same. All are forged under a single banner of 'warfare', but they have distinctly different attitudes. The Army will intuitively defend the fighting man above the potential that technology offers to substitute for him, whilst the other two will never completely comprehend the inherent friction in land operations that requires so much manpower. The Army might think that it has seen the most combat in the last fifty years, but that belies the courage and nerve to fly a fast jet daily or the tactical skill and coolness of character needed to tail a Russian submarine from only yards behind. As a result, their subconscious preconditioning—their bias—will be markedly different as they get into discussion, as will their approach to problems, their positions in debates and their instinctive answers to questions.

Since the end of the Cold War, a tussle has existed between the Army and Navy over who was dominant. The Army would claim that land forces had seen most combat since 1969—it frequently proselytised the idea that 'in the end conflicts are decided by who occupies the ground'—whilst the Navy cautioned that this was an aberration and that, as a maritime nation, investment in the fleet should be the UK's first strategic priority, as it had been 200 years previously. On the Navy's part, this took the form of continually challenging the manpower strength of the Army as being too large, whilst from the Army's point of view the programme for the naval aircraft carrier seemed both unaffordable in a time of restrained resources and inappropriate for the battles being fought—Afghanistan being a long way from the sea. To the side, the Royal Air Force attacked the flying professionalism of both, suggesting that the Army should not be entrusted to fly the complex Apache attack helicopter and that the Royal Navy lacked the 'air-mindedness' to operate the new F35 Lightning efficiently from its aircraft carriers, tasks it suggested were better suited to the RAF.

There is a part of the arrangements of the modern MoD that exposes these differences of approach and biases cruelly. Strongly preconditioned by their experience of how things work in their own service environments, officers moving to joint appointments are now required to understand the nuance of the tactics of their sister services. Some manage that effectively by consulting widely; some are damagingly incapable of doing so.

Working with a joint, three-star Director of Operations in the MoD demonstrated to me the collision between strongly held previous experience and the demands of a joint appointment. This officer had many years of sea experience, giving him an acute concern for the mechanical state of the Royal Navy ships then deployed to the Adriatic in support of the UN operation in Bosnia in 1994. It was what he knew about. In briefings, he would ask for a daily report on the delivery of some generator part or valve to the fleet and track its progress with concern, knowing from hard experience that a ship would be compromised without it.

By contrast, his understanding of messy land operations was distant from reality. He would ask why the troops took so long to get from A to B (across a mountain range), he was impatient with the inevitable complexities of supply and he had the notion that officers lived in considerable comfort in the field. He was a gifted, strong-minded and effective officer, but he was dominated by his previous experience and in these circumstances this knowledge did not serve him well. Likewise, an Air Force or Army officer would show exactly the same incomprehension if he or she were asked to direct an anti-submarine campaign.

But it is worse than that. When 'jointness' gathered pace in the early part of the decade, it became common for the two-star Joint Force Commander deployed to hotspots by the new Permanent Joint Headquarters (PJHQ) at Northwood to be selected from any service (i.e. he could be a rear admiral, major general or air vice marshal). These would all be very high calibre officers, who had been competitively chosen. They would have attended the Higher Command and Staff Course at the Defence Academy, where they would become agile at the sequencing of operations in the different environments of land, sea and air in combined operations practised in war-games. Crucially, however, they were learning about units, ships and air squadrons as represented by coloured counters on a screen, or as 'icons' on a map.

One such two-star Joint Force Commander explained to me how he was 'fighting' his brigades down a 'wadi' (dry watercourse) in an arid area during a command post exercise. It became clear that he gave very capable orders, could report the movement of the icons on the electronic map with clarity and he could correctly interpret the deftness of the synchronisation of units in time and space, but he had no real idea about the relative difficulty of the land units' task because he was from another service. He lacked that hard-won, innate, instinct for when to encourage and when to chide, when to support and when to leave well alone, or when the moment had come to commit the reserves. Again, it was not his fault; it was just as completely outside his previous experience.

This was to bite back during the wars in Afghanistan and Iraq, when a number of officers in senior posts in the MoD lacked what the Germans have described as the *Fingerspitzengefühl*, the fingertip feeling, for land operations. These officers were not bad or uncaring, nor Luddite towards change or over-obsessed by technology. They were just conditioned by the things that they had seen and done over long years previously.

Officers Behaving Badly

All of this so far has been about well-intentioned officers, behaving well. But in human nature, and in organisations created by humans, there is always a darker side, where the cynical and self-serving can be seen behaving badly.

Lieutenant General Sir Graeme Lamb was a special type of officer: tough, unconventional, widely read, naturally optimistic, inventive, cunning and artful. In 2006, he reflected rather colourfully on his brother officers, comparing them to his own standards thus:

'the majority I would rate as fair … a few I would gladly join with and assault hell's gate … and some I wouldn't follow to the latrine.'[47]

Of the latter, he went on to say:

'Well … the world for us is made up of two extremes: war and peace, which are unsurprisingly very different activities; activities that draw out and expose for better or worse two quite different characters.

In peace, the measure of one's business success is to be found in compromise, consensus, what the market will bear, management, the gains associated with clever debate, personal ambition (which should be made of sterner stuff, but seldom is) and, oh, so clever arguments crafted to support a master's voice, selected arguments that are seductively eloquent, compelling arguments that brief well, constructed by wordsmiths whose object is simply to win the case, much like the legal profession at any cost—and, if you succeed and win the proposition for your leader, then it is onward and upward limitless promotion.

So in peace it is superficiality, spin, image, short-termism not substance, which more often than not will do nicely.'

His key point was that officers were not being honest in what they were saying or doing, but anticipating their master's wishes largely for the purpose of their own advancement. Lamb also deplored the eternal pursuit of consensus.

This does not describe the behaviour of the average officer on the average day, or even 95 per cent of officers for 95 per cent of the time. They are all very much better than that. But what Graeme Lamb, a man in love with the poetry of words, does describe so well is what can appear at the edges: fringe personalities, or the fringes of normal personalities that are under great pressure. Here he is spot on, for officers find themselves under great stress in the MoD, which can distort their personality. The most malign pressure is the obvious and public reward for success: advancement in rank, with all its benefits in esteem, reward and public recognition, which would turn even the most humble head; but also the notion that not to be promoted was failure, with all its shame. Matt Kavanagh, Special Adviser to the Defence Secretary 2006–8, described these antics as 'truly shocking'. There is also intense peer pressure to deliver work (whether it was right or wrong), or else lose respect.

Major General Andrew MacKay, who commanded the 52nd Infantry Brigade in Helmand in 2007, was equally critical of some of his brother officers, but MacKay was much more focused on their ability to perform in battle:

'A cull should be instigated of the senior commanders not fit for their role in the war at hand … promotion systems should be torn up and replaced with those apt for a war; those fit for command should not be kept waiting to assume responsibility.'[48]

Where this is true, poor decision-making is, literally, lethal for the troops being commanded. But the services are pretty ruthless about weeding out those who are temperamentally unsuited to command a long way before they can be so destructive. Nonetheless Frank Ledwidge observed that, both in Iraq and Afghanistan, no UK commander was ever sacked.[49] Thomas Ricks in his book *The Generals* makes the same argument about the modern United States Army and, with typical American directness, lists all those who should have been let go.[50]

Norman Dixon in *The Psychology of Military Incompetence* (a piece still read with rising anxiety by most officers) offers some ideas about how this can come about.[51] He proposes that a strongly hierarchical structure, such as the military, can catch the fancy of inadequate personalities and then develop further dysfunctional traits within them. He suggests that hierarchy bestows comfort through rank and privilege to those who were socially uncertain and to the intellectually stunted. The paradox is that the least able to perform in the stress of battle are the most attracted to the organisation that would actually have to fight, the military. Such a personality could find himself very much at home in the bureaucracy that is the province of the Ministry of Defence.

Nicholas Heaven, who retired from the Royal Artillery as a captain, said he regarded the Army system as 'flawed' with, he believed, 'too much sucking up to the level above going on'. His experience was that each layer might add its own twist, so that the person at the top was fed a distorted picture. He also said that he observed that promotion was not entirely on merit or ability.[52] He went on that, whilst in industry even the most junior would be prepared to say 'hey, that won't work', in the Army everyone just kept under cover and rallied around to try to make it work. Putting a different view, Dr Rob Johnson (now a distinguished Oxford academic, who had once served as a junior officer in the British Army) recounted how he was dismayed to meet officers who were 'ambitious, ruthless, class-conscious careerists'. This remark struck home hard because Dr Johnson was serving as a captain in the Devonshire and Dorset Regiment, one of the infantry battle groups in the brigade I was commanding at that time, 6th Armoured Brigade, when these views were formed. I had remained blissfully unaware of such undercurrents.

Colonel Christopher Davies, another retired officer, was asked whether he agreed with those views and he came back with an answer that is worth including:

'Growing up in Liverpool where the local culture is underpinned by strong Irish–Catholic traits of aggression and "bolshiness", it never occurred to me that criticism, denigration and "facing up" were anything but normal ways of confronting new people, novel ideas and alien cultures. In the city of my nurture, such traits may be looked upon as strengths. It took me a while to realise that head-on confrontation was seen as aggressive opposition in the Army. My "masters" didn't like it and I was the loser: the "system" is simply too strong to be overcome by a headstrong individual—and that is one of its strengths.'

Of course, as is often the case in life, both sides had a point. I like to think that I learned wisdom as I got older. I even came to recognise that some of my "masters" were actually quite smart and deserving of my loyalty and obedience. I suppose, in the end, it all comes down to honesty. But we are dealing with human beings.'[53]

The Culture of the MoD

'The first thing he noticed was that Las Vegas seemed to have invented a new school of functional architecture, "The Gilded Mousetrap School" ... whose main purpose was to channel the customer-mouse into the central gambling trap ... whether he wanted the cheese or not.'

Ian Fleming, 'Diamonds Are Forever'

The MoD is both the supreme headquarters of the Armed Forces and the UK Department of State for Defence; it therefore has two heads: the Chief of the Defence Staff and the Permanent Under Secretary. This is a unique situation in UK government departments, and few other nations have such an arrangement either.

The Chief of the Defence Staff (CDS) leads the generation of combat power, whilst the Permanent Under Secretary (PUS) is responsible for the correct use of expenditure in accordance with the wishes of Parliament, for guidance to ministers and for legal issues. These two princes need a strong hand above them to coordinate their efforts, a role played in the structure by the political head, the Secretary of State for Defence and his ministerial team.

Despite the best efforts of all CDSs and PUSs the MoD remains an instinctively schizophrenic organisation. Because there are always two fiefdoms—military and civil service—there are always two chains upwards for staffing decisions, so decisions zigzag back and forth between them. A paper for a military issue would not succeed unless there was a parallel Civil Service endorsement for the necessary expenditure. Conversely, a budget adjustment proposed by a civil servant would be unlikely to be carried unless the military had also signed up to it. An elaborate dance of 'socialising' problems 'around the bazaars' takes place in order to get things through. As Des Browne, Secretary of State 2006–8, commented:

'As everything was staffed up through the MoD, everyone had to put their DNA on it. So it only ever came to me as a polished civil service/military paper, with everything in it cleared across Whitehall beforehand. But I found it difficult to get to the person who actually knew the answers, the person who had drafted the paper in the first place. I felt that the bureaucracy worked well for the interests of the bureaucracy.'

Unfortunately, this is a necessary process to reach consensus given the size of the staff and the twin staffing chains. Sometimes one side will try to bounce an issue on the other, but it is rare and scores might be settled elsewhere to destructive effect.

It is a surprising fact that there is not enough real work to do in the MoD and many people slave away at, frankly, invented tasks. The reasons for this are many. The military headquarters structure is designed to cope with the stresses of war, so inevitably it is under-stretched in peace. By one measure, power is decided by the size of the staff effort that can be harnessed, so large staffs represent power. There is scant reward in public service for getting things right, but blame soon appears if things go wrong, so there is a need to have the staff to cover every option, however unlikely. If a parallel branch in another service (or in the Civil Service) has a large staff, there is an inclination to match it so as to be able to bring equal horsepower to common issues. As joint branches are formed, sometimes the single services do not reduce their staffs to compensate. Senior officers in field units and headquarters are supported by substantial staffs out of necessity, so the idea of a brigadier or major general sitting alone at his desk in the MoD is not easy to imagine. Support staff accumulate over time, and the MoD is a recognised training organisation itself, so young officers are readily available.

Whilst many would agree that the MoD is overblown as a whole, few admit that it is their own branch that needs the cull. It would result in being caught out if a conflict happened, in losing a staff battle or having a budget reduced. So optional work is embraced as though it is essential, issues are over-staffed and debates continue long after they have reached a natural conclusion, all clogging up the system and camouflaging the really key work.

There is also human nature, in all its colours, at work in the MoD. People have 'agendas' that they pursue openly or covertly within the trading-pit of the Main Building, offering to support such-and-such a scheme if their own is supported in return. Ideas are floated out like balloons around the corridors to see where they might land, with no clarity of whose hand has released the string. People authoritatively quote their masters on matters, with their masters being completely unaware of the subject—especially when their masters are politicians. People form strong views on snap or lazy judgements, and then refuse to be argued out of them. Hallowed names are cited in defence of emotive issues—'so-and-so would just not allow it to happen'—especially when the issues are dealing with royal matters and the Household Division. People fudge their figures to get programmes into the overall budget, hoping to hide the real costs until it is too late. Alternatively, some people exaggerate their costs to show how it would be impossible to cancel a programme after so much had already been spent. Spurious or even dishonest reasons are invented to support ideas or to defeat others. Some people take positions because it gives them a personal advantage. Others just like playing poker.

Vice Admiral Sir Jeremy Blackham went further. In his experience, putting such an extravagance of civil servant and military intellectual talent into a head office with too little to do led to:

'… people playing games. It became … a game of wits where it was easy to forget what you were really there for. People got fascinated by The Game. Victory was gaining the policy hand, not the delivery of it.'[54]

To make this meshing together work at all, an elaborate committee structure has evolved; all to the good for producing consensus, but it leads to a lack of focus and responsibility. A problem is not owned and solved by any individual, but by *a committee*, which of course is an absurdity. Everyone rails at the committee system: the civil servants think the military are sloppy or opportunistic in their preparation (especially about finance), whilst the military think that civil servants are obstructive, obsessed with trivia and process, and wilfully detached from the reality of the front line. When looking into the bottom of their glass at the end of another long and tedious day in the Main Building, where issues had seemed to go nowhere or just stood still, the military would even accuse the civil servants of believing that simply the act of convening a meeting was the measurable output. But the committee system is an awful necessity in a large, diffuse structure with two parallel chains of command.

As a result, the real decisions are often taken in side conversations (whilst the committee could blunder on unaware that it had been usurped and, on becoming aware, its members are resentful). Too often the enormous staff horsepower of the MoD, and it is very great, is used *to justify a decision already taken*, not to analyse the factors and propose the options for sensible courses of action.

The culture in the MoD deteriorated towards the end of the decade as the strains of insufficient forces to fight two different wars in two different theatres began to take its toll. Matt Kavanagh, Special Adviser to both the Defence Secretary and to the Prime Minister, saw the situation as follows:

'By 2009, the problem was that the military and the politicians were talking past each other. ... The MoD accused the Prime Minister of being indecisive, while the Prime Minister felt the MoD was not being strategic. Relations between the two sides deteriorated to an extent that they were unable to have constructive conversations, not just about the issue of troop numbers, but many other equally important issues as well.'[55]

Did it Matter?

'The MoD is intensely tribal. It is almost as though the MoD has been designed to create a system of mutually opposing forces, optimised to cause a lack of any forward motion.'

Amyas Morse, MoD Commercial Director 2006–9[56]

The complaints most often heard about the MoD is that it riven by inter-service rivalry, that MoD civil servants appear incompetent or self-serving, that the politicians at the top of the MoD are not up to the job and that the MoD resembles a bear-pit of parochial interests. That it is a battlefield of warring clans slugging it out, or is just impenetrable and perverse.

Pausing to reflect, those making these remarks should not be surprised, for the MoD is arranged to be all of those things. Good, well-intentioned public servants behave in the way they do because the MoD 'system' demands such behaviour from them. The Service Chiefs come into constant collision with one another because they are defending their part of the budget and aggressively fostering the public profile of their service to secure it. This parochialism compromises their collegiate role of formulating joint military advice. Civil servants are constantly chasing the freer-wheeling military to be more exact with their spending, conscious that the wrath of Parliamentary committees is close by ready to deplore financial inexactitude. The Secretaries of State are without previous military experience and, in the decade 2000–10, they succeeded each other with alarming frequency, so it is hard for them to challenge military expertise and they are in some respects innocent of the MoD processes. Lieutenant General Sir Rob Fry explained how he was sorry for his Secretary of State, Des Browne, 'who was trying to follow ever-changing military advice and valiantly doing his best'.

There are simple organisational reasons for two of these problems. Money has been allocated only annually to the MoD for centuries, as a necessary democratic restraint on a too-powerful military; this makes efficient long-term budgeting very difficult indeed and overseeing that expenditure is rightly the obsession of the appropriate Parliamentary committees. However, the people who hoped *to spend* the public defence monies (the military) were not the same as the people who had *to account* for them (the Permanent Under Secretary and his civil servants). This sets the groups against each other and represents a separation between responsibility and accountability. Moreover, the 'spenders' are in competition with each other to secure the biggest chunk of the finite resources, since there is never enough to satisfy everyone's requirements and all go short to a greater or lesser extent. This makes the Service Chiefs budgetary rivals; intensely so.

Second, deploying the military instrument offers evidence of its usefulness to the nation, and hence ensures a continued funding stream. So the services are instinctively eager to respond to a call to arms for every deployment, whether appropriate or not. The Army was determined not to be left out of the order of battle for Iraq in 2003, which was one reason that the much larger Package 3 option was chosen.[57] In Afghanistan the RAF exchanged the existing Harrier aircraft (which could loiter, fly slowly and was well suited to supporting Army operations) for high-speed Tornado bomber aircraft; this spread wear and tear across the whole UK air fleet, but it was strongly suspected that it was being used to demonstrate the utility of the Tornado and perhaps to exclude the Navy's pilots who only flew Harriers. Lieutenant General Sir Rob Fry recalls, as the head of the Royal Marines, helping his First Sea Lord, Admiral Sir Nigel Essenhigh, at a policy conference with the Chiefs of Staff and the Prime Minister in 2002 to confirm the planning for the invasion of Iraq. They both came away elated, delighted at the institutional triumph of getting the UK's Commando Brigade included in the order of battle for the coming operation to overthrow Saddam Hussein. But there had been no discussion about whether the strategy was correct, or what they would do if things turned out poorly.

It is no wonder service officers are seen to be leaning forward for their branch to be used and to have rivalries between them; the MoD system sets them up to be like that. It no surprise that civil servants are focused more on the cost of doing things and less on how to achieve outcomes; they are constantly being wire-brushed by Parliament and the press about things they can't completely control. It is no accident that politicians are bemused by military complexity, because it is outside their previous experience and expertise.

You might even conclude that nobody was really in charge. The politicians were always selecting the cards that looked the most politically attractive from the weekly events, with less concern given to whether it was right or wrong militarily; they would then defer to the weight of military advice rather than making the decision that their office of state demanded, as illustrated by these quotations from Secretary of State Des Browne: '[I always followed] the … military advice' and John Reid: '… the advice of the Chiefs, which I always take'. The military would only propose what they thought the 'market would bear', although some of their subordinates were running around in frustration trying to goad the system into action and in the process overstating their case to get things moving. The civil servants were forever trying to increase their institutional powers and influence but then, as Jeremy Blackham observed, would demur if it looked as though they would be held accountable.

Well, these behaviours do matter. The catastrophic mismanagement of the Defence equipment budget in the decade 2000–10—a separate subject from this book—showed the consequences clearly enough.[58] All decisions in the last decade were influenced to some degree by malign imperatives within the MoD system, well beyond the circumstances that caused them or that they served. Proper analysis was not always undertaken and the right decisions were not always reached.

6

SETTING THE CONDITIONS FOR SUCCESS AND FAILURE

The Cold War made defence a simple calculation, as each side tried to over-match the military, political and economic strength of the other. As it drew to a close, difficult questions began to appear about how military force should be used in the future. The conflicts of the Cold War (for the US in Korea and Vietnam, and for the Russians in Afghanistan) had left deep imprints in the United States and a certain wariness about ever again becoming embroiled in protracted operations. To give some forward direction, the US Secretary of Defense Caspar Weinberger laid out his six principles for the use of American military power in a speech to the National Press Club in November 1984.[1]

The Weinberger Doctrine

Weinberger wanted to prevent the US from sliding into wars which it was unlikely to win, such as Vietnam, or where the interests were temporary, so he stated unequivocally that the American military instrument was only to be used for fighting wars in pursuit of vital national interests, where the reasons for going in had been well thought out beforehand. He championed six principles: US forces should only be committed in pursuit of vital national interests; with a clear intention of winning; within clearly defined political and military objectives; there should be regular reassessment of the forces needed and appropriate adjustments made; there should be public support; and the commitment of troops should be a last resort.

The disintegration of the Warsaw Pact military alliance in 1989 presented the West with a dilemma not completely answered by the Weinberger Doctrine. Whilst warfare involving major combat operations was still a theoretical possibility, there was no visible opponent who could pose such a threat, questioning the need to retain forces for major combat at all. Military chiefs, summoning all the warnings of history to substitute for any visible danger, urged instead that it was essential to retain the capability to win major wars. They proposed that the West's armed forces should be designed around the worst theoretical case, with the same capability adapted downwards to serve lesser purposes as they arose.[2] This preserved the existing framework of the Cold War—armoured divisions, fast jets, carrier strike fleets and nuclear submarines—but it encouraged the USA and her allies to approach warfare in that way, rather than appropriate to the threats that actually appeared. The result was firepower and technology at the expense of manpower—the idea was to crush, rather than persuade or police. Although the UK had been schooled from hard experience in the manpower-intensive military operations needed to overcome a bitter insurgency in Northern Ireland 1970–96, and should have known better, James de Waal correctly observed that too often 'fashionable American military thinking [was] quickly picked up and echoed in Britain'.[3]

The USA continued to modernise and update its forces at a prodigious rate, absent any peer competitor. It was as though Eisenhower's warning of a military–industrial complex with a momentum entirely of its own was true; the military enjoying new equipment and industry reaping the profit of producing it.[4] To stay alongside the USA as the remaining superpower, its allies were obliged to equip themselves likewise, so as to mesh in with the forces of the alliance leader. The result was a rather absurd 'arms race' within a friendly alliance (NATO) as everyone struggled to keep up with the US, with modernisation of defence forces being made because it was possible to do so, not necessarily because it was particularly needed.

These muscular armies were ill-prepared to counter the enemies that appeared and chose to fight. A succession of foes, watchful of the West's strengths, avoided attack in a matched competition and probed points of weakness instead. They did this with insurgency, terrorism, using menacing rhetoric, or by cocking a snook and jamming up the works of important global institutions such as the UN. Iran, Zimbabwe, Iraq, North Korea, Syria and Libya demonstrated this approach with varying success. As Sir Roderic Briathwaite, a former ambassador to the Soviet Union and the Russian Federation, commented later when looking back over the period: 'our failures in Iraq, Afghanistan, Libya, Egypt and Syria …[have] dramatised an unattractive truth: even the West's overwhelming military power does not enable us to shape the world according to our wishes.'5

Then, in 1991, Iraq suddenly invaded Kuwait. Saddam Hussein's old-fashioned land-grab took the West completely by surprise and seemed incredible in an increasingly interconnected world. But he was not in Kuwait for long and very soon his armed forces were efficiently and expeditiously ejected from the stolen territory by a US-led coalition, using the complete spectrum of military capability, from fast jets to special forces.

The Powell Doctrine

Seeing Saddam Hussein's forces smashed and fleeing northwards appeared to endorse the efficacy of designing combat forces for the worst case and adapting downwards for other wars. As the operation drew to a close, General Colin Powell (as Chairman of the US Joint Chiefs of Staff) took the moment to articulate an even more restricted vision for the use of US military power. Powell felt that he should apply a brake to political sentiments that were getting carried away with what military force might achieve; he needed to remind people of the dangers inherent in its use. The Powell Doctrine that followed derived many of its points from the previous Weinberger text (not surprising, since as a young officer Powell had helped to draft that) but Powell went further.6 His new emphasis was on having a clear exit strategy, full international public support and a limitation on costs.

It was also a time when the ways that wars might be fought were changing rapidly. New technologies turned military base metal into gold by combining precision targeting with stand-off attack—munitions fired from a distance—all made possible by secure and reliable communication links. Now it was less the stab of bayonets, more the hurling of high explosives with exquisite precision from a distance. It seemed that combat power could be more precisely applied, so that the military resources were more effective and less collateral damage would be inflicted. But it was not all one way. With significantly fewer soldiers required to deliver the same raw explosive effect on an enemy, armies reduced their manpower and, with that, diluted their ability to do other manpower-intensive military tasks, such as peacekeeping and counter-insurgency.

No Useable Doctrine

As ever, weaknesses were soon exposed. Powell's ideas were vigorously challenged because of his insistence on an 'exit strategy' before deployment, which was seen as unrealistic in a messy world. US Secretary of State Madeleine Albright asked in 1992: 'What's the point of having all this superb military that you're always talking about if we can't use it?'[7] Then, in a defining moment, a small but sophisticated US force helping the UN in Mogadishu, Somalia, in 1993 had to be suddenly withdrawn after nineteen US helicopters were lured into a small-arms ambush and two crashed during 'Operation Gothic Serpent', resulting in 18 US deaths (later immortalised in the film *Blackhawk Down*). It showed that US forces were powerfully and extravagantly equipped for the wars they thought they would fight, but were poorly adapted to fight the insurgencies that presented. The US had machines but a limit on the casualties that they were prepared to suffer; the warlords had wild men and an urban jungle.

This experience exposed the limits to the ways that technology and firepower could overmatch determined fighters, especially if dispersed amongst a civilian population. It demonstrated how casualties were a powerful indicator of failure in a non-vital intervention, how a democracy's resolve to continue was weakened in an 'optional' war when significant casualties occurred.

Soon afterwards in 1993 violence erupted in the former Yugoslavia on a scale and with such brutality that the West just could not ignore. As the inter-ethnic fighting in the Balkans intensified and mistreatment of civilian populations and prisoners became widespread, public outrage forced the UN to deploy a 'peacekeeping' force. The UK was keen to be involved in this, with Foreign Minister Douglas Hurd hoping that the UK would be able to 'punch above its weight' in military terms. The following year in Sarajevo under the command of a British officer, Lieutenant General Michael Rose, the UN adopted the policy of placing small detachments of UN soldiers around the disputed areas to 'shine a torch into dark corners'. Rose was an original thinker but a contrarian character and he resisted the idea that NATO, with all its firepower, should become involved.[8] Instead, he believed that the violence would be moderated by the presence of soldiers from the international community as observers. For a while this seemed to settle things down, but it ran its course spectacularly when the Serb entity called the UN's bluff and took many of its detachments hostage (including, as already discussed, a whole battalion of the British Army in Gorazde), using them as shields to deter NATO bombing. The intention of peacekeeping was obvious from the words used, but the way that 'peace' might be 'kept' (if none existed in the first place) was not addressed. Instead, people drifted into talking about 'peace enforcement', implying military coercion. But to enforce a peace, a greater military capability to overmatch the protagonists was needed, as well as the readiness to use it. Bosnia was not stabilised until Rose's successor, Lieutenant General Rupert Smith, adopted a hard-headed attitude and progressively brought in all the isolated UN detachments—clearing the battlefield of UN 'peacekeeper' soldiers—and began a coercive bombing campaign, which was very soon successful.

There were some warning signs here too. Against a ruthless enemy, even one equipped only with ageing weapons, isolated detachments were merely that: tokens and vulnerable to capture. Just 'doing good' did not solve problems that had deep and vicious roots within a community at war with itself. Playing at being soldiers—carrying weapons without instructions to use them—led to confusion and created a battlefield that was neither cleared for battle, nor safe to occupy.

Blair's Doctrine

In 1997, the newly elected Prime Minister of the United Kingdom entered this arena with firm ideas for change. Tony Blair led his New Labour movement to power with a fistful of initiatives to modernise the UK, from the economy, to education, and to the banking system. He also sought a profoundly altered use for military power, in addition to the traditional ones of defending the homeland and promoting stability in the international system. In a speech in Chicago in 1999 just before a major NATO summit, Blair outlined his ideas for a globally interconnected world. Towards the end, he suggested conditions under which nations might intervene to resolve a situation, if necessary by the use of military force.

Blair espoused a doctrine of 'liberal interventionism', which had its roots in British nineteenth-century foreign policy under Lord Palmerston and, later, President Woodrow Wilson's commitment to the expansion of democracy throughout the world. It was to be developed by others later and would emerge as the UN concept of 'R2P', or 'Responsibility to Protect'. Blair had discussed the speech in the margins of an event a few days before with Professor Sir Lawrence Freedman of King's College, London, and Freedman had given Blair a number of thoughts. From this outline, Blair constructed a major departure from the tautness, focus and self-interest of the Weinberger and Powell Doctrines.[9]

To use military force, Blair made five new proposals: that the West had to be sure of its case; that it should have exhausted all diplomatic options; that it should have explored whether military operations could be sensibly and prudently undertaken; and that it should be committed to the long term.[10] Only at the end did he say, 'Finally, did we have national interests involved?' Blair followed this up in 2002 by putting forward the idea of using military power as a 'force for good'.[11]

Blair made no mention now of restricting the use of military force to vital national interests, counting the cost before leaping into armed intervention, obtaining domestic and international support, or having an acceptable way out in the event of the unexpected, all the bulwarks of the Weinberger and Powell Doctrines. Instead, Blair questioned a whole-of-campaign approach by saying that '… in the past we talked too much of exit strategies'.

Blair was reacting to the pressure that 'something must be done', putting it above proper consideration of what could be done. In the circumstances of the day, it did not look too odd. The West had become frustrated that bad leaders were exploiting and preying on their own populations, recklessly threatening their neighbours or dangerously upsetting a regional peace. Sitting around a camp table one evening in a damp, abandoned villa in Vitez, central Bosnia, cold and frustrated, discussing the latest atrocities of thuggish gangs, the hugely experienced BBC war correspondent Martin Bell poked the nearest military representative in the chest and said:

'… You have got to do something!!'
I hesitated and replied: 'So … what should be done?'

Martin Bell had no answer, neither did anyone else and the conversation petered out. Bell's intense frustration at what he had seen and his moral outrage that the world was not a fairer place was filed daily in his reports, helping alongside others to frame the mindset of the policy-makers in the West.

In the face of such emotional pressures, Blair was now proposing that military force should be used as a device to solve wider world problems, alongside its traditional role as the measure of a nation's last resort. Blair proposed that the military could be used as policemen, as a substitute for the judiciary, and as humanitarian assistance in order to rebuild shattered and failed states. In a surprising twist, this 'liberal interventionism' was also adopted at the opposite end of the political spectrum by 'neo-conservatives' in the US, who wanted to promote Jeffersonian democracy if necessary by military means.

These pressures resonated with the military too, faced by the constant struggle to show their utility to taxpayers. As the Cold War drew to a close and with it the decline of a European continental threat, the UK Chiefs of Staff (with General Sir Edwin Bramall in the lead as Chief of the General Staff (CGS)) had argued for the requirement to be ready to conduct unspecified 'out-of-area' operations.[12] This was a sensible contingency in the light of an indefinite threat, but it fell straight into the arms of a political class edging towards using armed forces for less-than-vital interests. This trend reached its conceptual nadir in the 1998 UK Strategic Defence Review, which included the hymn that the UK forces would 'Go first. Go fast. Go home.'[13]

Both the politicians and the military had been heavily influenced by recent events. The wars of 1992–4 in the Balkans had ended when heads were knocked together at a conference at Dayton, Ohio, and a very powerful NATO land force sent to ensure compliance. In Kosovo in 1999, the UK government persuaded Europe and the NATO alliance to compel the Serbian government by military means to cede control of the province to the majority Albanian population, with Blair's Chicago speech about the need for liberal intervention delivered at the height of the crisis.[14] The intervention also forced an historic change in the UN charter (that had previously specifically protected the sovereignty of nations) when, under the authority of being a 'force for good', it was shown that sovereign states could be invaded in pursuit of humanitarian ends.

Finally, Sierra Leone was delivered from a brutal civil war when the UK military intervened in May 2000 to support President Kabbah, beleaguered in his capital Freetown by the rebel Revolutionary United Front.[15] Later, in September of that year, the UK demonstrated its strategic reach (a key tenet of the 1998 Defence Review) by rapidly sending a substantial airmobile force all the way from the UK to Sierra Leone in order to rescue a group of British soldiers that had been taken captive by a rebel faction, the 'West Side Boys'.[16] These operations left potent impressions about the effectiveness of the timely use of armed force.

Problems for the Military

But the armed forces were uneasy. Whilst these interventions could work spectacularly well, as happened in Sierra Leone and in Kosovo, there were also problems. Politicians seemed unknowing of the absolute nature of armed conflict, with too much subtlety and finesse ascribed to armed action—use it a bit, dial it up and down like a thermostat, turn it on and off at the switch—whilst forgetting that introducing further violence into a problem would cause the situation to take unexpected turns. Governments proved lazy about providing the complete range of instruments—economic, judicial, educational and policing—which would take advantage of any security pause imposed by the military. And, as we have said, the forces that the West had to hand were configured to fight major combat operations, not manpower-intensive counter-insurgency or counter-piracy engagements to bolster failed states.

There were also unfortunate spill-overs for the military. In wars of choice, politicians were ever ready to negotiate or accommodate, whereas for the military compromise or lack of success was viewed as defeat, rotting its self-esteem. Second, commitment instantly ratcheted up when a soldier was killed, with any idea of withdrawal seen as abandoning that soldier's life for little purpose. To the military mind, there was no going back short of success, once a deployment had been started.

SETTING THE CONDITIONS FOR SUCCESS AND FAILURE

What did the Changes Mean for the UK?

Britain's armed forces had moved since the end of the Cold War in 1969 from being focused on defending the European Central Front and the North Atlantic against the Soviet Union (where, if things had gone badly, nuclear release would have occurred) to a world where large-scale war, and nuclear war in particular, had become difficult to imagine. The UK armed forces remained well equipped and, through downsizing, were able to continue to acquire excellent equipment as they got smaller. They were also entering a technological revolution where precision attack, guided from the other side of the planet if need be, became a reality.

As the bipolar world dominated by two superpowers disintegrated, the restraints imposed by it dissolved. Military force might now be used to resolve lesser problems, championed by Prime Minster Blair under the doctrine of being 'a force for good' in support of liberal interventionism. Politicians thought that 'punching above your weight' cleverly leveraged available military strength, ignoring the consequences of such hubris if it were challenged. Whereas Weinberger and Powell had laid down strict conditions emphasising that armed forces were for the defence of vital national interests, opinion now moved towards using them more readily for solving less clear-cut problems, short of all-out war.

The next decade was to expose those weaknesses, as things developed rather differently under the twin stresses of the rise of al-Qaida and a non-compliant Saddam Hussein.

7

A LONG PEACE IS SHATTERED

'A magpie, seeing some light-coloured object conspicuous on the empty slope, flew closer to look, but all that lay there was a splintered peg and a twisted length of wire.'

Richard Adams, 'Watership Down'

The new Millennium began benignly enough and even the 'Y2K' computer bug proved to be a will o' the wisp. If anyone bothered to think about it on the Millennium night, they would have been satisfied at the way in which military power had been adapted to help solve the world's problems in a modern way. Bosnia was now peaceful to the surprise of many, the Albanian Kosovars were free from Serbian oppression and Sierra Leone's civil war had been brought to an end, pleasing the public mood 'to do something' and satisfying the armed services' eternal need to demonstrate their utility.

Events soon shattered that. On 10 March 2000 world stock markets collapsed by 10%, as the 'dot com' financial bubble evaporated in a cloud of microchip fairy dust.[1] Eighteen months later, on 11 September 2001, in a much more terrible event than any of the previous decade, a catastrophic terrorist attack using hijacked airliners demolished the huge structures of the Twin Towers in New York and severely damaged the Pentagon Building in Washington. These events left the US in particular doubly traumatised.

Political change was in the air too. The Clinton presidency was replaced in 2001 by a more nationalist-inclined elite under President George Bush

(2001–9), guided by the 'new conservative' ethic of proselytising democracy. Bush was bequeathed the US's largest-ever budget surplus ($237 billion in fiscal year 2000), but by 2008 the national debt had ballooned from $5 trillion to $11 trillion. The UK followed a parallel route. The Blair government came to power in 1997 with the UK economy in rude health and projecting a budget surplus, but a combination of excessive spending on public services and the expansion of the UK banking sector meant that its public finances were to become dangerously over-exposed to financial turbulence.

In 2008 the world suffered an economic heart attack, giving a recession at least as deep as the Great Depression of 1931. This limited the capacity of both the US and the UK to fight wars that were to go on for much longer than had been initially expected. For the UK, reducing its military commitment became a dominant theme towards the end of the decade and grievously reduced any chances of success.

The US and UK had reached the same parlous state under governments of distinctly different hue: the US was led by right-wing Republican neo-conservatives, whilst the UK had a centre–left-wing New Labour administration. Both were looking outwards to solve the world's problems: the US was the unchallenged super power conferring as it did a mantle of leadership, whilst the UK was unique amongst European nations in having such a global perspective. Both the US and the UK shared strong perceptions of right and wrong and a common conviction to address problems beyond their borders, in contrast to the much more pragmatic 'realpolitik' of previous decades when the Cold War had forced nations more readily to accept things as they were.

The Twin Towers

The sensational attack on buildings in American cities by al-Qaida was an infinitely more serious shock for the West than any for a generation. And it was far more serious than the issues that the West had been dealing with using the formula laid out in Blair's Chicago speech of April 1999, because it was an attack on the homeland of the US.

Western leaders coped well with the initial trauma and shock; they managed to settle their populations and displayed an impressively united and determined front to resist terrorism. There was great support for America from around the world, as Jean-Marie Colombani observed in the Paris newspaper *Le Monde* on 12 September 2001: '*Maintenant, nous sommes tous Americains*'. However, terrorism was an abstract thing, difficult to grasp, only evident by its murderous and destructive effects and was perpetrated by a very small number of people. It was extremely difficult to bring the traditional instruments of state power to bear on terrorists—shadowy, slippery and few in number as they were—and even more so to do it with conventional armed forces. Tom Brokaw (a reporter for NBC and an observer of the collapse of one of the towers) even asserted that 'there has been a declaration of war by terrorists on the United States' and the public mood was very much with him.[2]

So, nine days after the Twin Towers were attacked, Bush took charge of events and emotions by declaring a 'war on terror'. President Bush felt that there had been such an elemental assault on the liberty and the way of life of the US that it demanded the strongest response. Declaring war on an abstract idea such as terrorism was a challenge, but Bush wrote his blueprint for the coming years in an address to Congress on 20 September 2001, with the military clearly playing a leading role:

'Americans are asking: How will we fight and win this war? ... This war will not be like the war against Iraq a decade ago, with a decisive liberation of territory and a swift conclusion. It will not look like the air war above Kosovo two years ago, where no ground troops were used and not a single American was lost in combat. ... Americans should not expect one battle, but a lengthy campaign.

Every nation, in every region, now has a decision to make. Either you are with us, or you are with the terrorists. [Applause] From this day forward, any nation that continues to harbor or support terrorism will be regarded by the United States as a hostile regime.'[3]

He then went on to place the 9/11 attack alongside the other great events that had threatened American civilisation:

'Great harm has been done to us. We have suffered great loss. And in our grief and anger we have found our mission and our moment. Freedom and fear are at war.... we will not tire, we will not falter, and we will not fail.'[4]

It was fearsome rhetoric and, whether the President's view was correct or not, the style used and the emotive reaching back into previous times of threat shaped the views of the American population. Peace had been shattered and the underlying beneficence of the West challenged. A sense of being able to tame disorder by sensible cooperation between nations had disappeared. Instead, uncertainty and fear emerged, winnowing down the confidence of the West and igniting more basic instincts of self-preservation and defiance. So started the 'War on Terror', with its military element riding under a banner of 'Operation Enduring Freedom'.

As happened to all British prime ministers when they came to power, Tony Blair had to make up his mind where he would position the UK's foreign policy with respect to Europe and to the United States. In his early years in office, Blair decided to be neither in nor out of the European project; for instance, whilst deciding not to join the European common currency, he strongly supported the expansion of EU membership. As for the relationship with the US, Blair was much more single-minded and very firmly aligned himself and the UK government alongside the US, declaring in his memoir that 'our alliance with the US gave Britain a huge position [in the world]'.[5] In his speech to Congress on 17 July 2002 he put it thus:

'And our job, my nation that watched you grow, that you fought alongside and now fights alongside you, that takes enormous pride in our alliance and great affection in our common bond, *our job is to be there with you.*

You are not going to be alone.'[6]

So where the US decided to go, the UK would follow; hoping to influence the senior partner 'as Greece to Rome', but solidly in there. A recommitment was made by the UK to its 'special relationship' with the US and it was to mean that if the US went to war, the UK would go to war.

8

WAR COMES TO AFGHANISTAN IN 2001

'No one knew what anyone else was doing ... we entered both countries oblivious to how little we knew.' [1]

Robert Gates, 22nd US Secretary of Defense

Hunting al-Qaida

This change of mood, principally in the USA, soon found hard expression. Intelligence confirmed that the 9/11 attacks had been the work of Osama bin Laden, using his militant Islamist organisation, al-Qaida ('The Base'). Indeed bin Laden admitted as much on a chillingly unemotional video released soon after the event. The United States already regarded al-Qaida as a serious irritant, but perhaps one only to be contained and marginalised. Following the destruction of the Twin Towers, this sentiment changed dramatically and a messianic struggle to eliminate al-Qaida was to dominate the US domestic psyche for the next decade until Osama bin Laden was finally killed during a raid on his secret compound in Abbottabad, Pakistan on 2 May 2011, whilst every event and foreign policy issue seemed to be filtered by or tested against it.

Al-Qaida was operating openly from sanctuaries within Afghanistan, a country recently taken over by the Taliban (a fundamentalist Islamist party originally set up to confront the excesses that Afghani warlords visited on their peoples). The US asked Afghanistan to expel al-Qaida, echoing President

Bush's speech to Congress 'either you are with us, or you are with the terrorists. From this day forward, any nation that continues to harbor or support terrorism will be regarded by the United States as a hostile regime....' The Taliban government refused the demand (although there is evidence that a more subtle approach might have had more success), whereupon President Bush decided that the US had no alternative but to eliminate al-Qaida itself. Supported by US special forces and firepower from US aircraft, the Taliban were attacked by a dissident Afghan faction—the Northern Alliance—under US guidance. The UK was there too, sending special forces, a naval task group, a commando battle group and tanker, reconnaissance and surveillance aircraft.[2]

The Taliban were overwhelmed in battle within weeks and toppled from power. They fled with the remaining al-Qaida elements across the southern border with Pakistan into Waziristan. Meanwhile, the population of Afghanistan, already-traumatised following years of civil war, was freed from the fundamentalism of the Taliban but returned instead into the hands of warlords, all loosely coordinated from Kabul under the weak central authority of Hamid Karzai, the leader of the majority Pashtu group.

ISAF

As the Taliban departed, the coalition of interested Western nations quickly set up the International Security Assistance Force (ISAF) in Kabul to secure the Afghan capital and the immediate surrounding area. The UK played a important part, providing the first military commander and headquarters, the UK's 3rd Division under Major General John McColl. This was everything to do with Britain's policy of 'go first, go fast, go home' being played out. But at the same time, Britain also offered to lead the West's counter-narcotics effort in Afghanistan, a much more long-term task and one that would have profound effects later on. At the end of the first six month deployment, other nations came forward to replace the British lead and in turn ISAF was commanded by German and Turkish generals. There was still occasional violence, but the Provincial Reconstruction Teams deployed by ISAF to the north and west of the country were welcomed and increasingly effective.

WAR COMES TO AFGHANISTAN IN 2001

A Limited Success

President Bush had had little difficulty in getting approval to invade Afghanistan, given the threat that al-Qaida clearly posed. In one sense his campaign had been very successful, with al-Qaida scorched, the Taliban toppled and the remnants driven over the border into the wild tribal areas of Pakistan. But the initial energy devoted to overthrowing the Taliban soon petered out and what followed was done at no great speed, and always proved to be just behind what was needed. The Taliban regrouped and gradually reappeared in strength, leading the UK Director of Operations Lieutenant General Sir Rob Fry to observe later that the failure to capitalise on the victory over the Taliban was the single greatest strategic failure of the decade.

It also opened a box of slippery and venomous questions. How to govern the newly liberated Afghanistan? What should be done to improve the almost medieval conditions of rural Afghanistan? What could be done further to eradicate this abstract thing 'terrorism'? What to do about the huge collective insult delivered by the West to Islam by appearing to attack its culture and its tenets?

Unfortunately, the US and its partners were already looking elsewhere.

9

THE WAR ON TERROR OPENS IN IRAQ IN 2003

'Iraq is unquestionably one of the world's most difficult countries to govern ... Few other countries are so seriously divided in language and religion, with no natural majority. Few have such a powerful system of local, clan and family loyalties still flourishing beneath the formal political and administrative structures. Hardly any have so deeply entrenched a tradition of violent intrigue at every level...'

Gwynne Dyer in 'World Armies', 1979[1]

America's blood was up. Whilst the problem of al-Qaida in Afghanistan seemed to have been settled, a new threat in the US's 'War on Terror' was emerging in Iraq. Here Iraq's President, Saddam Hussein, was baiting the US by appearing to possess chemical weapons of mass destruction (WMD), in contravention of United Nations Resolution 1441. President Bush saw this behaviour as a threat to the region and to the US, so he set in train plans to overthrow the regime in Iraq if it failed to comply with the UN inspectors. John Scarlett, Chairman of the UK Joint Intelligence Committee, reported on 23 July 2002 that President Bush wanted 'to remove Saddam, through military action, justified by the conjunction of terrorism and WMD', but with Scarlett suspecting that 'the intelligence and facts were being fixed around the policy'.[2]

The story of the run-up to the invasion of Iraq by the US-led coalition in 2003, and the strong participation by the UK, is told extensively elsewhere, not least on the Chilcot Inquiry website.[3] Here, we address only the effects on the UK armed forces. Sufficient to say that they arrived in theatre capable and well-equipped—as yet undismayed by or unknowing of the consequences of war for the UK—and with a conviction that victory would be swiftly achieved.

The two nations collaborated closely when drawing up military options, with the UK trying to work out how to stay in touch and best fall in behind the US plan. As Brigadier Justin Maciejewski said afterwards:

'It was about the British political and institutional obsession with the British–US security relations; if the US was going to invade Iraq, the British would be alongside them; everything else was just military detail.'[4]

Overturning conventional wisdom, US Secretary of State for Defense Donald Rumsfeld estimated that a smaller force equipped with advanced technology could now defeat a conventional army in a pitched battle, reversing the historical calculation that an attacking force required a three-to-one superiority. Rumsfeld collided head-on about this with his Chief of the US Army Staff, General Eric Shinseki, the latter believing that 'hundreds of thousands of troops would be required to police post-war Iraq'.[5] Intelligence showed that Shinseki's plan had involved 'a slow build-up of 250,000 US troops'.[6] Major General Tim Cross, a UK officer attached to the US and assigned to help plan for post-conflict operations, supported Shinseki's assessment, but was frustrated later to find that the US and his own MoD in London moved away from it. To Cross, it was clear from the beginning that far too little attention was being given to preparing for what would be needed after the guns fell silent, a situation which he thought could easily collapse into chaos.[7]

The invasion was launched and, initially, Rumsfeld was right. After a short, intense air- and sea-launched bombing campaign, Baghdad and the other major cities were rapidly invested. A week after that, all military resistance ended, as the Iraqi Army collapsed. An economical victory, with the coalition armed forces choreographed forward by their commanders, had indeed been rapidly achieved. It was a remarkable feat of arms.

THE WAR ON TERROR OPENS IN IRAQ IN 2003

Aftermath of the Invasion

'The people of England have been led in Mesopotamia into a trap from which it will be hard to escape with dignity and honour. They have been tricked into it by a steady withholding of information. The Baghdad communiqués are belated, insincere, incomplete. Things have been far worse than we have been told, our administration more bloody and inefficient than the public knows ... We are today not far from a disaster.'

T. E. Lawrence, 'Report on Mesopotamia', The Sunday Times, 22 August 1920

As the fighting against Saddam Hussein's forces died down, looting and a general breakdown in law and order soon followed. In a letter to *The Times* it was suggested that now was the time to seize the moment and airlift in four acclimatised light infantry divisions from bases in the southern USA. This was a commonly held view and it was remarkable only in that the US found it impossible to do the obvious. After all the discussion about keeping the force technological and small, and with inter-departmental battle-lines drawn, it was never going to happen.

Long-held cultural instincts almost immediately resurfaced and the coalition was viewed as invaders. To its cost, the US Army was only configured for fighting high-intensity wars, not patrolling and protecting civilian populations. With too few numbers and the wrong equipment it often had to resort to firearms or the threat of violence to exercise control over a restive and traumatised population. In one awful event an army captain, billeted with his troops in a local school, felt himself justified in opening fire on 200 protesters, who were defying a curfew but only demanding to be allowed to re-open their school, with the result that 15 Iraqis were killed.

At this point, the coalition made some serious miscalculations. The command arrangements were untidy and reflected the long-term antagonism in Washington between the State Department (responsible for external affairs) and the Pentagon (which directed the military and which, up until that point, had been very much in charge). Senior military commanders fell out with the newly appointed civilian head of the Coalition Provisional Authority, Paul Bremer III, as their two departments of state in Washington jockeyed for supremacy. Meanwhile, the UK believed strongly that the role of nation-rebuilding was not the task of either organisation; that it lay more properly with the United Nations. With the UK lobbying hard for it, President Bush agreed to setting up a UN special representative and staff in Baghdad under a very capable Brazilian diplomat, Sergio Vieria De Mello. On 19 August 2003, this encouraging development for international civil control was snuffed-out when extremists blew up the UN headquarters in Baghdad, killing De Mello and 20 of his staff; as a result, the UN withdrew and, with it, the engagement of the wider international community.

As its internal divisions became deeper, the US appointed Bremer from the US State Department as *primus inter pares*. Unfortunately, Bremer was to fail to consult his military opposite numbers sufficiently about his plans, or to inform them of his actions. Soon trust between the civilian and military groups collapsed entirely. The US Army compounded this by withdrawing its well-resourced fighting headquarters and commander, General Tommy Franks, replacing it with a much smaller unit to act as a static corps headquarters. This was led by a newly-promoted officer, Lieutenant General Ricardo Sanchez, who was judged by the American author Thomas E Ricks to have struggled mightily but unsuccessfully with his task.[8] In less than a year, Sanchez had to be replaced by the much more capable, and wiser, General George W. Casey.[9]

Given vice-regal authority, Bremer could rule by decree. In his Coalition Provincial Authority Orders 1 and 2, Bremer disbanded the defeated Iraq Army and forbade any members of the Baath Party (in effect, the complete civil service) continuing in public service. From their army, 400,000 soldiers were sent home without pay yet retained their weapons, and the civil ministries were emptied of 50,000 officials. These actions quickly made Iraq ungovernable—for there was nobody qualified, paid or capable of running the country—and increasingly Iraq fell to the mercy of armed gangs. As Justin Maciejewski, a UK battalion commander at the time in the invasion force, said: '… people stared into space as they tried to work out what to do next with no one to talk to! There was a sense of utter despondency and disbelief.'[10] Bremer allowed little flexibility for local initiatives, for instance over-ruling a plan by the local British commander in Basra, Major General Robin Brims, to use the command structure of the Naval Academy to establish a local security apparatus, to the latter's intense frustration.[11] The coalition also misread the religious cohesion of Iraq, falsely seeing it as a homogenous Islamic state, and old enmities between Shias and Sunnis quickly surfaced.

THE WAR ON TERROR OPENS IN IRAQ IN 2003

Paul Bremer decided that he would need to hold formal elections before handing over power to the Iraqis, a process that would take two years, until 2005. The UK's senior political representative in the country, Sir Jeremy Greenstock, pressed for a much more rapid transfer of power to locals to give the Iraqi people a sense of early ownership of their liberated country. But Greenstock was over-ruled; indeed he was marginalised thereafter in meetings with Bremer and no longer consulted because of the stand he had taken. It is easy to see how that hiatus of nearly two years before authority was transferred allowed the virus of insurgency to be nurtured in that warm bed of dissatisfaction, but it must have been a difficult decision to call and there will have been compelling arguments on both sides, not helped by the coalition's poor understanding of the local factions and politics. As it turned out, the country was in armed uproar by the time elections were held, and the delay in handing over control to Iraqis had contributed significantly to its descent into turmoil.

Violence erupted early on in the centre and north of Iraq. The newly freed Shia population rushed to settle scores with the minority Sunnis, who responded by arming themselves and forming protective militias. As the Shias tried to cleanse Baghdad of Sunnis, an inter-ethnic conflict erupted. Meanwhile the Kurdish population fought to carve their own independent state in the north. To their enormous frustration, the US soon found itself antagonising both sides in trying to quell the violence and, as the foreign invader, became the primary target. It is unlikely that al-Qaida was present in Iraq before the invasion, but it rapidly moved to foment the growing insurrection, taking advantage of the changed circumstances. Only in the south was there relative calm, largely because almost the whole population were Shia.

So as President Bush was declaring 'Mission Accomplished' on 1 May 2003 on the flight deck of the USS *Abraham Lincoln*, the situation in Iraq was already sliding rapidly out of control and the coalition forces, particularly in the US sector, were coming under attack. In July, President Bush declared that American troops would remain in Iraq in spite of the increasingly violent attacks, challenging the insurgents with: 'My answer is, bring 'em on!'

By the next year, 2004, and with only 130,000 US troops in Iraq instead of the several hundreds of thousands that US Army Chief of Staff General Shinseki had wanted to deploy and with steeply rising casualties, the Commander of Multi-National Force Iraq, General George Casey, put together a

'Transition Bridging Strategy'. After the elections due in December 2005, the coalition would withdraw from centres of population and hand over to the new Iraqi security forces, encouraging the Iraqis to take ownership of their problems and responsibility for their own security. In parallel, General Casey initiated a programme to 'embed' US Army trainers within units of the nascent Iraqi Army to guide and advise them. But events were flowing in the opposite direction. As the difficulties increased many times over and a successful campaign plan seemed ever more elusive, it descended into a plan to hand over to the Iraqis whatever progress was being made—and to head for the exit.[12]

The scale of violence in the north and south of Iraq were poles apart, with the UK having a much easier time. The UK had been assigned to the right flank of the main US thrust coming north, so remained in Basra afterwards. The situation there was sufficiently settled for Lieutenant Colonel John Donnelly to report that Basra could be held by a single battalion using soft-skinned vehicles and wearing berets rather than ballistic combat helmets, markedly different conditions to the mayhem that was emerging further north in Baghdad.[13] With unyielding instructions from London to scale back, British dropped her force levels rapidly from 42,000 to 9,000 soldiers. Using those remaining behind as a protective security screen, the British set about the task of forming a new security and government apparatus from locally prominent people.

The UK also volunteered to command the south by leading the coalition Multi-National Division South-East, or MND (SE). This was a subordinate division of the overall fighting command, the Multi-National Corps Iraq, which in turn was under Headquarters Multi-National Force Iraq. Both of the latter were based close together in Baghdad, whilst the British HQ MND (SE) was more than a hundred miles away. MND (SE) had troops from the UK, Norway, Italy, Japan, Australia, New Zealand, Romania, Denmark, Portugal, the Czech Republic and Lithuania. As well as Basra city, MND (SE) was given security responsibility for the surrounding 'governorates' (roughly provinces) of Al Muthanna, Maysan and Dhi Qar. Although Basra remained peaceful, these surrounding provinces (especially Maysan and Al Muthanna) were populated with independently minded tribesmen and they soon proved difficult to police with thinly spread forces. In June 2003, only three months after the invasion started, six British military policemen were besieged by a mob in the police station in Al-Majar Al-Kabir and killed. It was an omen of things to come.

The British Army had several generations of counter-insurgency experience to draw on, following the withdrawal from Empire and its critical role in quelling 'The Troubles' in Northern Ireland 1969–97. So it knew what it was required to do and how to do it, but it was to prove no better than the US at reading the situation correctly. Initially with a peaceful population in Basra, only made restive by the collapsed infrastructure and lack of amenities, the British continued to withdraw its forces back to the UK as quickly as possible and adopted a low-profile 'soft' approach on the streets. It appeared to the UK that it faced a 'hearts and minds' operation to establish local government and rebuild infrastructure. What the UK failed to calibrate was how much worse things could get if they turned bad. This left a city with a population of 2 million to be controlled and secured by a single infantry battalion.

On the front foot in their own area, the British were not shy of telling the US how the violence further north was largely of its own doing, without comprehending that the US were facing a complex Shia–Sunni armed confrontation, dangerously stoked up by al-Qaida into a far greater level of violence. As the violence around Baghdad increased and the US began scrabbling for solutions, it seemed that the British approach might deliver some answers, given how peaceful Basra city appeared. Typically ready to learn, General Casey set up a training school near Baghdad to explore how the US could adopt some of the British ideas and he asked the British to deploy its highly capable 16 Air Assault Brigade to Baghdad before it returned to the UK. But the UK MoD vetoed the idea and the brigade departed from Iraq soon afterwards, leaving British Army chief of the time, General Sir Mike Jackson, very disturbed: 'the apparent unwillingness … to correctly address the challenges presented … was pathetic'.[14] The admiration had already started to fade when Brigadier Nigel Aylwin-Foster—a thoughtful, rather shy, British armoured corps brigadier on attachment to the US—wrote an indictment of the US Army's tough approach, highlighting its perceived cultural insensitivity seen from the British perspective.[15] This was a well-argued paper and had been called for by a number of US officers including General Petraeus, but it was widely condemned in the US as being out of touch with the rapidly worsening situation and did nothing to bring the allies closer together.

The US also tried to persuade the UK to follow its lead in 'mentoring' the new Iraqi Army, but the UK would have none of it. It was decided in London that the UK had insufficient troops to protect any isolated groups of army trainers out on detachment with Iraqi battalions. It was argued also that the Iraqis had to stand on their own feet and be weaned off coalition support, not made eternally dependent on a UK presence. This was to have bad consequences for the UK later when it desperately needed help from a trained local force. Worse than that, the Iraqi battalions that the British did train were siphoned off from the peaceful south to contribute to the much worse security situation further north in Baghdad.

Britain kept its force levels perilously low and continued to patrol in lightly protected vehicles, turning a blind eye to the corruption of local police officers and officials. It was very much what politicians in London, fearful of getting their hands drawn into a mangle, wanted to hear. Significantly, the UK Chief of the General Staff General Sir Mike Jackson—a pretty hard-bitten warrior, with an alert mind and wide experience—visited frequently and continued strongly supporting the light-touch approach. It could be argued that whatever the local commanders reported back (especially the need for a substantial reserve force in theatre), political circumstances in London were never going to allow that to happen. If a mistake was made it was that judgements were built up on what they could see, not on what they should have imagined would happen.

Hard Fighting

'I think we recognised that exemplary was dead … adequate was not what most of us wanted, but was good enough.'

General Sir Michael Walker, UK Chief of the Defence Staff[16]

But it was not all quiet in the south. Out in the rural provinces, and largely unreported, things got pretty rough for the British. Major fire fights happened on most patrols and troops were beleaguered in their bases on return; soon patrols always deployed in Warrior armoured fighting vehicles, supported by Challenger main battle tanks. In al-Amarah Province in June 2004, during ambushes of great ferocity, Private Johnson Beharry gained the UK's highest gallantry award, the Victoria Cross, for saving his comrades' lives.[17]

Only a few Sunnis lived in the south, but the many Shia militias and armed tribal groups vied amongst themselves for advantage. Their aims were a mixture of garnering political support and criminal activity for profit. One group was centred on the Badr Brigade, enemies of Saddam Hussein who had found sanctuary in Iran for many years. They were well organised and disciplined, but mistrusted by the local Shias. Another group was Fadhila, or the Islamic Virtue Party, led by Muhammad al-Wa'ili who succeeded in getting elected as Governor of Basra in January 2005 but was seen by many as corrupt, wily and opportunistic.[18] As the political manoeuvring amongst the Shias increased, yet another group coalesced around the charismatic Muqtada al-Sadr (fourth son of the most revered Shia cleric in Iraq, Grand Ayatollah Mohammad Sadeq al-Sadr), who began to champion the withdrawal of coalition forces, 'the foreigners'. Quite suddenly things started to get much worse for the British in Basra, and in April 2004 they were caught off guard with far too few resources in reserve. Muqtada al-Sadr had built up a strong militia of the discontented, his so-called Mahdi Army, and was launching attacks in Najaf, Baghdad and Basra, killing significant numbers of coalition soldiers. Simultaneously, Sunni rebels staged a violent challenge to the coalition in Fallujah, to which the Shia Muqtada al-Sadr provided support.

From patrolling in soft-skinned vehicles with chat-up patrols on foot wearing only berets, overnight the UK was facing a full-scale and violent insurgency. As well as small arms, the enemy used armour-piercing shoulder-launcher RPG rockets, fired mortars and set up roadside bombs using artillery shells or Iranian-supplied IEDs.[19] The British leadership in Basra quickly realised how circumstances had changed and converted as many patrols as possible into armoured vehicles. But this cold realism emerged much more slowly in London. No reinforcements were dispatched to Basra to deal with the increased threat and the acquisition of proper mine-resistant vehicles was not accelerated.

Four months after it had started in April 2004, the violence in Basra subsided almost as suddenly as it had begun, following a miscalculation by Muqtada al-Sadr about the coalition's resolve. The Mahdi Army opted for pitched battle and soon found itself pinned down by US and Iraqi forces in Najaf, where it was defeated. On 5 August 2004, the Shia spiritual leader, Grand Ayatollah Ali al-Sistani, returned from a successful cardiac heart operation in England and immediately called for a truce, which was soon agreed.

The violence calmed down in Basra for a while, further confusing policy makers in London.

The US had been asking for some time for the UK to take on a bigger share of the security burden, but America was always brushed off.[20] As mentioned earlier, the UK's 16 Air Assault Brigade was repatriated instead of deploying northwards to Baghdad as requested, so the US pushed instead for the UK to take over all nine Shia-dominated provinces in the south and to lead a second Multi-National Division further north, once the current Polish commander came to the end of his tour. This made some progress and the Allied Rapid Reaction Corps stationed in Germany—the British-led headquarters commanded by Lieutenant General Richard Dannatt—was stood up to be the coordinating headquarters for both divisions in the south. But in time, this plan was also stood down in London.

Britain was in a bind: she was as eager as ever to be seen to be fostering her special relationship with the US and yet was determined to wind down her commitment in Iraq. However, the debate about who was really doing the heavy lifting would not go away, so at a NATO summit in June 2004 Tony Blair made an undertaking in principle for the UK to deploy a substantial force instead to Afghanistan alongside the US, sometime in the future, if the situation there demanded it. This had momentous consequences, because it led inexorably to the UK breaching its pre-eminent military planning guideline, i.e. of only committing to one 'enduring' (long-term) military operation at a time. General Sir Richard Dannatt as CGS the following year found himself scratching around to create ten brigades (five each to sustain rotations in two theatres) from only the eight brigades that the Army was structured to provide. Dannatt tried to find out how the decision to accept a new commitment of a brigade in Afghanistan as well as continuing with a substantial force in Iraq had been arrived at. He could find no record that it had been discussed by the Chiefs of Staff Committee in the committee minutes of 2004, where the hazards of such an undertaking would surely have been raised.[21] Who can know what was in the Prime Minister's mind at the time, but it would be easy to conclude that Blair hoped that an offer of future support would demonstrate good coalition behaviour, whilst in the short term avoiding any further commitment of forces to Iraq. But it demonstrated yet again that decisions were taken without the MoD assessing their military consequences, and it was to backfire seriously when the UK took on the security of Helmand Province in Afghanistan.

Instead, an assumption had been made that the UK commitment to Iraq would reduce dramatically by the end of 2005, included in a policy paper by the MoD's Director of Operations entitled 'Strategic Rebalancing', which circulated through the MOD in the spring of 2005. It was argued in the paper that Britain's commitment to Iraq could soon be down to a 1,500-man training team, whilst offering the opportunity to increase the UK's military influence in Afghanistan. This appealing logic was based upon a flawed assumption that Basra was in some way disconnected from the rest of Iraq (and Iran), and that the relatively benevolent conditions previously experienced in the south of Iraq would return, allowing an early handover to Iraqi control. Eventually, in July 2005, the London *Daily Mail* leaked the details of the MoD assessment paper, now signed off by the Secretary of State for Defence, Dr John Reid, and it exposed the UK's real intentions.[22] It contained the following prescription:

'The current ministerially-endorsed policy position is that the UK should not:

a) Agree to any changes to the UK area of responsibility.

b) Agree to any specific deployments outside Multi-National Division South-East.

c) Agree to any specific increases in the roughly 8,500 UK service personnel currently deployed in Iraq.

… This in turn should lead to a reduction in the total level of UK commitment in Iraq to around 3,000 personnel, i.e. small scale, by mid 2006.

(signed) John Reid'

With hindsight, it is easy to see that the last paragraph was simplistic and unrealistic, but it demonstrated clearly the political mindset in London, which was to get out. Focussing on Basra rather than Iraq, and subsequently on Helmand not Afghanistan, was a peculiarly British myopia that would come back to haunt policy-makers.[23]

Eventually, in November 2004, Washington telegraphed the UK (in terms that did not anticipate a rejection) that the US required UK support for a second major battle with Sunni militants in Fallujah. As a result, the UK sent north its Black Watch Battlegroup, a powerful armoured infantry force, to be part of the cordon sealing off the south-east of Fallujah city for six weeks.

Unfortunately for Britain, by early 2006 a virulent Sadr-inspired insurgency had re-appeared in Basra, this time openly supported by Iranian al-Quds fighters, and the city began to fall under the grip of al-Sadr's militia, the Jaish al-Mahdi or JAM, and others. The militias increased their penetration of the local police forces and a *de facto* JAM interrogation centre was established in a wing of the Jumait Police Station in Basra supervised by a notorious police thug Captain Jaffah. Violence against both British troops and Baswari citizens increased sharply and militia murder squads roamed the city.

In London, the mood in the military eroded further, from trying to leave Basra in a reasonably settled and ordered state into trying to extract as early as possible, accepting the inevitable damage to the British reputation as the lesser evil and, if necessary, tolerating casualties amongst the local population in the process.[24] Brigadier Patrick Marriott, commanding the soldiers on the ground in Basra at the time and later to be promoted to Major General and Commandant of the Royal Military Academy Sandhurst, was appalled by this and confided his frustration to his diary of 26–29 January 2006:[25]

'… but why must we reduce in such haste? Because of Afghanistan! This is strategic madness. History will prove this to be an error. The UK approach is wrong [and] I find [our] position embarrassing …'

Marriott continued in his diary with a note about a discussion with US General George Casey, still commanding the Multi-National Force Iraq:

'General Casey summed up our current situation during his visit by saying: "The US is setting conditions for Iraq, the UK is setting conditions for withdrawal." He is right—we are "cutting and running" from Iraq to reinforce Afghanistan, [which is] a strategic red "Herrick". But what is worse now is that we are trying to persuade the US that ours is a sound military plan. It is not.'[26]

[Note: 'Herrick' was the randomly generated codeword used to describe the UK's deployment to Helmand and used here as a play on the phrase 'red herring'.]

Whilst there had been enthusiasm for the invasion of Iraq, this was just not the case for the tasks that followed. Brigadier Justin Majewski concluded that Iraq was 'perceived as a political threat [rather than] an opportunity, resulting in the UK Government seeking to minimise political, military and financial exposure to the campaign'.[27] Given the rapidly deteriorating situation for the

British forces now also deployed to Helmand Province in Afghanistan, it had become the imperative.

But it was not a simple state of affairs. The situation had become increasingly complex once Nouri al-Maliki, a minority leader and a compromise candidate, was elected Prime Minster in the first Iraqi national elections. Al Maliki's grip on power was always tenuous and he needed support from other Shia leaders, such as Muqtada al-Sadr, so al-Maliki was reluctant to sanction moves to control al-Sadr's militia, the JAM. Moreover, there was antipathy between Baghdad and the elected governor of Basra, Muhammad al-Wa'ili, leading to stalemates that stalled or prevented many British security initiatives. For instance, Air Chief Marshal Sir Jock Stirrup was told by Prime Minister Maliki in 2006 that he would not sanction UK operations which were designed to target the JAM, removing at a stroke one of the primary objectives of the UK's Operation Salamanca/Sinbad.[28]

Meanwhile the body politic in Washington was waking up to the consequences for American prestige of a messy withdrawal and even the collapse of Iraq as a nation state. Violence in the centre of Iraq was increasing dramatically, teasing General George Casey's plan to transfer responsibility for security to Iraqis by 2007 under the 'Transition Bridging Strategy'.[29] A group of Americans, including the academic Eliot Cohen and the retired US General Jack Keane, urged President Bush to reconsider his options, arguing that it was unthinkable that an army as powerful as America's could not defeat an insurgency. A new approach and new ideas were needed. President Bush mulled over the issue for three months and, to the surprise of most, reversed the advice of his Chairman of the Joint Chiefs of Staff to withdraw, instead directing that considerable numbers of extra troops would be surged into Iraq in early 2007 under a new team led by General David Petraeus.[30]

Simultaneously, the US took a bold step to engage with the Sunni militias and wean them away from their alliance with al-Qaida. After a brutal six months, new tactics of swamping urban areas with US troops brought much more peaceful conditions to the troubled centre of Iraq, where the Sunni–Shia conflict was most active; however it did little towards regaining control of Sadr city, the very large Shia enclave in Baghdad. Here, raiding operations were still forbidden by the Iraqi Prime Minister, Nouri al-Maliki, a Shia himself.

Operation Salamanca/Sinbad and The Deal

The UK either failed to notice this change of direction by the coalition leader, or chose to ignore it; for the British, the end-game in Basra was already in view. Despite that, two successive British tactical commanders in MND (SE) tried to wrest back the rapidly deteriorating situation using distinctly different approaches.

Major General Richard Shirreff, a clear-thinking officer and outstanding leader, was earmarked to deploy to Basra in January 2006. He saw clearly enough the dire consequences of defeat for the British Army and its reputation in the deteriorating situation. Shirreff said to his commanders before deployment to 'be under no illusion about the enemy: he is ingenious, capable and determined to inflict an humiliating defeat on us'.[31] To reverse that, Shirreff arrived in theatre with a well-thought-out plan to take back Basra city, district by district, with British troops alongside the Iraqi Army (and with immediate reconstruction following up to consolidate the gains).[32] It was to be called Operation Salamanca, later Sinbad.[33]

His plan to achieve security, from which a political solution could emerge, was wholeheartedly supported by the coalition commanders, General Casey and General Chiarelli, who generously provided access to corps assets (such as surveillance drones) and $80 million of US funds in cash for reconstruction. The US even offered to detach a US battalion to help the British, although the idea was rejected back in London.

Shirreff had early success, especially in turning around the opinion of the people of Basra that the British Army was not protecting them against the militias. But this initial victory could never be consolidated because of the refusal of London to provide sufficient forces to carry it off, or to accept help from US ground troops, compounded crucially by inadequate Iraq governmental support and weak Iraqi security forces. As General Shirreff observed wryly in his testimony to the Chilcot Inquiry, 'in London ... there was no appetite for any kind of surge operation ....'[34] Brigadier Justin Maciejewski was blunter:

'General Shirreff wanted a winning strategy; Whitehall wanted an exit strategy ... he could barely disguise his view that many of the higher management in London were defeatists. He expressed particular frustration that PJHQ ... was more obsessed with force levels than designing a winning plan for Basra. His relationship with General Nick Houghton, Chief of Joint Operations [at PJHQ] … was particularly bad.'[35]

Many voices in London saw things differently to Sherriff (and they still do), as James de Waal from the Royal Institute of International Affairs argues when commenting on Maciejewski's view of events:

'Astonishingly, this operation seems to have been a personal initiative by the British commander, Richard Shirreff … what Maciejewski represents as a failure of determination by "defeatists" at home can equally be seen as a baffling reluctance by government to rein in an insurgent commander acting against national policy.'[36]

But this may not be completely correct either, because the Chief of the Defence Staff Air Chief Marshal Sir Jock Stirrup was clearly aware of what Major General Shirreff was proposing to do:

'I supported the approach I had discussed with Richard [Shirreff] just after I took over as CDS, and just before he [Shirreff] deployed, until the facts on the ground changed ….'[37]

By this time, the UK had entered Helmand, Afghanistan, in strength and was fighting hard on two fronts separated by a thousand miles and each several more from the home base. She was becoming seriously overstretched militarily. The 'light' deployment to Helmand had become a full-scale local war and, whatever the violence of the fighting in Basra, it was now even worse in Helmand. Halfway through Operation Sinbad, poor footwork by General Sir Richard Dannatt, the new Chief of the General Staff, led to the latter being quoted inadvertently in October 2006 as saying that the British Army had become more of the problem than the solution, that 'our presence exacerbates the security problem … and we should get out sometime soon'.[38] This was very badly received indeed by the UK troops fighting the battles of Operation Sinbad; one officer serving in Basra at the time acidly observed 'it definitely undermined us—confusing or what!'[39] Simon Jenkins commented in *The Times* that: 'for Dannatt publicly to question the wisdom of what his soldiers are doing is a breach of constitutional discipline … [he was] either daringly brave or totally naive'.[40] Prime Minster Blair noted in his memoirs: '… as you can imagine, I wasn't best pleased.'[41]

As Shirreff's campaign progressed, the British troops outfought the Shia militias in many pitched battles, leading one local newspaper to describe the

British as the 'Lions of Basra', but the militias would creep back as soon as the British moved on. The militias adjusted their tactics by using rockets, some fired from up to 10 km away, and laying IEDs. For a time the UK base at Basra Palace became the most rocketed location in the whole of Iraq. The British simply did not have enough troops to hold what they had taken or to suppress all the possible rocket firing points, despite some singular successes.

Denied the prize of retaking Basra, there was one positive outcome for Shirreff. He was finally granted permission to blow up the Jumait Police Station—so long a symbol of compromise and collusion by the British. This his sappers duly did for him 'with an exaggerated amount of explosives'.[42]

Operation Salamanca/Sinbad had fallen into a mire of the disunited Shia politics of the moment—permissions endlessly granted or withdrawn as the Shia leaders jockeyed for advantage at the expense of the coalition—and doing it properly was probably always beyond the capability of the UK without wholehearted Iraqi support and trained local battalions, both of which were absent. Air Chief Marshal Sir Jock Stirrup wrote to the Defence Secretary on his return from Iraq in late 2006 to report that it was Prime Minister Maliki himself who had said that 'he would not allow the kind of operations envisaged for Op Salamanca'; Stirrup concluded that the Iraqi political mood and consequent restrictions meant that the UK would have to change its approach. Air Chief Marshal Stirrup finished his report by saying that 'I then outlined the need to drive the Iraqi politics to the right place'.[43] As Operation Sindbad/Salamanca was winding down, Major General Shirreff was replaced after his six-month tour at the end of 2006 by Major General Jonathan Shaw.

Shaw had a distinctly different view. He was in many ways the opposite of Shirreff—more cerebral, more political—but just as tough-minded. Shaw had done his homework before deploying and saw the situation in terms of tribal clanship and armed criminal gangs, describing it as 'Palermo, not Beirut'.[44] Shaw reversed Shirreff's argument that achieving security was the essential precursor to a political solution[45] and he proposed the opposite: that security would only be achieved *after* a political solution had emerged from within the Shia population themselves. The formal order (Operation Zenith) to withdraw UK troops from Basra city back to Kuwait had already been given by the UK's Permanent Joint HQ in London in December 2006, just before his arrival and hugely limited Shaw's options. Nevertheless, he set out to find a way to hand over as much responsibility as possible to the Iraqi security forces, believing that with some 80–90 per cent of the violence directed towards his forces, a British withdrawal would force the local Iraqis to stop playing politics, sort out their loyalties to the Iraqi state (or not) and move towards proper governance.

If military progress had run its course because of insufficient troops, Major General Shaw decided that the next best option would be to broker a deal with the Jaish al-Mahdi militia for disengagement and conflict termination. Acting on a proposal by the UK's foreign intelligence service, MI6, Shaw made an agreement with the imprisoned leader of the JAM, Ahmed al-Fartusi, to release militia prisoners progressively and to withdraw the British out of bases in Basra city in exchange for a cessation of militia attacks. Security in Basra would be handed over to local Iraqi Army and Police forces, whose commanders assured everyone they could cope. As it turned out, Iraqi forces were too weak and divided to achieve anything and, in effect, the British handed over Basra and its population to a merciless fundamentalist militia. The plan was briefed back to London, where Air Chief Marshal Sir Jock Stirrup saw it as fitting his overall strategy, although serious doubts were expressed elsewhere, for instance by the Assistant Chief of Staff J3 (the Head of Operations) at PJHQ, who protested strongly that the plan would not work in the medium term, would be incomprehensible to the dependants of those who had recently died and that it was too early for the UK to deal with murderers.[46] Shaw maintains that the plan was fully visible to his superior US coalition commanders (Generals Odierno and Petraeus) and had been approved by them.[47] But as the situation deteriorated and as the intent of the UK to extract itself became clear, many in the United States were furious and worried.

The plan to make an accommodation with the JAM started well and there was a significant lull in violence for about three months, but it failed spectacularly in the medium term. On release of the last militia prisoner—al-Fartusi himself—and with the British forces withdrawn into the coalition base in Basra airport, the Jaish al-Mahdi reneged. The British came under relentless rocket and mortar attack at Basra airport and the Basra population became rightfully very fearful for their lives. As Jack Fairweather described in his book *A War of Choice*:

'From the British short term perspective, the deal with Al-Fartusi had been an extraordinary success—after months of incessant bombardment, attacks on the two remaining British bases had all but stopped.

But their Faustian bargain undermined the very institutions that the British had gone to Iraq to create … [there were] murders, rapes and abuse and the city was nothing like the peaceful oasis British defence chiefs were trying to portray in the media.'[48]

With the majority of the violence in Basra city apparently targeted against them, the British had reasoned that the violence would decline if they withdrew, seemingly not calculating that the violence was directed against them precisely *so as to get them to withdraw*. Instead, left a free hand and unchecked by too-weak Iraqi security forces, the JAM was able to tighten its grip on Basra by intimidation and the introduction of extreme Islamist laws. The British, in confronting their most immediate problem of being besieged and attacked, rather than facing their long-term responsibility for protecting the Basra population, had effectively connived in this and directly allowed it to happen. A note of caution is important here because, whilst there were many reports of the mayhem caused by the militias, they are largely anecdotal and authoritative sources such as the Iraqi Body Count do not give a clear picture of the scale of what actually happened.[49] But even after the Iraqi national elections in January 2005, the British were still responsible for the security of the Iraqi population in their area under international law,[50] for responsibility only passed to the Iraqi government once Provincial Iraqi Control was jointly agreed, province by province, between the coalition and the Iraqi government (this did not happen in Basra city until December 2007).[51]

Throughout the spring of 2008, the British remained confined to their base at Basra airport, relatively safe but detached from the insurgency that was raging around them. They had switched their effort to training the Iraqi Army and sitting in 'over-watch' as a ready reserve, but they were not embedded and mentoring with the Iraqis as the US was. A few embers of British involvement still glowed as a UK colonel detached to the staff of Basra Operational Command started to plan a new version of Operation Sinbad under the Iraqi leadership of Lieutenant General Mohan al-Furayji.

The UK's withdrawal to Basra airport had forced Iraqi Prime Minister Nouri al-Maliki to confront the issue of a breakaway Shia group establishing itself outside his authority in the south of Iraq. In one respect, this was exactly what the UK had set out to achieve: an Iraqi initiative to solve an Iraqi problem. On 25 March 2008, with very little prior warning to the coalition command, Prime Minster al-Maliki ordered General Mohan al-Furayji to carry out a UK-authored plan now termed 'Charge of the Knights' to move into Basra and defeat the Mahdi Army. The battle initially went against the Iraqi Army, which suffered considerable losses, but the situation rapidly improved when US air support and ground teams arrived from Baghdad. The JAM were defeated and fled. The British 4th Mechanised Brigade stood to one side out in Basra airport and were hardly involved, not least because of antipathy towards them from Prime Minister al-Maliki, who with astonishing political insouciance publicly held the UK responsible for the descent of Basra into banditry. London eventually gave permission for the British to 'embed' fully with the Iraqi Army and in the following weeks the UK under Brigadier Julian Free managed to re-establish a greater role for itself. At last the British Army was able to put right many of the things that had gone wrong since 2004 in its approach to the Iraq campaign.

The plan to accommodate with the JAM was initiated in Basra, but the decision to pursue it was then approved at the very top in London.[52] It fitted very well with the strategy pursued by Air Chief Marshal Sir Jock Stirrup as CDS of getting the Iraqis to sort out their own politics and for the British to withdraw rapidly from Iraq, so as to be able to concentrate more resources on the burgeoning commitment of the British in Helmand, Afghanistan. Stirrup gave the deal with Al-Fartusi and the JAM his full support, and he was not alone in Whitehall in this. As it was being activated, though, a change of domestic political leadership occurred as Prime Minister Tony Blair handed over to Gordon Brown and this seriously upset plans.

Having extracted British forces from the city, UK policy-makers in London had intended to present the new prime minister with a *fait accompli* that British forces were no longer materially contributing to security in southern Iraq, so they should be withdrawn as soon as possible and diverted to Afghanistan. Initially Prime Minister Brown was keen on as fast a drawdown as possible (and only restrained from doing so immediately by Air Chief Marshal Sir Jock Stirrup as CDS). However, when Prime Minister Brown made an early visit to Iraq in September 2007, he was pressured by both Iraqi political leaders and US commanders about the importance of the UK remaining fully engaged as members of the coalition, just at the moment when the US surge was showing tangible signs of success. From that moment onwards, Britain was on the horns of a dilemma: unable to influence the situation in southern Iraq but also unable to get out, so they had to sit it out alone in Basra airfield.[53]

The retaking of Basra marked the end of Britain's involvement in Iraq and the US had to step in to add Basra to all its other responsibilities in 2009. The British might have been right in the long term that prompting the Iraqis to solve their own problems was the best solution, but it was at the cost of huge reputational damage for the British and the lives and disruption of many Baswari citizens.

Out of Step

'So the aftermath was more bloody, more awful, more terrifying than anyone could have imagined. The perils that we anticipated did not materialise. The perils we didn't materialised with ferocity and evil that even now shocks the senses'. [54]

Prime Minister Tony Blair

The Iraq intervention was a painful story of the coalition being both out of step with events and within itself. As Major General Mungo Melvin observed, the 'US and the UK got in together, acted individually and left separately'.[55] There were insufficient troops on hand to deal with violence once it occurred and this allowed latent enmities in the Iraqi population to spiral out of control. The coalition took its time to transfer power back to the Iraqis, trying for a perfect political solution through democratic elections, rather than licensing a rough and ready answer much earlier on. This allowed malcontents to foment dissatisfaction against the invading force. With each miscalculation, both the scale of the challenge facing the coalition ratcheted up and the scale of resources needed to meet it was amplified. Until 2007, the coalition was forever out of step with reality on the ground; following the problem rather than being in front of it.

Worse still, the primary coalition partners (America and Britain) were also out of step with each other as circumstances conspired to put them travelling in opposite directions. Early on the US was challenged by a violent insurgency, whilst the UK had much more benign conditions in the south and was caught musing rather primly that the violence against the Americans might be as a result of too-tough a US approach. The US planned to train up a new Iraq army as soon as possible, allowing for early handover, disengagement and exit—but the UK wouldn't make the same commitment. Whilst the UK was just as eager to leave Iraq, it would not provide sufficient numbers of soldiers to put the same effort into training the Iraq Army and, as a result, continued to carry too much of the security burden in its area without local help. When the UK was suddenly facing a surge in violence, it failed to provide quickly the extra forces needed to master the violence; instead, it accelerated its plans to exit, leading to an ignominious withdrawal to Basra airport. The UK made a strategic miscalculation about the type of forces the situation demanded; for too long, they were lightly equipped and thinly protected, deployed in inadequate numbers, and the UK was critically short of specialist capabilities such as helicopters and surveillance drones. Instead of fleeing as casualties mounted, the US reversed its intentions and surged in extra troops to face down the insurgency. Bizarrely, as things began to improve in the US sector, they deteriorated sharply in the UK area because the will to dominate the situation was absent in London. Substantial damage was done to the UK's reputation and to its aspiration of 'a special relationship' with the US, caused by this lack of resolve on the part of the UK at the critical moment. Faith in the British Army as a competent organisation withered in Washington and Whitehall. US General Jack Keane reflected on the events later, showing all the bitterness felt by the Americans (even though they were fully involved in the key decisions):

'And then we had the famous al-Fartosi deal! You know how the deal went: "we'll pull out of the city if you don't bomb us". And of course Jaish al-Mahdi, lying through their teeth, not only continued the level of violence but increased it in Basra. The enemy was encouraged and emboldened … when they saw the [British] troops withdrawing. Iraqi citizens were being attacked, mauled and terrorized. Lawlessness was taking over. The Iraqi military … lost respect for the British.'[56]

The UK field commanders were also consistently out of step with their strategic masters in the MoD in London, where responsibility lay for setting a strategic direction and tasking them. As Tony Blair said:

'Back in late 2006, there was a pretty acute sense amongst the senior command in the Army that we had done all we could do in Basra.'[57]

Damningly, both Operation Sinbad and the subsequent deal with the Jaish al-Mahdi—surely, issues of national strategy—were conceived in Basra and not in London. As Major General Shaw painfully concluded:

'as the British Commander in Basra in 2007 … a tactical position which should have simply been executing orders … it fell to me to take on responsibility for generating the strategic plan'.[58]

Air Chief Marshal Sir Jock Stirrup challenged this by saying:

'the idea that [Major General Shaw] was having to "freelance", as it were, is simply untrue. What it is true, and in my view appropriate, is that the ideas of the commander on the ground were accorded considerable weight in our considerations.'[59]

What is certain is that there was high political interest in London when the invasion of Iraq was being planned—Tony Blair holding a long session with all the Chiefs of Staff to discuss the invasion plan—but it waned very significantly as the occupation seemed to go on without end, especially once the Prime Minster diverted his attention to re-election. It may only be a crude indicator, but in his 700-page memoir, Tony Blair devoted 110 pages to the circumstances surrounding the invasion of Iraq in 2003, but only 21 pages to discussing the much longer and more challenging conflict that followed until 2009.[60] As for the commitment of UK troops to Helmand in 2006, he speaks of the deployment in a single half page and the word 'Helmand' does not appear in his index, yet this was arguably the defining military decision of the decade for the British and was a decision taken squarely in his premiership.

Instead, in the world-view revealed through his memoir, Prime Minister Blair brackets his short passages dealing with the aftermath of the invasion with much more detailed accounts of his struggle for re-election, and with his ongoing conflict with his heir apparent, Gordon Brown. Blair makes no mention of the deal done by the British with the Jaish al-Mahdi to release prisoners in exchange for a safe evacuation of British forces out of Basra, except obliquely in a passage where he regrets its consequences:

'We had, in effect, entered into a *modus vivendi* with the governor and militia there. The economic conditions of the people had improved, but the security situation hadn't. The question was: were we a provocation or a support? There was an increasing opinion that we might have been the former.

I confess that I was always very doubtful about this … I was deeply sceptical of the notion that Iraqis or indeed anyone else preferred to live like this.'[61]

This begs the question why Prime Minister Blair distanced himself from the decision-making and also, if the statement is correct, why the Chief of the

Defence Staff did not require the Prime Minister to give direction on such an important issue. Given the wide-ranging military, political and reputational consequences of this for the UK, it was surely the most *political* of decisions, which needed to be taken at the highest level. All this speaks of a Prime Minister far too detached from the war that he had led his country into—when warfare is usually the issue of highest national importance for a Prime Minister.

Likewise, commenting on the denouement in Basra in his memoirs, Mr Blair said:

'I had a feeling that, had we believed in our mission more and not despaired so easily—as indeed our soldiers on the ground showed—we would have played a far greater part in the final battle [for Basra].'[62]

In summary, after the initial success in helping to overthrow Saddam Hussein, the British involvement in Iraq had ended in failure. When the British found themselves up to their necks in a problem very much greater than they had first anticipated, they lacked the political and institutional will to resolve it, either by reinforcing with sufficient combat forces to master the insurgency or by deploying sufficient cross-government capability to exploit military success where it appeared. Sometimes there were three conflicting strategies about Iraq running at the same time: in the Basra theatre, in the UK MoD and in the Prime Minister's office in 10 Downing Street. The military cannot ignore their part in failing to resolve these contradictions, for instance in stiffening the government's resolve to see things through to a better conclusion. As General Jack Keane said, when giving his view of the British withdrawal from Basra:

'There will be times when we are going to face a lack of will on the part of our national leadership, because of the political pressures that are on them. It's going to be more troublesome … in the run-up to … elections. I think that we, as military leaders, bend too much to national leaders. We answer to them, in terms of civilian oversight of the military. I am not challenging that. But what I am challenging is our reluctance to be completely honest with them, if need be to the point of being brutal. We have to have some spine. We have to be tough but loyal. They have to feel that strength from us. They have to understand that this really matters—that it isn't a game—that people are going to die. And although we won't say so directly, they have to understand that we are holding them accountable to us, that it is unacceptable for them to ask us to implement policies, and then deny us the resources which will make success possible. We have to find the words to say that—and we have to get inside their heads and their hearts with those words.'[63]

Furthermore, just as the UK MoD attempted to take a more strategic view under Air Chief Marshal Sir Jock Stirrup, perversely the final order was given to become seriously over-stretched by promoting a demanding commitment in Helmand before the UK's obligation in southern Iraq had unwound (the flawed logic in the MoD's 2005 'Strategic Re-balancing' paper). As Brigadier Patrick Marriott, commander of the UK's 7th Armoured Brigade in Basra at the time, recorded balefully in his diary, 'the lunacy of fighting on two fronts [at the same time] is beyond me'.[64] He went on later to say that 'strategically, the significance of Afghanistan in comparison to Iraq is piffling. The Middle East is pivotal. Afghanistan is peripheral.'[65]

Another very senior British commander serving in Iraq in 2007 (and still serving at the time this book was published) echoed this in a short piece he wrote at the time to record his thoughts:

'In effect, they wanted to divest from the strategically important to the side show. Reducing the capacity of terrorists to find a sanctuary in Afghanistan was important, but, in the global scheme of things, Iraq was always going to be far more important to the UK. The immutable facts about Iraq at the time bear re-stating: it was a country at the very heart of the Middle East with enviable natural resources and potential—the second largest known reserves of oil and natural gas in the world; almost uniquely in the region it was capable of feeding itself and exporting food thanks to the irrigation of the Tigris and Euphrates rivers; though there was poverty, no one was starving, despite the gloomy predictions of the aid agencies; finally, Iraq was more secular and had a larger educated sector of the population than most of its Arabic neighbours.'[66]

These are clear and powerfully phrased views expressed by British Army commanders serving in Iraq at the time, and their frustration at the direction of events coming from London is very clear. The Chiefs of the Defence Staff and their strategic planners in the MoD should have recognised the importance of Iraq in comparison to Afghanistan. Instead, it was the Ministry of Defence that was keenest to leave. As Des Browne observed, 'when I arrived in the MoD on 5 May 2006 it was clear that the MoD leadership wanted withdrawal from Iraq'.[67] Britain got the fighting right but the politics and the strategy wrong.

Finally, it is worth remembering Clausewitz's prescription that the successful prosecution of a war required a trinity of purpose of the government, the army and the people. Public support for the Iraq expedition was never strong and it got weaker as the casualties mounted (both military and civilian) and as the government failed to demonstrate a successful route forward. It was something of a miracle, and to their eternal credit, that the armed forces' morale did not falter for this lack of support from home, especially given the danger, discomfort and the ever-deteriorating situation.

10

BATTLE RETURNS TO AFGHANISTAN IN 2006

NATO Expands its Role

Events were also about to take a dramatic turn for the worse for Britain in Afghanistan. The ISAF force defending Kabul had grown to 4,650 troops and command had rotated successively through Turkish and German generals, but this ad-hoc arrangement was unsatisfactory and the North Atlantic Treaty Organisation (NATO) agreed in 2004 to assume leadership. By 2005 it was clear that the Taliban was regrouping and reinforcing, whereas enthusiasm for many of the contributing NATO nations to be part of a full-scale fighting force to confront the Taliban was only lukewarm at best.

NATO had been created as a mutual defence alliance designed to protect Europe from Soviet aggression, but it was now attempting power projection into a distant continent—poles apart from its founding charter. It is no coincidence that this happened when a British politician, George Robertson, was NATO's Secretary General. Robertson had been the first Secretary of State for Defence in the Blair government when all the ideas of liberal interventionism and of armies being a force for good had first taken root. Robertson believed that deployment to Afghanistan would simultaneously bind the alliance together more strongly at a moment when its founding purpose was less evident and give the Europeans a greater say in current coalition operations. As NATO troop numbers increased, ISAF started to roll out security around the central Afghan mountain range, deploying teams to the north-west (completed 2004), the west (completed 2005) and the south (completed 2006).[1] ISAF's campaign plan under NATO command was to extend the authority of the Kabul government into what had become a hinterland of drugs gangs and warlords. As the journalist John Ware suggested:

'Protected by troops, civilians would build up the economy and the justice and education systems. The idea was to win the hearts and minds of ordinary Afghans away from the Taliban, who were setting up their own shadow local administrations.'[2]

Unified Command

Although the US was the lead member of NATO and contributing support to ISAF, it was not directly involved with ISAF operations engaged in *counter-insurgency*. Instead and in parallel, America deployed a *counter-terrorist* force, specifically dedicated to hunting down al-Qaida remnants under Operation 'Enduring Freedom'.[3] The fact that ISAF and the US were effectively hunting the same people in the same theatre was clearly unsatisfactory. In December 2005, NATO Allied Foreign Ministers meeting in Berlin had agreed to an extended role for ISAF, giving it command of all coalition forces and absorbing the US-led Operation Enduring Freedom. The UK pushed hard for this to happen, not least because the first NATO headquarters to deploy in May 2006 would be the British-led and administered NATO Allied Rapid Reaction Corps (the ARRC).[4] The ARRC was a much more substantial headquarters than hitherto and more suited to the task of commanding the expanded ISAF responsibilities. Indeed, by October 2006, the ISAF force had grown to 31,000 troops and it had taken responsibility for the entire country (with an additional 8,000 US troops continuing to hunt for al-Qaida). At the end of his nine months' tour, the ARRC commander, UK Lieutenant General David Richards was replaced by US General Dan McNeil and, from then onwards, a single American commanded both ISAF and Operation Enduring Freedom.[5]

The high profile that the UK had adopted in the discussions that made all this happen left Britain exposed to sweeping up the tasks that nobody else wanted to do, so the UK emerged from the horse-trading with responsibility for reconstruction and security in Helmand Province. This was a cruel twist, for Helmand was neither an important regional centre of political influence—that was in nearby Kandahar—nor was it strategically located, but it was an area infested with war-lordism, sharp tribal tensions and an historical resentment of British rule going back a century. It was also unfortunately here that the British were leading the West's efforts to dismantle the local economic engine, the opium crop. It was a gigantic task to attempt in the allotted time frame of three years, and many doubted from the very beginning if parts of it were achievable. Worse still, Britain somehow thought her job in Helmand would be about local development and improving governance, protected by a light military force, even though it had been reported by the UK's recce teams as one of the most challenging military areas of all.[6]

Although Britain commanded the whole NATO effort for six months in 2006, she struggled to establish a proper national structure for her own troops in Helmand Province. You will see later how the result was a lack of a coherent strategy to govern what the UK was trying to achieve, with the approach flip-flopping back and forth every six months according to the view of the local tactical commander, a Brigadier, as he arrived or handed over. Eventually this was corrected in November 2009, three long years later, when Lieutenant General Nick Parker was appointed as both Deputy Commander ISAF and Operational Level Commander of all British troops deployed in theatre. But by then much damage had been done and many early opportunities squandered.[7]

In his evidence to the House of Commons Defence Committee as Deputy Chief of the Defence Staff (Operations) at the time, Lieutenant General Sir Rob Fry gives an insight into why the UK felt so strongly that it had to take this path:

'Had [the UK's move to Helmand] and not happened, there is a chance that NATO would never have gone into the south of Afghanistan, with untold consequences for the [NATO] alliance. We would also have created, de facto, the very ungoverned space that we went there in the first instance to deny. What we as a nation achieved during that period was a very large, bold and imaginative stroke, which has been lost because of subsequent events.

I would even make one greater claim. I think that we probably made the Americans think more about counter-insurgency than counter-terrorism [and] played a role in the general intellectual mindset of America, with consequential results in Iraq....'[8]

HIGH COMMAND

The decision to accept responsibility for bringing peace and reconstruction to Helmand would eventually challenge the UK beyond its imagination.

Helmand

Helmand is an area about three times the size of Wales, and is dominated by a broad river flowing from the high mountains in the north to the open desert in the south. The northern mountains start just north of the national circular arterial road, Route One, and are bisected by the deep valley of the Helmand Rud (river). To the south of Route One the province widens out into open desert, eventually leading to the border with Pakistan. Under a 1960s US Aid irrigation programme, the river had been diverted and canalised to create a very fertile and productive strip some ten miles wide either side of it. The newly-greened desert was settled by a multitude of tribes from across Afghanistan, but the disparate population of about 1.5 million gives little central cohesion to the area. The climate, topography and irrigation made it an ideal landscape to grow narcotic poppies and, at times, Helmand has been responsible for 42 per cent of the world's total opium production. From opium totally disproportionate wealth, in Afghani terms, was to be found.

The British had been there before. Just to the east of Helmand was where the two brigades of British and Indian troops under Brigadier General George Burrows had been defeated by the Afghans at the Battle of Maiwand in 1880, during the Second Anglo-Afghan War.[9] In the unwritten, story-telling culture of Afghanistan, this is recent history.

The UK was concerned that it would be supporting legitimate authorities and insisted that the existing warlord, Sher Mohammed Akhundzada, be replaced by Mohammad Daoud. Daoud was a well-respected and able civil engineer who had worked as a link to the UN and Non-Governmental Organisations (NGOs) during the Soviet occupation. However, Daoud was obliged by President Karzai to accept Amir Muhammad, the brother of Sher Mohammed Akhundzada, as his deputy. Daoud set about attempting to reform Helmand and control the narcotic production, which was probably why, after less than a year, President Karzai replaced him as governor in December 2006 with a less principled nominee, Assadullah Wafa.

The UK deployment to Helmand had been under consideration for well over a year before the deployment was made in 2006 and a full assessment and plan prepared.[10] To get to that point, a detailed civilian–military reconnaissance had been carried out, coming up with a plan to occupy a limited lozenge of territory between the towns of Gereshk, Lashkar Gar and a proposed base out in the desert just south of Route One—Camp Bastion. The civilian planning team leader, Mark Etherington, commented that 'they were confronted with a challenge on the ground of "biblical proportions" that bore no relation to what people in Whitehall had in mind'.[11] Indeed, the Helmand Plan identified a number of very serious challenges including: illiteracy; an opium economy; an untrained, uneducated, unprofessional, drug-taking and corrupt police force; local government dominated by patronage networks; and a deteriorating security situation.[12]

The UK Helmand force was to be based on 16 Air Assault Brigade, commanded at the time by Brigadier Ed Butler. Butler was given the mission to support the region's reconstruction and development, yet out of a total strength of 3,300 fewer than 600 were fighting soldiers (found from 3rd Battalion Parachute Regiment). The remainder were logistic and support elements. The force itself would be commanded in Helmand by a UK colonel reporting to a Canadian brigadier in Kandahar, with the Brigade Commander, Brigadier Butler, parked in national over-watch in ISAF headquarters in Kabul, a day's travel away. In the months before deployment, Brigadier Butler expressed considerable misgivings about the small size of the fighting echelon of his force and lobbied hard for it to be substantially increased, particularly with helicopters, but to no avail.

The original aim had been to deploy in late 2005 outside the summer 'fighting season', in order to give the force time to settle in during the quiet period of the year. However, the Secretary of State would not authorise the deployment until all of the other NATO contributors had agreed to their part of the overall plan, so departure was delayed until the Dutch government gave assent for their forces to go to the neighbouring Uruzgan province in January 2006. The result was that the UK force arrived in late spring towards the end of April 2006 just as the anticipated fighting season was beginning.

The Taliban Attack

The deployment of the British force coincided with—or more likely triggered—a Taliban onslaught.[13] The British soon found themselves under sustained pressure throughout the 'security lozenge' and areas that they hoped could be lightly garrisoned came under relentless attack. Captain Doug Beattie recounts in his book *An Ordinary Soldier* how he was assigned to secure the peaceful town of Garmsir, only to find him being attacked on all sides.[14] The officer mentoring the local Afghan Army force in Garmsir, Captain Timothy Illingworth, was awarded the Conspicuous Gallantry Cross for his exceptional leadership and bravery in seven days of desperate fighting against the Taliban.

Governor Daoud believed that he was about to be overwhelmed by the Taliban and demanded military assistance to secure government offices, particularly in the towns north of Route One up the Helmand valley (but outside the UK security 'lozenge'), without which he assessed that they would be over-run. This left Brigadier Butler in a perilous situation, where he would be damned by some if he did, or lynched by others if he didn't.

His mission had been to support the Governor, whose governance was now about to collapse, and the doctrine of 'mission command'—where commanders are told what to achieve and are then left alone to decided how to achieve it—dictated that he should modify his actions in the light of changed circumstances. In late May, Brigadier Butler decided to deploy small detachments of fighting soldiers to secure the main government offices in Sangin, Now Zad, Musa Qala and Kajaki. What was not so well considered was the provision of the resources, equipment or political support needed to make such a change. He probably assumed that London would come to the same conclusion as he had done. He was soon in deep trouble, because London didn't. Moreover there is evidence that the Commander of Combined Joint Task Force-82, Major General Benjamin C. Freakley, had offered American forces to secure the beleaguered government offices instead, but Butler declined the offer.[15]

One detachment from the Parachute Regiment was dispatched to Sangin, a centre of population and commerce. They had taken over the government office and were filling their first sandbags when local leaders appeared and asked the paras to go away. The elders knew that the Taliban would soon attack and the resulting battle would destroy their town, displacing or even killing some of the civilian population. The young para commander protested that he had come to protect the people … and continued with the task of fortifying the government office.[16]

In the ensuing battle over the next thirty days, the paras defended their post with great fortitude and at considerable risk to themselves, but in doing so began the destruction of the area around the post. Over the following years a significant number of civilians were killed or wounded, property was destroyed and a proportion of the population displaced to refugee camps. As the strength of the Taliban rose, the platoon base was replaced by a company and eventually a battalion base and further destruction ensued. As Jack Fairweather observed in *A War of Choice*: '… the town itself lay in ruins, a sad testimony to how badly a reconstruction mission can go wrong'.[17] On 18 June 2006 a former district provincial chief, Jama Gul, was killed in Sangin along with four body-guards and 25 relatives.

It is clear that Butler had not taken the decision to establish platoon bases—'houses'—in the northern Helmand valley in isolation, and that his intentions were well known in London before the operation was launched. General Sir Nick Houghton, who was at the time Chief of Joint Operations, stated this clearly in evidence to the House of Commons Defence Committee in a report published in 2011. He stated that Brigadier Butler's plan had been briefed to the Chiefs of Staff on 24 May 2006, two days before the moves took place. Houghton also noted 'in the minutes of 3 May [it was stated] that there might be a requirement for an earlier than planned and more significant deployment to the north of Helmand to support the governance of Governor Daoud'.[18] Furthermore, the Deputy Chief of Joint Operations, Major General Peter Wall, representing the Operational Commander at PJHQ, was in Helmand at the time that the discussions with Governor Daoud were going on.

The detachments became known as the 'platoon houses' and were soon besieged in strong and repeated attacks by large numbers of Taliban, making their very survival dependent on support from heavy weapons (artillery, attack helicopters and close air support) with resupply difficult and dangerous. In the attacks many Taliban foot soldiers were killed, although the casualties to the British were mercifully few.

This was a very changed situation and the local civilians—who were meant to be the object of a 'hearts and minds' campaign—were caught in the middle of it. Indeed many of the Taliban soldiers were simply out-of-work opium farmers given 'a dollar a day' to fight, so their deaths were an added tragedy to the local Afghan families.

The deployment out of the security lozenge northwards up the Helmand valley was a strategic tipping point for the whole campaign and it was to frame operations for the British for the rest of the decade. The British Army fought some ferocious battles with the greatest fortitude, but they also lost a lot of soldiers: 19 Infantry Brigade suffered 81 dead in one six-month tour, and 14 were from a single battalion, 2 Rifles[19]—a very high price to pay for a war that was not of vital national interest.[20] Because of a lack of military resources—troops, helicopters, surveillance drones—they became 'fixed' in military terms. The UK force was spread so thinly, over so large an area, that too often it could only react to enemy attacks, rather than prevent them; they had lost the initiative to the enemy. When an area was cleared, the UK lacked the forces to provide long-term security, allowing the Taliban to return. This was mournfully described by Commander 12 Mechanised Brigade, Brigadier John Lorimor, as simply 'mowing the grass'. To protect themselves when attacked, the UK soldiers resorted to heavy weapon systems, substituting firepower for a lack of troops on the ground and catching the civilian population in the crossfire.

This situation was only retrieved when the extra troops of President Obama's surge to Afghanistan arrived in 2009. Now 33,000 ISAF troops (mostly US Marines) patrolled an area that had been occupied first by 600 UK parachute soldiers in the initial Helmand deployment and then by an all-up total of 8,000 British troops. Moreover, the UK's Major General Nick Carter was given command of ISAF's Regional Command South in Kandahar. This was the first UK commander in either Iraq or Afghanistan to be given a properly resourced force for the task required and, not surprisingly, he achieved considerable success.[21] But it had taken too many years to get to that state of affairs.

Why Helmand?

The choice of Helmand rather than another province has been hotly discussed since. There were many arguments for the UK to go somewhere other than Helmand: Kandahar was the Pashtun capital and where the future of the south would be decided; in Afghan culture the narrative of the British defeat at Maiwand was still very much alive; Britain's leadership of the anti-narcotics programme meant that pursuing 'hearts and minds' presented an almost insuperable challenge at the same time that the local opium economy was being destroyed. More than anything, Helmand was a political backwater in the eyes of Kabul. What was rather chilling to discover afterwards was that the significant parts of the military command—who would pick up all the consequences for the choice of Helmand—were not fully involved in how the choice was made. Air Chief Marshal Sir Jock Stirrup, later to be CDS, said of his time as Chief of the Air Staff, 'I am afraid that I was not party to the conversations and dynamics that led to the decision that it should be Helmand for the UK.'[22] The Army's Chief at the time put it more pithily, when asked why it was Helmand not Kandahar, saying to journalist Deborah Haynes of *The Times*: 'Search me, guv.'[23]

The final decision to deploy to Helmand had been taken at an awkward time for the top leadership in the MoD. It spanned the handover of both the Secretary of State for Defence and the Chief of the Defence Staff, with many other key staff in the process of leaving or settling in. The planning process had dragged on for more than a year and, as the plan was refined and coordinated with other government departments, it lost some of its early simplicity and clarity of purpose. The planning was started when General Sir Michael Walker was Chief of the Defence Staff and was well under way when Dr John Reid succeeded Geoff Hoon as Secretary of State for Defence in May 2005.

But whilst Dr Reid was in post when the initial deployment was ordered, he had moved on to the Home Office before the fateful decision was made to expand the operation to the upper Helmand Valley in June, leaving the new Secretary of State for Defence, Des Browne, to sort out the consequences. Reid professed later that he was astounded that the move north up the Helmand valley had happened only a matter of weeks after he had left the MoD. A further mis-timed event was the changeover of the Chief of the Defence Staff at a critical moment. General Walker had directed all the planning and preparation for the deployment, but retired as CDS in April 2006. The force was deployed to Helmand under his successor, Air Chief Marshal Sir Jock Stirrup, then very new to the job. Stirrup said that, as Chief of the Air Staff previously, he had not been part of the detailed planning for Helmand:

'Clearly, we debated those issues in the Chiefs of Staff Committee, although I was not directly involved in the planning … I am afraid that I was not party to the conversations and dynamics that led to the decision that it should be Helmand for the UK.'[24]

Yet fate required him to execute the plan as Chief of Defence Staff, days after he assumed the appointment.

It is worth pausing to try to capture the mood of the decision making at the time. Dr Reid, who had been Secretary of State for Defence when the preparations were being made, gave compelling evidence about the issues to the Chilcot Inquiry on this. He explained that he had probed the Chiefs of Staff's plans, through the Chief of the Defence Staff, but always took military advice once it was given.[25] Reid said 'I ... asked ... the advice of the Chiefs, which I always take ....'[26] Instead, he said his role was to lay out questions for the Staff to answer. He continued that he had initially refused to sign off the Helmand plan until three specific conditions had been met:

'First of all, that the military configuration which had been decided upon by the Chiefs of Staff was financed in full by the Treasury.

Secondly, that the configuration of [other nations'] troops around the British [deployment to Helmand] which had been promised by NATO was delivered.

Thirdly, that the alternative incomes money be produced by DfID; and that the $100 million the Americans were already spending there stayed there. Because I did not want us to go in trying to take away poppy money from farmers, giving them nothing in return, and therefore turning them into subversives against us. Because, in my experience, people do not elect to starve to death in a state of grace. So if you take away their income, they will demand an alternative one.'

Dr Reid then conceded to the Chilcot Inquiry panel that he had agreed to the plan going ahead, even though *only two* of his conditions were met (the first two, not the requirement about narcotics substitution).[27] He had, though, taken the plan to a full meeting of the Cabinet for a decision, chaired by Prime Minister Blair. Once the plan had been explained to the Cabinet ministers, the Prime Minister had gone around the table to poll for views. As it became apparent that there was general approval for Dr Reid's scheme, Gordon Brown, as Chancellor of the Exchequer, abruptly stood up and departed without giving a view either way, saying, 'Well that means that I shall have to find the money from other programmes.' As someone present observed, 'that is not really the way that a chancellor of the exchequer of a great country making a fundamental decision to deploy to battle should behave'.

Dr Reid recalled that he was also worried about the overstretch that might occur if the operations in Iraq did not conclude as quickly as was hoped. He had a memo sent to the Chief of the Defence Staff to probe this issue before agreeing to the plan:

'The Secretary of State recalls … he queried whether in the event of a slower than expected drawdown of United Kingdom forces in Iraq, our planning assumptions for deployment in Afghanistan would be achievable. His recollection is that CDS confirmed to him that our current commitment in Iraq would be sustainable when set against a deployment to Afghanistan.'[28]

Chief of the Defence Staff, General Sir Michael Walker, replied thus:

'The short answer is yes, but to provide further reassurance for [the] Secretary of State we have taken advice from the Chief of Joint Operations [Lieutenant General Houghton]. He is clear that our plans for Afghanistan are deliverable, even if events slow down our Iraq disengagement. Furthermore, Deputy Chief of the Defence Staff (Commitments) [V Adm Style] has factored the possibility of such a slippage into the MoD's strategic planning for Afghanistan and our strategic intent for future commitments.'[29]

Dr Reid declined an approach from this author to discuss these events but, taking his evidence at face value, superficially the decision machinery seems to have been working as it should have been. The well-prepared and forceful politician had probed the military experts' plans and set conditions to be met. The MoD staff consulted internally about the questions raised before making an unequivocal reply. It had been discussed formally in Cabinet and the Cabinet had agreed to the scheme as presented by Dr Reid.

However, Dr Reid (along with other senior MoD staff) still had responsibility to challenge the intelligence assumptions and to explore what would be done if things went wrong or if circumstances turned out differently. As General Sir Michael Walker observed later, 'We did not have any clear intelligence picture on Helmand … it was an empty hole … an ungoverned space ….'[30] Dr Reid's subsequent surprise at the move northwards up the Helmand valley indicates that it was the last thing that he had expected to happen, but you could easily make a case that the north and south of Helmand were militarily joined at the hip and a threat from that direction simply could not have been ignored.

This was a failure of strategic imagination. As Major General Andrew MacKay bitterly commented:

'It resulted, I believe, in the upper echelons of government (political, civil and military) going into Helmand with their eyes shut and their fingers crossed.'[31]

Although there is cast-iron evidence in General Houghton's statement to the HCDC that the subject had been fully discussed in the Chiefs of Staff Committee beforehand, Brigadier Butler was largely left alone to make the key decision of the UK's Helmand deployment—whether to respond to Governor Daoud's request, or stick to the original plan? The consequences of that decision were neither anticipated in London, nor was guidance given about what to do when the Taliban attacked in unexpected strength. Furthermore, no provision was made for an adequate reserve, meaning that when things got very hot indeed for Brigadier Butler's force, there were no substantial reinforcements to bail them out. Michael Clarke discussed this in interviews in September 2011 and revealed:

'Senior ex-officers have confirmed that no detailed staff work was available to give substance to the belief [that Iraq would be drawing down according to plan and releasing resources for Afghanistan] … there was no detailed planning for how two simultaneous theatres of operation would be managed and supplied.'[32]

When asked why a bigger reserve had not been earmarked, General Walker (who was CDS until just before the final decision was taken) said:

'This was us supporting a NATO corps operation. It was up to NATO to find the reserve [to support our forces in Helmand]. They had plenty of assets at their disposal. With a bit of effort they could have created a reserve.'[33]

Given that the total NATO force in theatre in 2006 was 20,000 troops and NATO was about to assume responsibility for the internal security of a country with a dispersed population of 32 million suffering a virulent and active insurgency, this was probably an unrealistic assumption. It was not the view shared by the other key British officer, Lieutenant General David Richards, who was just about to take his headquarters of the Allied Rapid Reaction Corps (ARRC) to Kabul to command the NATO troops. Following extensive analysis and war-gaming over the summer before they left, the ARRC staff officers had realised that they were critically short of certain combat assets, particularly a dedicated reserve. Richards initially tried to get NATO to provide this through the normal channels, but was consistently rebuffed by his immediate NATO commander, an officer whose speciality lay with transport airlift rather than the Operational Art. He then tried to persuade the UK Ministry of Defence to make up the shortfall, including one very heated exchange with the Director of Operations, Lieutenant General Rob Fry, but again nothing was forthcoming. Soon after he got back to his headquarters, he was told plainly enough by a visiting senior UK general at the end of a cordial supper that any further protest would mean that it would be the last job Richards would get as a serving officer. Even then Richards did not give up and arranged to have a private side discussion with Dr John Reid, the Secretary of State, in the margins of a meeting in Berlin. As a result, Dr Reid made sure that some additional artillery and helicopters were provided, but they were not enough as events soon proved.[34]

More than anything, this indicates the bind that the UK found itself in: how to be an active Alliance member showing leadership, without being drawn into shouldering the disproportionate burden of troop contributions? It also shows the acute challenge of truly judging circumstances on the ground from London. The officer at the head of the MoD's own internal think tank (the Defence Operational Capability Directorate) was of the opinion that with the Helmand operation, 'they had been sold a dodgy car, by those who planned it …where the engine and gearbox were not connected'. He told the Chiefs of Staff in his first review of the Helmand operation in July 2006 that:

'No reserves had been allocated. It was designed like the raid on Dieppe in 1942, which ended in complete failure, when given the right effort it could have been like D Day in 1944. I think that we have got Afghanistan profoundly wrong—history will judge you.'[35]

At least Dr Reid's replacement as Secretary of State, Des Browne (now Lord Browne of Ladyton), seemed to arrive at the correct perspective commenting afterwards about a situation that he had had little influence over and which had so dramatically escalated within a few days of his taking office:

'When Ed Butler created the platoon houses he took a tactical decision which changed our strategy. It was within the range of decisions that it was legitimate for him to make, since everyone was conditioned to believe that supporting Governor Daoud was crucial to our strategy. So I told Ed that I took responsibility for his decision.'[36]

The UK Parliament's House of Commons Defence Committee later examined in detail the circumstances surrounding the decision to deploy.[37] Their conclusions are difficult to disagree with:

'Given the demanding nature of the situation in Iraq, we do not consider that the implications of the decision to move UK Armed Forces into the South of Afghanistan in early 2006 were fully thought through, in particular, the potential risk to UK Armed Forces personnel. We consider that this criticism applies equally to the international decision to deploy into the South, in that all decisions made at such a level inevitably involve tensions and delay, which contributed in this case to the difficulties subsequently encountered.

… we are concerned that the MoD did not anticipate that the presence of the [UK] Armed Forces in Helmand might stir up a hornets' nest, especially as much of the intelligence was contradictory.

[that] … senior military advisers should nonetheless have raised serious concerns about the unpredictable nature of the conflict on which they were embarking. This briefing should have drawn clear attention to the need for force levels to be sufficiently robust to cope with an unpredictable conflict.'

So how did this come about? The answers lie deep within the way the war was commanded from the UK and the way the people in the Ministry of Defence organised themselves, which will now be explored.

11

EMERGING CRITICISM AND FLAWED STRATEGIES

'Hindsight is always easier than the dreadful moment of decision.'

Richelle E. Goodrich, 'Eena, The Return of a Queen'

A Capable Army

Even though the British armed forces didn't seem to be winning the wars of 2000–10 in Afghanistan and Iraq, paradoxically few criticised their fighting prowess. Evidence of this is found aplenty in the dozen or so books written by journalists that chronicle the events, either there in person or speaking to those who had been involved in the fighting, and some of whom were actively seeking the worst. They describe the hard conditions, harsh fighting and unremitting tension for young soldiers, nurtured as they were in towns and villages far away in the developed world, completely absent from the pitiless realities of primitive living and clan bloodshed. These are recurring ideas in all the books: that the soldiers showed toughness, competence, courage and, more often than not, a patent humanity and considerable restraint; that the company and battalion officers were efficient and professional, astonishingly wise heads on surprisingly young shoulders; that they all stood their ground. These were well-trained, highly motivated, staunchly courageous military units who endured much privation cheerfully and faced danger with confidence and steadiness.

But darker themes are there too. Each soldier had a crucial personal demon to slay on first going into combat—spooked or bloodied, would he or she run away? At the moment of test, passing the rite was infinitely more important to them than any destructive effects that might be caused by wild or indiscriminate shooting in the process. Soldiers frequently became detached about the fate of the enemy they had just killed and were callous about the citizens caught in the crossfire—the enemy 'just kept coming'; contact with citizens was infrequent and without much understanding. Soldiers who had been trained using battle simulators and who were used to playing video war games in their spare time could confuse the game with real life, becoming detached from human suffering and distress. The unremitting heat and dust led to short fuses and ill temper. The insidious but devastatingly effective IEDs (improvised explosive devices—booby-trapped bombs) seemed 'the work of cowards who would not face the fight' and made soldiers vengeful over the casualties inflicted on their comrades. There was a sense of abandonment by the nation at home, who seemed to have no comprehension about how tough it all was. Not all the time, but enough times. These scars are part of the record, but the commentators understood rather than criticised.

Someone Was to Blame

But then there is a gap. Above the level of the soldiers and their battalion officers, and in contrast to it, sharp criticism is universally directed at the performance of the UK's higher commanders. The books are littered with emotive descriptions of muddle, incompetence and ineptitude at the top. For instance, Dr Roger North alleges that there was a criminal failure to provide the deployed forces in Iraq and Afghanistan with the right kind of equipment, or enough of it.[1] Stephen Grey asks important questions about the inconsistencies inherent in what the commanders and soldiers were being asked to do in Helmand.[2] Jack Fairweather describes a drift in policy guidance and a lack of understanding of the complexities of the local situation in Iraq which resulted in dreadful consequences.[3] James Fergusson forensically dissects the muddle over the UK's entry to Helmand.[4] Sir Sherrard Cowper-Coles, the UK's Ambassador to Kabul, believed that the British Army was too eager in looking for action in Afghanistan so as to justify its existence and that 'at almost every stage, the expansion of our military mission in Afghanistan … had been agreed by often skeptical politicians on the basis of [too] upbeat military advice'.[5] The pre-eminent UK military think tank, the Royal United Services Institute, published a series of papers ('The Afghan Papers'[6] and 'The Afghan Decisions'[7])in which commentators tried to explain the UK's military decision-making in Afghanistan, and much of it was critical in tone and conclusion. Condemnation of the higher leadership reaches a crescendo in Frank Ledwidge's book *Losing Small Wars* where, after a very authoritative account of the ground wars, he gives the impression that he thought that all the generals were stupid.[8] Whilst some of the writing tells a good story and is thrilling, the reader is left in no doubt about how universally angry the authors felt about the errors that they sense occurred at the top. And it is certainly convincing, for most of them had been in Iraq and Afghanistan for long periods as first-hand observers, making their comments raw, authentic and believable.

Tactical leaders were criticised repeatedly for having a 'can do' military mentality and for being far too aggressive, but without perhaps also considering the ineffective flock that an army that 'wouldn't do' would be, or one that lacked a winning spirit in its veins. It is worthy of note too that the senior officers and military system that were criticised so strongly were also the ones who created the admired forces that deployed to Helmand and Iraq, so at least they knew how to train a fighting force. A more detached interpretation of the lack of success by senior tactical commanders is provided by others, for instance Professor Anthony King.[9] He starts from a different viewpoint—that those British commanders were very competent overall—but he comes to a parallel and similarly baleful conclusion. Professor King explains how British commanders got the fighting in Helmand right and were very mindful of the civilian population, but failed to concentrate their forces sufficiently to be effective because they were too ready to seek battle (which, in other circumstances, would have been an excellent military instinct); how their activity would be successful for a day, but was wasted without enough forces to hold what they had seized. As quoted earlier, they were simply 'mowing the grass'.[10]

Of course, armies are great lumbering beasts and getting them synchronised and moving in a coordinated direction is a huge achievement of willpower and skill by a field commander. He must exhibit a cool and optimistic face, whilst at the same time suffering the same terrors (or worse) as those whom he commands. Tactical situations can be very fast-moving and the facts are often unclear, yet sharp and lasting decisions are demanded. He has to keep a clear and analytical mind, whilst being surrounded by the intense noise, distraction and clutter of an army on operations. He must be neither hostage to his worst fears, nor reckless in his desire to win. And, at the end of the day, it is onto the commander's conscience that the butcher's bill of the casualties and the dead will fall. These are not easy things to get right and it is remarkable that, given the many different brigades that deployed into the two theatres, so few tactical mistakes were made. This is not to deny that things did go wrong, because the overall results were not what were being sought. But if the commanders were doing largely what they had been trained to do, and doing it well, the focus must shift to whether they had orders that were achievable—and whether they were working to a correct long-term framework.

The Chilcot Inquiry into the circumstances of the UK's involvement in the Iraq War took statements from many of those responsible for the prosecution of the wars.[11] They are very revealing. A common impression comes through from senior British military commanders that somewhere, outside and above them, the campaign strategy was incomplete and the policy wanting. Yet if you asked any politicians of the era, they would counter by saying that they consistently followed the military's advice and gave them everything that they asked for. So there is a disconnection here. Everyone agreed that things did not go well, but none of those involved seemed to believe that the fault lay with him or her.

Further evidence has emerged. The series of papers entitled 'Britain's Generals in Blair's Wars' gives an account of what it was like to command in Afghanistan and Iraq.[12] It would be difficult to read the chapter by Major General Andrew Stewart, commanding the Multi-National Division in the south-east of Iraq in 2003, without being hugely impressed by the subtlety, restraint, creativity and intelligence that he brought to the task.[13] These commanders were mostly generals who would recognise all the complaints made against the British Army's activities in Iraq and Afghanistan by the authors previously, but who felt powerless to do much about it, given the constraints of political will and lack of resources under which they were operating.

The problem seems to have been the strategic structure in which the tactical instructions were set. To explore this idea further, the strategies handed down to the tactical commanders have to be examined and the inconsistencies exposed: if commanders were asked to do one or more strategically incompatible things at the same time, where they were bound to fail, however good they were. But first it is necessary to unravel what strategy is and what good and bad strategy looks like.

Strategy

'Strategy is designed to make war useable by the state, so that it can, if need be, use force to fulfil its political objectives.'

Professor Sir Hew Strachan, 'The Direction of War'[14]

Much is made of the need for an organisation to take a strategic approach, but the term is often used too loosely and confusion occurs. Strategy is derived from the Greek words *strategos*, a general, and *strategia*, generalship. Entrusted with the challenge of defending Athens against the Persians in 480 BC (a policy objective), the Athenian general Themistocles planned to abandon the city of Athens to the Persian Army and concentrate on defeating the Persian Navy in battle at sea, destroying the sea line of communication back to Persia and hence forcing a general retreat (his strategy). His tactical plan within that strategy was to lure the Persian Navy into an ambush in the Bay of Salamis, where the cramped space denied the Persians the advantage of their numerical superiority. He won.

Reflecting on his experiences of the fighting in the later Napoleonic Wars of 1806–7 and 1813–15, the renowned strategist Carl von Clausewitz defined strategy in his book *On War* as the process of deciding how battles could be used to support the purposes of the war (note: not of warfare, but in support of the general's conduct of the war). A contemporary of his, the Austrian Archduke Charles, said, 'Strategy is the science of war: it produces the overall plans … and decides the general course of the military enterprises; it is, in strict terms, the science of the Commander-in-Chief.'[15] More recently, J. C. Wylie defined strategy in his book *Military Strategy* as 'a plan of action designed in order to achieve some end; a purpose together with a system of measures for its accomplishment'.[16]

In later generations, the meaning of the word widened even further and its sense became corrupted. Today, strategy often gets conflated with the policy aims above it, which should be giving strategy its purpose. Worse still, it gets entangled with the operational plans below, which should be deriving their guidance from the strategy. Indeed, in a looping movement, strategy is used now as the description of the government policy of which, in its classical meaning, it is supposed to be the servant. An indication of this in the period was that the MoD maintained a senior civil servant as its *policy director*, whereas no one was appointed as a *strategy director*. The MoD had no mandate to make government policy for the armed forces, so did not need a policy director, but it was surely expected to create strategies to serve the government's policy. That post was absent.

The essence of this is that military commanders need the ability to develop stratagems in order to deliver the policy objective that they have been directed to achieve. A useful framework is to consider strategy as the middle layer in a scaffold of ends, ways and means. *Ends* are the policies—what you hope to achieve. *Ways* are the strategies or grand plan—how you will achieve the policy aim. *Means* are how the strategy will be carried out (note that, in this sense, this is not just the resources that you would require). This is where we are going, here is the plan and this is how we will carry it out. Professor Sir Hew Strachan described the process by which military strategy should be framed as follows:

'In the ideal model of civil–military relations, the democratic head of state sets out his or her policy, and the armed forces coordinate the means to enable its achievement. The reality is that this process—a process called strategy—is iterative, a dialogue where ends also reflect means, and where the result—also called strategy—is a compromise between the ends of policy and the military means available to implement it.'[17]

An adversary will have a strategy too, to which the strategist must continually respond; as Strachan says, strategy is iterative. The two wars considered in this book were at their most challenging during their insurgency phases, when the insurgents soon realised that they would lose if they attacked the government's security forces head-on because the latter were invariably better equipped. So their plans were to avoid battles and attack potential weaknesses: supply lines, isolated detachments, the morale and legitimacy of the government. As a result, insurgents came together in strength infrequently, preferring to attack across a wide area, thereby dispersing the security forces' strength as it tried to protect the population. By scattering to cover the ground, the security forces dissipated their superiority of numbers and created vulnerable supply routes, which could then be ambushed. The insurgents tried to limit their opponent's freedom of movement even further by placing improvised explosive devices against vehicles and troops on foot and by sniping with rifles and mortars, on every occasion melting away before they were counter-attacked. The insurgents attempted to goad the security forces into violent reactions that would antagonise the local population, attacking the symbols of government legitimacy and authority, such as schools, courts, transport links, police forces and government offices. Confronted with this, the security forces needed a *counter-strategy* that protected weaknesses and attacked the insurgents' vulnerabilities, all the time resisting the insurgents' provocations. As things turned out, a successful counter-strategy to the insurgencies in Iraq and Afghanistan proved elusive to the UK and, as was explored later, the strategies that Britain did adopt often contained such stark internal contradictions that they rotted the overall strategy from within.

A successful strategy should give enough freedom for the tactical commander to fight his battles imaginatively and with the least constraints; however, it must focus him remorselessly on to the policy aims that his military actions are serving. It should provide crystal-clear guidance, from which every inconsistency and contradiction has been ruthlessly purged before it is issued. In absolute terms this is not overly difficult to do if the policy aims remain constant—which of course they don't—but what seems to be a much greater challenge is to become a good strategist in situations where policy is shifting, about which Colin Gray has written extensively.[18] He highlights the point that plans can only be completely relevant at the moment of their birth and that they need constant updating and re-appraisal by the strategist as events unfold, in order to ensure that they continue to serve the chosen policy objective. Hew Strachan equally emphasises Clausewitz's view that 'the most important single task for strategy is to understand the nature of the war it is addressing'.[19]

Herein lays the rub for the strategist. How to put aside preconceptions and correctly unravel the woven fabric of the current war, in order to discover its true warp and weft? How to retain a firm eye on the policy, whilst adapting a strategy for circumstances as they develop? This is even more difficult—indeed it might be impossible to achieve—if the high-level policy that the strategy sets out to serve is unclear, or if the policy continually morphs under the buffeting of daily circumstance. Often these changes in policy fail to be declared openly, because politicians wish to retain a certain ambiguity in order to escape being hemmed in by circumstances. To do all this within a massive and consensus-seeking head office bureaucracy such as the UK Ministry of Defence takes unusual skill.

A major problem for Britain in the wars in Iraq and Afghanistan was that the UK's pre-eminent policy objective for the decade was to support its 'special relationship' with the US, where fighting wars alongside each other was a visible token of the vigor of its relationship. This was always more than just the UK being a poodle to its stronger ally, because America had become the leader in both voice and action for all the ideals that Western nations generally had come to regard as fundamental. However, it drove the UK's policy aim to be at war, if the US was at war. Inevitably and fatally, the UK's subordinate military strategy evolved in turn to be in combat for as long as the US was in combat—as Prime Minister Tony Blair said after the Twin Towers, 'our job is to be there with you … you are not going to be alone'. What that combat was supposed to achieve for the UK was always of lesser importance. So it is not surprising that, whilst the policy aim of supporting America remained clear and simple, the UK's policy aims for the wars in Iraq and Afghanistan were much more imprecise and bounced around amongst a clutch of different ones. Moreover, UK strategy was contingent on changes in US strategy, which were themselves buffeted around. Over the decade it was declared variously that the UK was involved to defeat al-Qaida, to deny al-Qaida a sanctuary, to give the local populations security, to prevent terrorist attacks on the streets of British cities, to further democracy, to bring better governance, to defend the rights of women, to stop drug production, and so on.

With a policy objective that had become being at war because the Americans were at war, it is no wonder that British field commanders were left to puzzle out what tactical success would look like in both Iraq and Afghanistan and why the interpretations of how to achieve it changed so frequently and radically. When the UK decided that it could no longer find enough resources to be at war—and therefore had to withdraw from Basra, for example—it put great strain on the overall policy aim of maintaining the 'special relationship'. Likewise, when the UK underestimated the scale of effort needed to occupy Helmand, the subsequent failure to pacify the province only added to the damage. Strategists should have worked all this out beforehand.

Air Chief Marshal Sir Jock Stirrup made 'strategy' the main theme of his annual lecture to RUSI on 3 December 2009, although he did not go so far as to expose what his chosen strategy might be.[20] He expressed his frustration at the lack of a strategic approach and went on to explain how he was improving its teaching and application in the UK armed forces by courses and focus groups. This left the audience questioning because the initiative for all strategic behaviour in the MoD lay with him, the chief strategist of the organisation, and not with his subordinates who would follow his lead. By his questions, directives and example, good strategy would evolve and the strategic instinct would be developed.

Good Strategy

There were a number of events that showed that the UK was perfectly capable of crafting good military strategy and forging effective campaign plans, if the circumstances were right. Moreover, many individuals showed an inherent 'instinct' for good strategy. In contrast to later developments, the campaign planning for the UK's part in the initial invasion of Iraq in 2003, for instance, was excellent. It was a huge and complicated task. The collection and dispatch of forces went exceptionally smoothly, coordinated by PJHQ. The Chiefs of Staff Committee worked well together and posed the correct strategic question to the government about the legality of the war. Prime Minister Tony Blair found the time to spend half a day with his military chiefs talking through the options and listening to their concerns. Without arguing for the rights or wrongs of the decisions here, the UK government had arrived at a clear policy for the invasion itself and the MoD had developed a good strategy to implement it. This was the Whitehall machinery working as it should.

During the fight northwards, Major General Robin Brims halted the UK 1st Armoured Division for a week outside Basra, instead of rapidly assaulting into the city as he would have been taught to do. Rather, he waited at a distance for the Baathists to melt away, which they duly did. The alternative would have been a hard slog in close, urban terrain, with much destruction of the civil infrastructure and consequent alienation of the population. Brims's decision had strategic consequences and gave the very best chance for a good policy outcome to Britain's occupation of that city.

In the chaotic aftermath of the invasion, the UK's lead in Iraq, Sir Jeremy Greenstock, immediately spotted the danger inherent in Paul Bremer's chosen strategy of sequencing a protracted handover of power in Iraq. Greenstock fought exceptionally hard for a different strategy of early elections and early handover of power to the Iraqis, giving the Iraqi people responsibility for their own affairs before discontent against an occupying power could find shape and gain momentum. That he was unsuccessful does not undermine the fact that here his—and the UK's—strategic intentions were correct.

As the situation deteriorated sharply in Iraq in the unsettled days before the US surge of troops in 2006, Lieutenant General Graeme Lamb (as the UK Deputy Coalition Commander) championed a way to nudge the Sunni insurgency out of the hands of al-Qaida and into supporting the Maliki administration, which bore fruit in the 'Al-Anba Awakening'. He had correctly identified an unorthodox opportunity in rapidly changing circumstances and against much other background noise; moreover, he had the clarity to see how it supported the overall policy and to push it hard.

Major General Richard Shirreff, as GOC Multi-National Division South-East in Iraq, devised a comprehensive strategy to drive the militias out of Basra with Operation Sinbad. Shirreff had risen above the daily distractions of the conflict and come up with a plan to deliver the UK's policy objective of orderly withdrawal from a pacified province.

Colonels Andy Bristow and Richard Iron provided invaluable strategic advice to General Mohan al-Furayji—the Iraqi commander in southern Iraq—about how the Iraqi government forces could retake Basra. It was Bristow and Iron's plan that became the successful 'Charge of the Knights' operation to defeat the Jaish al-Mahdi militia.

In Afghanistan the UK seized the initiative for the West in December 2001 by creating ISAF in Kabul and then sending in Major General John McColl—a clear-thinking, wise and reflective soldier—to support President Karzai early in the new President's term of office. McColl was so successful in this post that Karzai asked that McColl return when he rejected Lord Ashdown as the proposed UN High Representative several years later. The UK was behaving strategically here in bringing in the right person to support the local leader so as to serve the policy objective of a stable Afghanistan.

Brigadier Jeremy Thompson, commanding 3 Commando Brigade in Afghanistan, realised how the first brigade had gone into Helmand with too few resources and had become 'fixed', so he changed the strategy. His strategy was to draw in his forces and reduce his tasks, thus he was able to regain the tactical ability to manoeuvre and wrest back the initiative from the Taliban. Later, Brigadier Andrew MacKay, leading the UK's 52nd Infantry Brigade, re-orientated the campaign in Helmand away from an early emphasis on killing insurgents towards protecting the people, echoed later by General McChrystal. In 2009, Major General Nick Carter as ISAF Regional Commander South successfully parsed out the different Afghan power groups in the area and then followed a strategy that would separate the population from the Taliban, by physical barriers if necessary.

Whilst the tactics—the fighting—was consistently successful and the UK never came close to being defeated in battle, eventually Whitehall could no longer ignore the lack of a effective strategic script to give meaning to what the UK was doing in Iraq and Afghanistan. In his second year as CDS, Air Chief Marshal Sir Jock Stirrup became very exercised by this problem and initiated a number of measures to generate a greater strategic instinct in the MoD Main Building. He could see clearly the penalty of performing discrete military operations without a cohering strategic theme to give them overall purpose. He should be given considerable credit for this because he was challenging established practices head on. The UK was, late in the day, trying to string actions together to give better shape and form to what it was attempting to do.

It is revealing, though, how so few of these examples of good strategic behaviour occurred in Whitehall.

Contradictions in UK Strategies

'We go through the present blindfolded … only later when the blindfold is removed do we realise what we've been through and understand what it means.'

Milan Kundera

Other parts of UK strategy never looked so good. Lieutenant General Sir Rob Fry, looking back at the gap between policy aspirations and applied military strategies for Iraq and Afghanistan during his time as the UK's military Director of Operations, would say later '… grand strategy [or policy] and military strategy passed as ships in the night'.[21] At almost every turn there were inconsistencies in what people were being asked to do. And inconsistencies between aspirations and the resources provided. To illustrate this, some of the instructions given out from Whitehall will be examined in more detail, highlighting the problems that resulted from them.

The allegation that the coalition won the war but then lost the peace is clearly true and the US has been excoriated for this failing, but the UK made exactly the same mistake. Attached to US military planning teams, UK military officers Major General Tim Cross and Major General Albert Whitely found that they were consistently speaking to tin ears when they reported back in London about the lack of preparation for post-conflict stabilisation.[22] It seemed impossible for them to attract attention to the issues involved, above the noise generated by the focus on defeating the Iraqi Army and institutional hostility to the war from some important corners such as the UK's Department for International Development.

With the invasion complete, the UK's deployed forces quickly reduced from a large division down to a single fighting brigade. This was insufficient to calm down the tribal areas of Maysan and Al Marrah as well as to police Basra city and Britain was soon driven out of the outlying provinces through a lack of resources. This was excused by saying that if Basra was pacified, the outlying areas would settle down.

But there was worse to come. The military force that could be deployed on the streets of Basra at any one time—once guard duty and sleeping were taken into account—was never more than an infantry-heavy battle group, that is to say about 500 men. As the Shia insurgency boiled over in Basra, the absurdity of expecting such a small force to confront an armed insurrection in a city with a population of nearly 2 million people was evident. In strategic terms, this offered two courses: reinforce to win, or withdraw as quickly as possible to prevent further loss of life. The UK was unable to decide which to do and it effectively asked its tactical commanders to 'make do'. By this, London abrogated control of the design of the campaign going forward and was too influenced by the immediate ideas of the commanders on the ground. Yet 'Phase 4'—post-conflict operations—was a key part of any overall war plan, indeed it is prescribed in the UK's own doctrine and it had been included as one of its campaign objectives.[23] How was so little done to prepare for it by the UK?

Almost unbelievably, an identical situation emerged later in Helmand, where a misappreciation of the scale of the security challenge that the UK's Task Force Helmand would meet nearly led to the UK being defeated in battle by the early Taliban assaults. Brigadier Ed Butler, the initial Brigade Commander, was allocated a single battlegroup for the task, although he managed to get that increased to a force of 3,200 before deployment. He had recommended a force of 14,000 troops, for which he was ridiculed.[24] Eventually the UK would treble the size of the Helmand force, but even this was never enough to get on top of the situation: a point evidenced by the tenfold increase later under the US Marines who eventually brought some stability in the area. By attempting to cover too large an area for the forces it was prepared to commit, the UK became 'fixed' in both Basra and Helmand, in military parlance, and were devoid of the resources to take the initiative. Ironically, it was a British field commander, Lieutenant General David Richards as commander of ISAF, who came up with a scheme for limiting operations to smaller, discrete 'Afghan Development Zones', areas that were restricted to the size that the available forces could defend. So the right instincts were there in the British military psyche, but could not surface.

The lack of enough security forces also had sinister effects on the security of the local population. James Quinlivan suggests from historical analysis that successful counter-insurgency operations require about 20 security personnel per 1,000 population, about ten times what is required for policing a tranquil situation.[25] This was never achieved in either theatre. In Basra, Operation Sinbad fizzled out because there were never enough troops to secure all the areas that had been taken back from the militias, who simply filtered back to terrorise the population after the Army had moved on. In Helmand, the UK was always capable of matching the Taliban in battle, but it was too small to prevent the Taliban from operating. Crucially, the numerically-weak UK force could only defend itself by using heavy weapons such as mortars and artillery, attack helicopters and air support. The 'collateral' damage caused by these heavy weapons to the lives and property of the Helmandis was very great, as they were inevitably caught in the crossfire.

Furthermore, the UK allowed the battles with the Taliban to be fought *amongst* the population that the UK had set out to protect, destroying their towns and livelihoods and killing them in the process, the exact opposite of its policy intention. If the UK was not prepared to send enough troops to swamp the area, why did it pretend that it had done so and still occupy the towns with inadequate forces? For attempting the right solution with the wrong resources carries the hope that the enemy will make an even greater miscalculation and, in this case, the Taliban read the UK's weaknesses correctly. The UK should have been much more careful about where it chose to fight its destructive battles—as it did in Malaya, where the UK managed to separate the local populations from the fighting by moving it wholesale into defended villages and driving the insurgents into the jungle, where the fighting took place.

Somewhere a better analysis of the cause and effect of the pain imposed on the local population in both Basra and Helmand should have been made. Good strategy is not about leaping to the obvious or conventional solution, but about having a plan that correctly balances the competing priorities. Killing a large number of Taliban foot soldiers—success—at a terrible price to the population that the UK set out to protect—failure—was never going to be the correct balance. As Churchill observed, when rejecting a proposal to bomb railway yards in France for which there was a strong military imperative but which carried the potential to kill many French civilians, 'you are piling up an awful lot of hatred'.[26]

The contradictions did not end there. A basic tenet of successful counter-insurgency campaigns is achieving the closest interaction between the military force and the local population. If that exists, intelligence will flow and understanding develop, with reassurance about motives on all sides. In Malaya and Kenya, the UK twinned its regiments with local forces and a significant proportion of the British officers and NCOs gained the ability to converse in the local dialects. Almost all the officers and SNCOs seconded to the Sultan's forces to defeat the insurgency in Oman in the 1970s could speak some Arabic. In Northern Ireland, the soldiers had the same language as the inhabitants and patrols always included a chat-up element.[27]

This simply did not exist in Helmand, or Basra. The UK brigades lacked understanding of the local circumstances and were unable to talk to the population except through interpreters or sign language. Of course, gaining these skills was always going to be testing: Arabic, Pashtu and Dari are challenging languages to learn, when a six-month tour was but a blink of an eye in a British officer's career. But it makes chilling reading to witness the poverty of the cultural and language preparation conducted in accounts of British operations. Sam Kiley's story of 16 Air Assault Brigade's time in Helmand in 2008 in his book *Desperate Glory* shows that communication was at best a cheery wave and more often a scowl. As a result, the British troops involved had poor interaction with the local population and very little understanding of their culture, largely because neither side could comprehend what the other side was saying.

As well as language, awareness of the traditional arrangements in Iraq and Afghanistan was very superficial. The UK got a bit closer in Iraq, where people like Major General Jonathon Riley and Major General Andrew Stewart placed a greater emphasis on their political/military responsibilities—Stewart worked out that he represented the 'Sheikh of Sheikhs' in southern Iraq and tried to operate through the existing sheikhly tribal system.[28] Even so, Rory Stewart's account as deputy governor in Maysan Province, Basra, showed how inept even this effort appeared to him in cultural terms.[29] Ram Seeger and Rory Stewart show how the coalition (and the governments in Afghanistan) blindly worked *across* the grain of the traditional tribal structures, instead of through the existing pathways,[30] with spectacularly poor results.[31]

So it was with intelligence. Britain was repeatedly surprised by events in Iraq and Afghanistan, often failing to understand and anticipate the dynamics of what was going on. This was not because the field commanders wanted it that way, but their short time in theatre was too brief for them to gain a nuanced or enduring picture and their local intelligence was so poor that they struggled to achieve anything beyond a superficial understanding. It was not until 2008, two years after entry into Helmand, that the Army's Intelligence Corps started engaging academics who had a detailed knowledge of local circumstances.[32]

The failure to understand what was really happening in Helmand was to have far-reaching consequences. As the shooting started, the UK believed it was facing a monolithic Taliban insurgency. Instead, there was a complicated four-cornered struggle taking place between the local Nurzai, Achalzai, and Barakzai tribes against the Alizai,[33] with the Kabul government's writ only exercised through these tribal fiefdoms.[34] The Taliban had initially appealed only to smaller groups and households, who were beyond the protection of powerful tribes. By forcing President Karzai to dismiss the principal warlord in Helmand, Sher Mohammed Akhundzada, as Governor, the UK completely upset the local power balance without properly comprehending the consequences of what it was doing. An armed conflict emerged where none had previously existed. Maybe it needed upsetting and certainly the UK could not be involved in supporting corruption and banditry, but at a stroke Akhundzada transferred his 3,000 local fighters under Taliban control to fight what had by then become the common enemy—the British. The Taliban leadership in Pakistan recognised the opportunity conveniently presented to them by the British invasion and sent reinforcements into Helmand. In effect, the British had created a hornet's nest and then vigorously stirred it.

Lack of good local intelligence meant British forces ended up fighting blind, shooting at those who shot at them. In both Iraq and Afghanistan, they did not realise the complex pattern of clan rivalries that they were getting involved in and the intensely negative effect of their operations on people who might once have supported them. The bloodshed that resulted created violent geometries of its own, as happens in any war, and the British became the unifying, single enemy for all factions.

Good strategic analysis is meant to tease out these truths and give proper status to them. Until far too late, the strategic planners did not recognise the crucial part that language and culture played in successful counter-insurgency. That, without them, interaction would be so poor and the flow of intelligence so minimal that a successful outcome would be impossible. The baleful result was that the UK's good intentions were locally misunderstood and resisted, and knowledge of what the enemy was planning to do was at best only thin.

Another particular problem for the UK in Basra and Helmand was the endemic corruption in the local police forces and the absence of the rule of law.[35] In Basra, the police were linked directly to militia groups coercing the population with thuggery and by slaughter. The UK tolerated the murderous Basra police cell under Captain Jaffa in Jumait for far too long until 2007. In Helmand, the police were so corrupt that the local farmers often accepted the writ of the unloved Taliban—because their justice was swift and clear, rather than delayed and arbitrary. The UK allowed itself to be stained by association with these corrupt elements, undermining good work done elsewhere. We were seen as no better. The UK had met this challenge before and knew what was needed to counter it. In Malaya, a well disciplined police force was created which upheld the law. In Northern Ireland, one of the first actions by the government in London was to disband the discredited 'B Special' reserve constables and make the Royal Ulster Constabulary institutionally incorruptible by very strong supervision. So, with such previous experience, it is a mystery how the UK ever expected to gain the support of the local Basrawi and Helmandi peoples whilst it was blatantly tolerating local police forces that preyed on their own citizens.

The local UK commanders in Iraq and Afghanistan probably felt that the problem of the police was beyond their grasp and tried to operate around it, but Whitehall should have worked out that a strategy that did not challenge the existence of corrupt local police forces and the wholly inadequate justice systems was a strategy missing its keystone. It is too simple to say that that was the ways things were.

The lack of a high-level 'comprehensive approach' (or pan-government coordination across all UK government agencies) also had devastating consequences.[36] In Helmand, the UK found itself in particular trouble by simultaneously championing two completely incompatible strategies: counter-narcotics through poppy eradication and winning the support of the population through 'hearts and minds'. General Sir Mike Jackson remembers one company commander asking him on a visit to Helmand, 'How can we burn this farmer's fields and expect to win his heart and mind?'[37] Of all the NATO programmes undertaken in Afghanistan—justice, education, civil service, economic matters, etc.—it was only the poppy eradication programme that had a negative effect on the local population. All the others carried the promise of improvement. To be seen in a positive way by the local population, poppy eradication would require imaginative measures to substitute for it in the local economy: they could have been helped to plant alternative crops; they could have been given cash substitutions; by buying the poppy crop under controlled circumstances for pharmaceutical purposes.

Yet Britain had willingly offered to lead the poppy eradication programme when discussions for splitting up the tasks of stabilising Afghanistan were taking place in NATO in 2002. Four years later, the UK volunteered to provide the 'hearts and minds' security force in the epicentre of poppy cultivation in Afghanistan. The first task fatally crippled the second. As the eradication programme progressed, many of the out-of-work opium farmers would become a source of dollar-a-day foot soldiers for the Taliban. When these amateur soldiers were killed in battle, the resentment against the British amongst the dead warriors' families only increased.

The MoD strategic analysis failed to highlight the utter incompatibility of these two actions. It should have demanded a much more energetic poppy *substitution* programme, crucial as it was to the success of the military campaign, especially as it was meeting the greater cost of sending the military force.

Finally, the events that led up to the withdrawal of the British forces from Basra exposed further strategic inconsistencies. When the UK withdrew from Basra city to the airport compound, under the fig leaf of 'over-watch', it abandoned the Baswari population into the hands of an unmerciful militia, who coerced them into submission by banditry, kidnap and murder. Their property was plundered and many were killed.[38]

The UK was certainly aware that this would happen. Nobody could justify that this was acceptable behaviour by a government that set out to be a 'force for good', especially as the UN Secretary General Kofi Annan had publically reminded Bush and Blair on the eve of invading that, by the act of invasion, they became responsible under international law for the lives of the civilians.

So what discussion took place that concluded that this was an acceptable strategy? If the decisions were taken in theatre, as some suggest, why were the operational commanders orphaned to take decisions of strategic consequence with insufficient guidance?

EMERGING CRITICISM AND FLAWED STRATEGIES

How were these Strategic Inconsistencies Left Unchecked?

'We were less interested in strategy, more concerned with delivering the strategy.'[39]

Des Browne, Secretary of State for Defence 2006–8

It is all too easy to write about these questions after the events. Daily, the staff in the Main Building of the MoD would have been striving to do their best, often faced with unpalatable options of recommending the extraction of the UK armed forces, with horrible loss of face, or reinforcing apparent failure. In those circumstances, soldiering on in the hope that something better would turn up would look attractive. As will be explored later, given the consensual approach but institutionally divisive structure of the MoD, having a detached relationship from the rest of Whitehall and with the UK being a junior partner in a coalition, this would have pushed the big issues to the side to be solved another day. So they did what they could to address the most pressing problems.

Furthermore, an institutional laziness crept in, excused by repeatedly deferring decisions to the 'commander on the ground'. The contradictions they left in their orders showed that the MoD was failing to think through the tough issues, to energetically forge a coherent long-term strategy or to provide strong leadership from above. This was a distortion of the doctrine of Mission Command, where delegation, not *dereliction*, of authority is required. As Major General Mungo Melvin observed later, the MoD 'was managing the situation rather than leading it; the absence of clear strategic thinking was the watchword of the decade. It was a conspiracy of optimism.'[40]

It is instructive to look at the questions raised in the previous section, for they are not the ones that you might initially have chosen. Apart from the cliff-edge of withdrawing from Basra, the others would be regarded as second order at the time and their strategic importance was probably not properly weighted. But they were key questions. They loop back to the fact that whilst strategy may be easy, being a good strategist is very much more difficult. How to raise these issues to their proper importance amidst all the other distractions? How to avoid choosing strategies flawed by such inconsistencies?

The result was undoubtedly strategic drift. In the case of the UK's withdrawal from Basra, it ended with the worst of outcomes: policy failure and reputational defeat. A population was left at the mercy of gangs and the UK deeply wounded its relationship with the US, paradoxically its most important foreign policy objective.

In Helmand, we chose to do battle with the Taliban in the centres of population whose protection was our policy intent, with terrible consequences for the inhabitants.

In Basra and Helmand, the UK got itself into the position of being seen by the local population to support corrupt security institutions that preyed ruthlessly upon them, even though the well-being of the population was the reason for the British being there in the first place.

From a lack of imaginative initiatives and clarity of purpose, the UK set itself 'mission impossible' in Helmand by combining the conflicting tasks of both *destroying* the existing (narcotics) economy and *constructing* a better life for the locals, all quite apart from the challenge of fighting the insurgent Taliban.

Without making the effort to gain close interaction with the population through language and cultural understanding, the UK was never going to receive the constant stream of low-level intelligence which is crucial to success in a counter-insurgency campaign.

There are common themes in all of these contradictions. The facts were generally known, but their consequences were not faced. There was confusion, a lack of will to see things through, a readiness to take a minimalist approach, and a reduction to a lowest common denominator that would satisfy the scripts of all the contributing government departments. Admiral Boyce's revelation that 40 per cent of the Chiefs of Staff's discussion in the run-up to the invasion of Iraq was about post-conflict issues demonstrates the paralysis that existed, because, as Major Generals Cross and Whitely testified, there was little useful output from spending nearly half the Chiefs' time talking about it.[41] John Reid's understanding that the Helmand expedition would be difficult, but might be conducted without a shot being fired, is in defiance of what he must have known or suspected about the Taliban's strength and intentions, both from the UK's own Helmand plan and the strong warnings put to him by Lieutenant General David Richards as the prospective in-theatre commander.[42] Strategic decisions continued to be taken in theatre and not in London and the will to grip the strategic inconsistencies did not appear. Major General Shirreff's strategy in Basra in 2006 was that there could be no politics without first achieving security; Major General Shaw, who followed Shirreff, reversed the strategy direction by stating that without first achieving a political solution, there could be no security.

Instead, the MoD and Whitehall suffered from group-think and dealing with problems bit by bit as they arose. They worried about 'what the market would bear' in terms of troop numbers and feared being left out of proposed military operations. They failed to see a global picture or define a strategic goal properly, so had nothing to work back from to craft coherent plans. The UK was 'punching above its weight', which by definition held inadequate forces in reserve. There was insufficient regard for the plight of innocent civilians and the cost to our own soldiers was not weighted properly in the calculations.

How dedicated people with excellent intellectual powers, supported by a lavish MoD staff machine, chose such courses and how the UK military allowed contradictions to go untrapped in their orders to the deployed forces will be considered by examining the nature of the system that handed them out. As Desmond Bowen, Policy Director in the MoD (2004–8), correctly observed:

'Too often the energy in Whitehall goes into handling the day-to-day detail, whereas the effort should be concentrated on achieving the big objective ... [it is] essential to keep the strategic purpose and end state in view.'[43]

PART 2

WHY IT HAPPENED

12

MAKING MILITARY DECISIONS

'You can't help but ... with 20/20 hindsight ... go back and say, "Look, had we done something different, we probably wouldn't be facing what we are facing today."'

General Norman Schwarzkopf

Sorting Out the Levels of Decision-making

Every organisation needs a structure for making decisions, where responsibilities are clearly laid out. Someone at the top of the organisation has to set the purpose of the enterprise and, from that, a means of its achievement will be worked out. The purpose and strategy must be reviewed and adjusted as events unfold.

Nearer to where things are happening, a subordinate is given the task of executing the strategy, matched with the necessary resources to do it. That subordinate should be given as much freedom as possible to veer and haul as circumstances develop, but he or she must be careful to report upwards accurately the progress of the task, with suggestions concerning any adjustments needed.

It really is as simple as that. Assign responsibilities; decide the strategy; issue the task; provide sufficient resources; review progress and make adjustments. Organisations which don't do all of that soon descend into a chaos of colliding interests, and confusion ensues.

For a military organisation, this is codified into a number of levels of command. The national policy/strategy function is termed the 'Grand Strategic level' and is primarily the responsibility of the Prime Minister. The agreed policies are translated into defined military objectives at the 'Military Strategic level'. Using them to organise and achieve success in the theatre of war is at the 'Operational level'. Battles themselves are fought at the 'Tactical level'. So, the Chief of the Defence Staff (at the Military Strategic level) receives the government's policy, digests it and issues his military strategy (task, plus resources) to the theatre commander, who decides the plan to achieve that strategy and synchronises the effort required to realise it, leaving the battle commander to choose the tactics, e.g. how the battles will be fought.

But the history of military arrangements in the UK shows that when dealing with matters of vital national interest (of life and death, or of public monies) the clarity of this ideal scheme becomes lost. Instead, caveats will accompany delegations, limiting the options of the commanders nearest the action. Tasks are set with inadequate resources and unrealistic financial exactitude demanded in messy circumstances. The freedom to act is curtailed once images of violence are broadcast back into the political homeland. Great things are expected, but many nervous strings of constraint are attached. Paradoxically, these controls make more likely the very things the constraints set out to avoid and reduce the chance of success.

The Defence Crisis Management Organisation (DCMO)

Before the MoD became an integrated headquarters in a single Main Building, Admiral Lord Mountbatten as the new Chief of the Defence Staff established a joint planning cell in Storey's Gate, Whitehall; an operation to protect Kuwait from invasion in 1961 was the first to be mounted from it. This provided the starting point for what became the MoD's Defence Crisis Management Organisation (DCMO), which moved to operating from nuclear-proof rooms many floors underground in the Main Building of the MoD.

Under this arrangement, policy and military strategy were decided first in London and then operational command assigned either to a NATO headquarters (such as HQ Northern Army Group in Germany) or to one of the static UK headquarters most suited to assume it: United Kingdom Land

Forces (Army), Headquarters Strike (Air Force) or Headquarters Fleet (Navy). Thus, the Falklands War in 1982 was commanded by the Royal Navy from Headquarters Fleet at Northwood; the first Gulf War in 1991 was commanded by the Royal Air Force at High Wycombe; the Bosnia campaign in 1994 by the Army from United Kingdom Land Forces at Wilton. The purpose here was to give a clear point of responsibility and to make the most economical use of the headquarters already funded and in being.

The arrangement worked well, but it was not 'joint'. Furthermore, each headquarters needed very considerable reinforcement when it was activated as a joint war headquarters, which meant they were not seen to be as responsive as they might be to unforeseen events.

There was also confusion about where operational command lay. For instance, during the UN phase of the Bosnian campaign in 1994 the Commander-in-Chief (C-in-C) Land Forces at Wilton was made the Joint Commander. As the Serbs began to close their hold around the British battalion protecting the Muslim population in Gorazde, Bosnia, CinC Land Forces one thousand miles away in Wilton felt obliged to give detailed instructions to the commanding officer of 1st Battalion Royal Welsh Fusiliers about keeping his battalion's defensive perimeter wide. The Commander-in-Chief was acting with best intentions and from his honest interpretation of his responsibilities, but the battalion commander's instinct on the ground was different; he thought that his sentries would be taken prisoner if they were spread out, as he was being ordered to do, which indeed they were. It was hardly an ideal arrangement and caused great tension in the chain of command. It was clear that some other design for an effective chain of command was needed.

To try to give clarity to the split between the two functions—command and political control—and to foster 'jointness', a new Permanent Joint Headquarters, led by a Chief of Joint Operations and working at the military Operational level, was added to the DCMO in 1995. It was located at Northwood, Middlesex, in buildings once occupied by the RN Fleet Headquarters. This was a journey of about an hour from MoD and Whitehall, but it was hoped there could be close liaison between the two locations. The new headquarters was generously set up with IT and buildings, although it suffered from its main command operations rooms being many floors underground in an ex-NATO Cold War hardened shelter, the 'bunker', offering excellent protection in the unlikely event of a nuclear attack. It made for a cramped, labyrinthine place to work and people only emerged from it at the end of their shift to experience fresh air and daylight, or starlight.

High-level Decision-making in Main Building

The task of formulating strategy for PJHQ to execute falls on that part of the Defence Crisis Management Organisation located at the MoD Main Building, an hour away in Central London. This is led by the Chief of the Defence Staff and it becomes his primary concern. Supporting him during 2000–10 were a Deputy Chief of the Defence Staff, Commitments (a three-star military officer and *de facto* the director of operations) and a Policy Director (a three-star civil servant), each with appropriate staffs, generally filled by gifted people at the top of their powers.

Advising the Chief of the Defence Staff and providing specialist input are the Single Service Chiefs. At this time, these met with CDS weekly in the Chiefs of Staff Committee. In attendance, with his own distinct responsibility for policy and finance, was the top MoD civil servant, the Permanent Under Secretary (PUS). In addition, senior members of the Foreign and Commonwealth Office and specialist logistic, medical, procurement, personnel and intelligence three-star officers were all on call. In the absence of a similar coordinating body elsewhere in Whitehall, the Chiefs of Staff Committee developed into a forum for cross-departmental coordination for the prosecution of the wars, with a much wider and more varied membership in attendance as a result.[1] The Chiefs also met more privately for an occasional 'Chiefs of Staff Committee Informal' (COSI) and they were briefed regularly by the Central Staff about the operational situation, in what became known as 'Op COS'. The Chiefs were also members of the Defence Management Board, chaired by the PUS, where defence business and finance were discussed. The Chief of the Defence Staff could use the Chiefs of Staff Committee to explore options and problems, but also had to carry the Service Chiefs with him if the MoD machine was to work effectively. This did not always happen for a variety of reasons.

Sometimes, security prevented it. When Admiral Sir Michael Boyce was told of the UK government's intention to invade Iraq, he was expressly forbidden by the government from passing that information on to his chiefs, although it leaked out anyway to the individuals by back channels. Admiral Sir Alan West, then head of the UK's active naval fleet, was told by his American contacts in June 2002 that war was being planned, so Admiral West himself put the Royal Navy on alert from July 2002 to be poised to deploy to the Persian Gulf by December, even moving a minesweeper squadron 'on the pretext of an exercise' to the Gulf in the late autumn.[2] None of this was on instructions from the Chief of the Defence Staff, who was emphatically disallowed from telling his chiefs anything. The consequence of all of this was that, in Admiral Boyce's own testimony, those responsible for standing up the UK invasion force had too little time to prepare for it, and those responsible for the logistics to support it had too little time to assemble the stores.[3] It also had a spill-over for the post-conflict preparations. Admiral West continued: 'We ... often asked about post-conflict operations, but there was never any clarity on Phase 4.'[4]

When things started to go seriously awry in Iraq, both Admiral West and the PUS (Sir Kevin Tebbit) recalled that they had the greatest difficulty in finding out what was happening, even though they were key members of the committee charged with prosecuting the military effort.[5]

West had a particular worry about the quality of information that was coming up from the deployed forces, the 'ground truth':

'We did not get a real flavour of the situation on the ground and never got a feel for how the situation was changing. One felt one was out on a limb [in the Navy staff]. The weekly chiefs meeting included an Ops briefing, but it was really an information meeting; we were never involved in a discussion.

In retrospect we were probably complacent [about it]. [Lieutenant General] Rob Fry (Director of Operations) did come to see me twice, but there was no further opportunity to debate it [in committee].'[6]

Where once there had been a constant and daily dialogue between the Service Chiefs and the Chief of the Defence Staff, now the discussion was more focused between CDS and PJHQ. Much of the discussion between the Chiefs was about how best to implement decisions already decided upon.

General Sir Michael Walker, who took over from Admiral Sir Michael Boyce as Chief of the Defence Staff in May 2003, recounted later that 'he felt certain' that all the important decisions had been discussed thoroughly at the

Chiefs of Staff Committee during his time as Chief of the Defence Staff.[7] Yet his Chief of the Naval Staff and his Chief of the General Staff both said that they did not know enough of what was going on. General Sir Mike Jackson reflected later:

'I often learnt about things after they had been decided and I often didn't know where a decision had been made ... but orders were orders, so you got on with it.'[8]

Admiral Sir Alan West, Chief of the Naval Staff, said:

'I never knew what went on between the Chief of the Defence Staff and the Prime Minister and I never felt that I was included in the strategic decision-making apparatus for the wars. I did not feel that I was part of the inner Cabinet where decisions were made.'[9]

He went on that, even though he was the head of the Royal Navy, he felt:

'... completely excluded from the ministerial circuit and in all my four years in post I was never invited to No. 10 to discuss the Navy or operations with the Prime Minister.'[10]

Admiral West contrasted this poorly with his previous experience when, as the three-star Chief of Defence Intelligence, he attended Chiefs' meetings under General Sir Charles Guthrie as CDS 'who insisted on making sure that all the Chiefs were properly briefed every morning [for the war in Kosovo] and fully included in the entire decision-making'.[11]

It has been suggested that on occasions an 'executive of two'—the Prime Minister and the Chief of the Defence Staff—was running the decision-making, with the results telegraphed back to Chiefs of Staff Committee for acceptance. General Sir Michael Walker reflected that this was an exaggeration, because it was the Secretary of State who invariably led discussions with the Prime Minister whilst he remained in support as CDS.[12] This is a vital point, because any lack of rigour in the process could lead to confusion about who actually had authorised a particular course of action. The Prime Minster might rightly assume that the chosen action was supported by the Chiefs of Staff, whilst the Chiefs of Staff might believe that they had no option but to accede because of a higher political need that was being telegraphed to them. Commenting on the style of discussions at the top of the MoD, Admiral Sir Alan West said:

'... you could ask a question at one of these top meetings, but it never sort of went anywhere and the question was just left hanging. There was really very little discussion in Chiefs [the Chiefs of Staff Committee] about the invasion of Iraq. If it took place at all, it took place elsewhere. We had two meetings with [Prime Minister] Tony Blair, but we did not debate the plan, we talked about how to execute it.'[13]

The last point West makes is crucial and is worth exploring further. Lieutenant General Sir Rob Fry, as Deputy Chief of the Defence Staff (Commitments), was the senior staff officer responsible for developing and presenting to the Chief of the Defence Staff and the Chiefs the strategic plan for the UK to send a military force to Helmand. I asked him if he had any difficulty getting his plan through the Chiefs of Staff Committee; he replied that it had been well received and there had been only a few questions. There were good reasons for this: not least that the planning had been going on for a year, so Chiefs would have seen much of the detail beforehand. Fry was an analytical, rigorous, forceful and creative officer, one of the most articulate at his level in the MoD, and with all those talents he enjoyed arguing a case. So the plan was fortunate to have such a first-rate advocate and I asked him how much probing about the wisdom of the proposed adventure had occurred; he replied 'none really'.[14] The result was that any discussion focused on the technical challenges of carrying out the deployment, not whether the deployment could achieve its objective, what the collateral cost of deploying to Helmand might be—or what to do if things went wrong.

Air Chief Marshal Sir Jock Stirrup said that he had challenged the plan to go to Helmand, as Chief of the Air Staff, saying 'we didn't know enough', but his protest seems to have had little effect.[15] General Jackson stated that he had no idea why the UK had gone to Helmand, even though he was Chief of the General Staff at the time the decision was taken.[16] This illustrates the fact that the Chiefs were not sufficiently included in the process to be able to make a decision about the deployment, when the appropriate military response should have been to double up the contingency reserve to match the scale of the unquantifiable risk. This was not done.

General Sir Richard Dannatt as Chief of the General Staff in 2006 felt that the decision for the UK to engage in Helmand whilst still drawing down from Iraq (when the United States had reversed its own policy and was surging in further troops) was very worthy of discussion, but he could find no trace of it in minutes of the Chiefs of Staff Committee meetings before he took over; he was unsuccessful in getting the subject on the Agenda when he became a member himself, leaving him intensely frustrated.[17] He came to the conclusion that the decision was taken outside the MoD, between the Prime Minster and the CDS of the time.

Taking all this evidence together supports the idea that the Chiefs of Staff Committee never analysed seriously these two key decisions of the decade: the decision to abandon Basra and the decision to scale up the armed operation in Afghanistan in 2006. Instead, in both cases the MoD worked away at implementing the decisions in the most efficient and effective manner possible, not dissecting the wisdom and the possible consequences of the choices taken. Likewise, there was certainly a lot of discussion about what to do about the aftermath of the invasion of Iraq, Phase 4, but little practical preparation for it.

Sometimes, other pressures crowded in to prevent wider consultation. Air Chief Marshal Sir Glenn Torpy suggested that when he was Chief of the Air Staff:

'it was not my place to question the conduct of a land war, when the Army officers (General Sir Mike Jackson (CGS), General Sir Richard Dannatt (Commander-in-Chief) and Lieutenant General Sir Nick Houghton (Chief of Joint Operations)) all seemed to be in agreement'.[18]

Admiral Sir Jonathon Band followed Admiral West as the Chief of the Navy Staff and was in post when the situations in Iraq and Afghanistan were at their most dire. He felt that the Chiefs of Staff Committee was kept informed about issues, but he did not think it was the forum for him to raise concerns about the consequence or conduct of the wars because, even if he had resigned on such an issue as civilian casualties, it would probably have achieved little, whilst it might have endangered his greater priority of nurturing the project for the Navy's new aircraft carrier.[19] This statement shows the cruel trap that the Service Chiefs found themselves in—support the MoD centre, or defend their own service.

Sometimes, as in all organisations, personality played a role. When Air Chief Marshal Sir Jock Stirrup became Chief of the Defence Staff, General Sir Richard Dannatt was dismayed to find himself kept at arm's length by his

CDS, even though he was the Army's Chief. On the other hand, it must have been uncomfortable for Stirrup to have a subordinate who knew more about the current land operations in Iraq and Afghanistan than he did, and he would have been on edge when dealing with General Dannatt's habit of using the media to exercise pressure. You can easily see how the second action provoked the first. Likewise Des Browne, Secretary of State for Defence 2006–8, commented on the lobbying that the Service Chiefs, including General Dannatt, undertook: 'on occasions they made a lot of background noise … and some of it was very loud noise, especially when they activated their support networks'.[20]

In the decade of the Iraq and Afghanistan wars, the Chiefs of Staff Committee could have been an essential forum in which the grand strategic questions were first identified and then teased and tested. Sometimes the task of keeping the group united prevented too deep a discussion of the key issues or the needs of secrecy prevented early disclosure of impending problems. At other times, the group was preoccupied by the incessant fight over resources, or the game-playing of the competing MoD staffs distracted or nobbled the group. The effects were pernicious and limited the effectiveness of the Chiefs of Staff Committee as a body to monitor and influence the formulation of strategy. It seems that, whilst there was considerable discussion about progress and it was well used for updating, the big questions were not addressed there but were decided elsewhere.

The Permanent Joint Headquarters (PJHQ)

Strategic plans are drawn up in the MoD Main Building by the CDS and handed down to PJHQ at Northwood for execution. PJHQ had great things expected of it and, in one way, it was very successful in bringing the efforts of the individual services into harmony. However, as a crucial point in the chain of command, it had also emerged as neither one thing nor the other. PJHQ had absorbed the three service operational staffs of the MoD and their function was taken on by a new operational branch at Northwood. The old operations directorates in the MoD had been responsible for putting together workable strategies and were in close physical contact with the CDS, Foreign and Commonwealth Office, the Cabinet Office, 10 Downing Street, civil servants and politicians, day to day and hour by hour. Out at PJHQ, these staffs were both physically and temperamentally separated from the centre of power, so they were absent in the magic hours when policy was taking shape and had too little influence on it. Freed from central London, PJHQ might have had a better opportunity to work alongside whichever service was the principal supplier of forces for operations. But that didn't improve either and, although Land Command was training the forces that deployed and received back the casualties, they still found themselves out of the loop.

But it was worse than that. Conceptually, the arrangement was optimised for when the UK might fight alone, where there could be clarity about who would fill the three levels in the scheme of appointments explained above: Military Strategic, Operational and Tactical. In coalition operations, however, the UK found itself as a bolt-on to someone else's chain of command. This fact of life of a coalition arrangement proved manageable at the top and at the bottom of the chain of command. At the Tactical level, the field commander just got on with the challenge of fighting on the ground; at the Military Strategic level (initially, at least) there were good links between London and Washington. But it seriously compromised the function of the Operational commander in the middle, whose role rested with the Chief of Joint Operations (CJO) at PJHQ, located back in a UK suburb, an hour from the centre of London and not forward in the theatre of operations alongside the US coalition leader. For, to be effective, an Operational-level commander has to be in touch with local circumstances, yet not become enmeshed in the actual fighting.

In the Iraq and Afghanistan wars Operational Command was vested in the CJO at PJHQ, with a two-star officer placed in theatre as the lead UK officer. This left everyone dissatisfied. The CJO had no chance to understand or influence complex local circumstances, since he visited the operational theatre only once a month or less, whilst the local commander was not empowered or encouraged to conduct a more long-term campaign to fill the gap. Nobody with national authority was alongside the coalition Operational-level command in Baghdad or Kabul either, until very late in the campaigns. Eventually, by the end of the decade under Air Marshal Stuart Peach as CJO, PJHQ confined its attention more to mounting and sustaining operations, although not before much damage had been done. Later General Sir David Richards was to reflect that:

'Operational-level command was being exercised by coalition commanders, not UK officers. It was the UK's failure to understand and reflect this in their own decision-making that often led to its biggest problems. In alliance or coalition operations, which most operations will be, PJHQ is *de facto* a glorified tactical HQ.'[21]

Lieutenant General John Reith was probably the most dominating personality to hold the post of CJO during the period and he did a very good job of catching the inconsistencies that could have disrupted the build-up and warfighting phases of the invasion of Iraq in 2002. But Reith was spared the complications that dogged his successors, for the political aspects of Reith's task were back in the Western capitals, not in theatre, and the UK's armed forces were well poised and structured for the coming battle with Saddam Hussein's army. Reith also had an immensely capable opposite number appointed as the Operational commander in theatre, Air Marshal Sir Brian Burridge.

Despite that, Reith defined the role of the CJO in PJHQ—not least because he was in charge of it when PJHQ had been really used in anger for the first time. He pushed to establish himself as an equivalent to the Combatant Commanders in the US system (such as CENTCOM, the four-star US commander of the Central Command), who were given greater delegation to run the war by their Commander-in-Chief, the President, and who did so largely without interference from the uniformed officers in the Pentagon. But Reith was unsuccessful in that move. That was probably right for the scale and circumstances of the UK, but in practice it left unresolved the problem of who was the true UK operational commander in the post-conflict phase.

Reith's successors coped less well with the complexity and nuance of the counter-insurgency that followed, not least because they were just too remote from the day-to-day events. Instead, the CJO became largely a transmitter of CDS's orders to the commanders in the front line and responsible for working up the military forces from the UK. Since the orders from the Chief of the Defence Staff were at the Military Strategic level, an important gap emerged which meant that the Tactical commanders began to have disproportionate sway over what should be done. As Lieutenant General Fry put it, 'there emerged a culture where there was just too much deference to the commander on the ground'. But PJHQ could not win either way in this situation, because many on the ground *also* complained of gross interference in the day-to-day minutiae of tactical operations by the staff officers in Northwood, many of whom were from the other two services and had very limited or non-existent experience of land operations.

This arrangement had a poisonous overspill, leading to consistently poor decisions for the longer term, despite the fact that all concerned might be acting from the highest and best interest. A brigade commander presented with a lawless situation in Basra or Helmand would rightly assume that his task was to crush those causing the lawlessness; likewise, to root out insurgents who were attacking his soldiers; or, if on operations with his brigade for only six months, to ensure that something measurable happened to mark the worth of their efforts. The fine balance between longer-term restraint and shorter-term offensive action would not have been the first part of his calculus, because his immediate challenge was to deal with the present, which was testing enough. Nor would he have been allowed the thinking and reflection time to do that, given the frenetic nature of day-to-day command of a fighting force. It is very much to the credit of the brigade commanders that, despite these pressures, they all tried to pin their daily operations into a longer-term framework. But it was inevitable that each successive vision adopted changed substantially on handover, not least because of deference from PJHQ and the MoD to 'the man on the ground'.

It is no wonder that Brigadier James Bashall, commanding the brigade in Basra just before the final withdrawal of British troops, decided that his primary purpose (in the absence of any better long-term intention being handed down to him) was 'to bring his brigade back in one piece … and not have individuals and equipment captured and displayed as had happened to the Americans in Black Hawk Down'.[22]

There was also a problem for the development and broadening of the senior British command caucus, given that the highest UK rank usually entrusted with field command was a major general, or its equivalent, i.e. at two-star level. Any more senior British officer deploying to the coalition's command structure was as a deputy in some sense or another. No doubt they had the innate skills—Lieutenant General Andrew Graham acquitted himself very well when he found himself commanding the Coalition Corps in Iraq for a precious week and organised the counter-attack into Najaf against the Mahdi Army—but the experience was so rare that habitual familiarity in higher command was only observed, not experienced, by UK senior officers. Several have commented in interview that the hugely talented and influential Lieutenant General Sir Rob Fry would have approached things differently as Director of Operations in the MoD if he had experienced high field command himself, which, through no fault of his own, was denied to him. Overall, British officers were less well-developed in this respect than their American counterparts in consequence.

Orphaned Commanders

The significance of control being exercised from a distant PJHQ (located a whole continent away) was that UK troops operated within a considerably less cohesive command structure than their sister US battalions. They could not plug into the resources of the Coalition Corps structure as easily as others, and anyway the British instinct was always to follow coalition instructions less closely than they should have done. Several British officers on the staff of the US theatre command in Baghdad were amazed to find the senior British commander in Basra acknowledging receipt of the Coalition Corps plan passed down to him, but taking very little notice of it.[23] This was fine in the early days whilst the Basra operation was containable by the small force that the UK was prepared to commit and whilst the US higher command still allowed the British Multi-National Division (South-East) to do its own thing; but as the challenge of the insurgency rose, the chance of being supported from within a larger organisation with greater resources was lost. That situation deteriorated rapidly and, to a certain extent unnecessarily, before the US theatre-level command was able to bring the full might of the coalition effort to bear in Basra under 'Operation Charge of the Knights'.

The unsatisfactory nature of the arrangement came to a head during Major General Richard Shirreff's time as GOC of the Multi-National Division (South-East) in 2006. Shirreff realised that the situation was deteriorating fast and that there was an urgent need to do something about it. He devised Operation Sinbad, which would have progressively flooded the Basra police districts one by one with military forces and wrested them back from the control of the militias. This was a sound concept, in concert with what the US was doing in Baghdad, and had every chance of success. However, it required a substantial surge in troops. Over the months that followed, a toxic and heated argument developed between Shirreff, who could see the problem on the ground and the opportunity presented to solve it, and the Chief of Joint Operations, Lieutenant General Nick Houghton, back in PJHQ, who was more aware of the political wish to get out of Basra. Yet when Prime Minster Blair visited Basra towards the end of Major General Shirreff's tour, it was as though Blair did not know of the request for extra troops and he seemed very surprised that the operation had been called off through lack of resources. It could be argued that if proper Operational-level command had been vested in theatre, close to the front line, a much clearer view of both the dangers and the good opportunities to solve them would have permeated through to the political decision-making level, with much better results. For, if you ask the politicians of the time, they will repeat that they did everything the military asked of them.

The dislocation in the command chain was not only between PJHQ and the theatres of operations. Because successive Chiefs of the General Staff were increasingly excluded from core decision-making by the CDS, discussed in more detail later, they tended to concentrate on what they were able to influence. General Sir Mike Jackson had an authoritative manner and self-evident fighting credibility, not least after commanding the land forces in the Kosovo War, so he had little difficulty in putting his view over, but even he felt excluded from the mainstream and settled his aim instead on what he regarded as the villain of the piece, the hydra of the Civil Service. His frustration only increased when, under the axe of a Central Staff directive, he was required to disband four of his infantry battalions. Jackson took the opportunity to begin a wholesale reorganisation of British Army infantry battalions on a scale not seen for a generation. This reorganisation was long overdue, but it generated a huge amount of steam and debate and it was a difficult time to have to carry it off when a war was being fought. As the arithmetic was crunched by his Director of Infantry, Brigadier Jamie Balfour, and the possible structures began to emerge, there was a serious push back from some regiments with histories going back centuries that appeared under threat; others embraced it. The matter was decided in the end largely by whether units could attract sufficient recruits and it emerged that his own tribe, the Parachute Regiment, would survive intact because they were comparatively well manned and provided over half of the candidates who went on to serve in Special Forces, who were very much in demand. This was a bruising battle and it required great strength of purpose to push through, inevitably competing for Jackson's attention as the war was deteriorating in Basra, but it did leave his successors with a modern, flexible structure for the British infantry.

General Sir Richard Dannatt succeeded Jackson in 2006. Having seen how the post of Chief of the General Staff had become boxed in, he was determined to do something about it. A month after taking over, Dannatt wrote formally to the Secretary of State laying out a list of problems that he believed needed to be addressed for the Army. At the receiving end, this letter looked suspicious and was regarded as a calculated act either to exert pressure from an institutionally weak position (which it was), or to prepare the ground for assigning blame later. What is probably true is that Dannatt was crucified by the public perception that as the Chief of the Army he was directing the wars, and was thus responsible for all their woes, whilst the actual authority of his position was much diminished in practice. Feeling out on a limb, Dannatt began to champion the important causes that he *could* influence—achieving much better homecomings for returning soldiers, better treatment of the wounded and increased soldiers' pay—but also ended up commenting unhelpfully where he could not. He felt that he 'needed to show some leadership by letting those in the Army, their families and those who cared about the Army know that the boss (me) understood the pressures and was doing something about it'.[24] However, his declaration that the 'Army was running hot' because it was fighting wars simultaneously in Iraq and Afghanistan, and that the Army was 'more of the problem than the solution' in Basra (a statement which was taken out of its proper context) caused shock amongst those on the front line, and a deep despair and feeling of being undermined from London. It also left the public hopelessly confused. If the Chief of the General Staff (as Chief of the Army) was saying this, the public, unaware that the CGS was lobbying from his relatively weak position on a flank, felt it must be true. Meanwhile, the other two Service Chiefs kept their heads down on the whole and concentrated on what was left for them to influence: keeping their future equipment programmes of aircraft carriers and fighters safely locked into the overall budget.

In interviews with his peers, the most common adjective used to describe Richard Dannatt was 'calculating', and calculation is certainly something that one would hope to find in a senior military general. The established route for the head of one of the armed services to challenge a government prescription or policy is to take the case in the first instance to the Secretary of State for Defence, which Dannatt did. If satisfaction is not gained, the next step is to seek a formal audience with the Prime Minister and, if the issue is still not resolved and is important enough, the chief should express his dissent by resigning. Richard Dannatt followed the first part of the process but he considered that he was talking to 'a deaf hierarchy in No. 10 and the MoD' and, as he explains in his autobiography, thought that he could do more to support his beloved Army by staying in post and applying pressure by other means. This broke the code of shared responsibility amongst the Chiefs and made his brother officers, the CDS and the Secretary of State very uneasy. Before leaping to criticism, it is worth considering what pushed Dannatt to do this. In the eyes of every soldier serving on the front line, Dannatt was their champion as the head of the Army. Every day his office telephone would ring to tell him the news that one or often more of his soldiers had been killed or wounded. His own son Bertie was serving as an infantry officer with the Grenadier Guards in Iraq. He felt himself morally and emotionally responsible for trying to improve things for the Army in a bleeding, hurting war that others seemed to have less concern about; when he tried to raise the issues, 'he got nowhere with Jock Stirrup [CDS]' and the other services seemed frightened that anything more for the Army would mean less for them.[25] He was incensed that the decision that had led to the Army being over-committed in two different theatres at the same time—breaking the conditions of the 1998 Defence Review—seemed to have been taken without properly thinking through the consequences. He was frustrated that an open and trusting interview with the journalist Sarah Sands, attempting to explain to the general public how their Army was under real pressure, had been hijacked by editors into becoming an attack on government policy. The final straw for Dannatt was that he judged that the Prime Minister had become distant from the wars he had led the country into; indeed, Blair only found the time to see his Chief of the General Staff briefly just once before he handed over to Gordon Brown.

Seeing the destructive consequences of Dannatt's actions, the next CGS, General Sir David Richards, used his appointment more deftly and shamed his colleagues on the Chiefs of Staff Committee into making achieving success in the ongoing wars the MoD's absolute first priority, something that Dannatt had started. This was to be called 'Op Entirety', and also ensured for the first time that the Operational Commander in theatre was included in the weekly Chiefs of Staff meetings. David Richards made adroit use of his position and his energies, but he was also building on the reforms of his predecessors. Mike Jackson had managed to push through a much-needed reorganisation of infantry structures, saving one battalion from being axed in the process, and Richard Dannatt had gained very significant improvements to the welfare, pay and status of the Army on operations. Most importantly, all three showed the inherent tensions present within the Ministry of Defence system and that its proceedings were not running smoothly.

13

THE CHIEFS

'For what art can surpass that of the general? An art which deals not with dead matter but with living beings, who are subject to every impression of the moment—such as fear, precipitation, exhaustion … at the same time this man, upon whom all eyes are directed, feels upon his mind the weight of responsibility, not only for the lives and honour of hundreds of thousands, but even for the welfare and existence of his country'[1]

General Albert Karl Friedrich Wilhelm von Boguslawski, 1834–1905

The Development of the Chiefs of Staff System

You may think it curious that in 1899, little over a hundred years ago, the joint commander of the forces that Britain sent to quell the second Boer rebellion in South Africa, with such disastrous early results, was individually chosen by the Prime Minister. It was to be General Sir Redvers Buller, an officer of outstanding bravery and popular appeal who had won the Victoria Cross in the Zulu War of 1879, who was (by his own admission) fatally unsuited to lead such a complex operation. Tactically very astute, Buller was strategically deficient and was outsmarted by the Boer command, suffering defeats at Magersfontein, Stormberg and Colenso.

This occurred because there was no such thing in Britain as a Ministry of Defence or a Minister for Defence; instead there were two individual service ministers, supported by a Commander-in-Chief of the Army (until 1895, a royal duke) and a First Sea Lord of the Admiralty. There were no central planning staffs to coordinate matters between the Army and the Navy and no staff to provide intelligence.[2] There were no centralised estimates to resource the armed forces and no mechanism for balancing the needs of the individual services. Instead, there was intense personal and institutional rivalry, as evidenced later by Admiral Sir John Fisher's remark, 'a penny more for the Army is a penny less for the Navy'.[3]

A Cabinet committee of sorts did exist to provide coordination for the defence of the burgeoning (and increasingly independently-minded) British colonies; it was called the Colonial Defence Committee. This examined and prepared plans for the defence of individual colonies, with the principle that the colonies would provide their own land forces supported within a sea security-zone provided by the mother nation's Royal Navy. A Joint Naval and Military Defence Group was in place to coordinate technical matters, such as the defence of ports. Finally, in 1895, the Cabinet established its own Defence Committee, but without a secretariat and supporting organisation it achieved little.

Britain had a schizophrenic view of its place in the world. In the late 1880s under Gladstone's Liberal premiership there had been a strong current of 'Little England'—a prosperous nation that sponsored colonies around the world for the betterment of the indigenous peoples. When Disraeli followed Gladstone, he promoted a grander idea of 'Greater Britain', creating imperial institutions and crowning Victoria as Empress of India in 1876. A grand Colonial Conference met in 1897, amidst the celebrations for Queen Victoria's diamond jubilee, resulting in 'an imposing ceremony of self-congratulation, marked by a great wave of flamboyant, emotional, Imperialistic feeling'.[4] But two years later the Boer War 'burst like a bombshell upon the British consciousness and the country was shocked to find itself so poorly prepared ... where defeat followed defeat'.[5]

The idea of creating a substantial defence committee had taken hold and, following the recommendations of the Elgin Committee which looked into the conduct of the Boer War, Prime Minister Arthur Balfour created the Committee of Imperial Defence (IDC) in 1902. This committee would be much more powerful than anything that had gone before; it was to be chaired by the Prime Minster, have a secretariat and would be tasked to create a strategic vision for the armed services and coordinate between them. In time, professional Naval and Imperial General Staffs were established to support the IDC so that, by the beginning of the First World War in 1914, Britain was in immeasurably better shape to help confront an expansionist threat from Germany.

The argument about Britain's role in the world also influenced views about the balance of Britain's armed force. The Navy held to the traditional 'blue water' vision of a global force able to provide security by controlling all the seas, with the Army being 'a projectile to be fired by the British Navy', according to Admiral Jackie Fisher.[6] The emergence of a supremely efficient land army in Germany and the passing of the German Naval Laws of 1899–1900, calling for a great shipbuilding programme, then led to a different view: that the country should instead be armed, poised and prepared for the 'bolt from the blue' attack by a continental European power on its homeland and/or to its colonies. This view, understandably held strongly by the Army, required the colonies to have large permanent garrisons and for the homeland to have a substantial anti-invasion force permanently in being, supported of course by a defensive Navy. By the time the First World War started, the Army had organised and trained itself well enough to be able to provide an effective British Expeditionary Force under Sir John French, and the Royal Navy had recognised the imperative of keeping an invincible Home Fleet in European waters.

By 1916, it was recognised that a powerful War Cabinet under firm political direction was required to coordinate efforts across all government departments. This proved to be a considerable success. Following that example, similar arrangements were created at the beginning of the Second World War under Prime Ministers Neville Chamberlain and then Winston Churchill, for the Falklands War (1982) under Margaret Thatcher and for the first Gulf War (1991) under John Major, but for the wars in Afghanistan and Iraq it was only ever a hollowed-out structure under Prime Minster Blair, even when it existed.

The Committee of Imperial Defence had met the need for a powerful central group with the highest political authority to coordinate the actions of the individual services. It served for almost four decades and was not wound down until the outbreak of World War II. However, it could not provide the right forum for the Service Chiefs to hammer out their domestic issues between themselves, especially with the arrival of a third service, the Royal Air Force in 1919. To address this, a new Chiefs of Staff Committee was formed in 1923. This was chaired by each service in rotation, with the chairman responsible for representing rather than forming the collective views of the other chiefs.

Further rationalisation was considered during World War II, but it was judged that a more centralised arrangement would be just too great a span for either a single military head or a single minister. Two important new functional posts did emerge, though: a Chief of Procurement and a Chief Scientist. These posts reflected the growing importance that technology and equipment played in achieving a combat edge, and inevitably some of the power of the individual chiefs ebbed away towards them.

The demands for greater coordination between the individual services were relentless and obvious. Bramall and Jackson[7] explain how developments in the command of UK defence forces were an eternal struggle to keep power matched to responsibility, to achieve balance between conflicting needs and to ensure a proper subordination of the armed forces to political will. In 1946 a single Minister of Defence was established over the three service ministers and, most importantly, that appointee was the only Defence politician to have a seat in Cabinet. In 1959 Marshal of the Royal Air Force Sir William Dickson was appointed to a new military post of Chief of the Defence Staff. Under the centralising enthusiasm of the second incumbent, Admiral of the Fleet Lord Louis Mountbatten, this led inexorably to a unified Ministry of Defence in a single building in 1964, with the merging together of the Admiralty, War Office, Air Ministry and the Ministry of Aviation.

Whilst Mountbatten was a serving naval officer, he also had an extraordinary breadth of wartime and political experience, both as Head of Combined Operations and as the last Viceroy of India. He attempted to shift the balance of power from the individual services into the MoD centre with him as a single point of military advice to the government of the day, but it was a step too far at the time. Nonetheless, he did institute a new central Defence Staff, with coordinating functions across all the single services.

The decades 1960–80 saw sustained downward pressure on the Defence budget as the British economy weakened, leading to changes in the top command structure to help meet savings targets. To save further money, Denis Healey, a Labour Party Secretary of State conducted a defence review in 1966 that realigned Britain's defence interests strongly towards the European Central Front, abandoning the ability to conduct operations east of Suez. A presence in the Mediterranean was removed a decade later and the Navy realigned to the defence of the North Atlantic sea routes.

During 1982 some of this was reversed, as lessons were drawn from the close-run war the UK fought to liberate the Falkland Islands following the invasion by Argentina. In its aftermath, the Chief of the Defence Staff, Admiral Sir Terence Lewin, put forward a plan to do what Mountbatten had failed to do, to make the Chief of the Defence Staff the principal point of contact with the government on operational matters, with the other Chiefs relegated to their own domestic fiefdoms as advisers. This was endorsed by the Service Chiefs at the time because it was seen to strengthen their military voice in government discussions, whilst for her part Prime Minister Margaret Thatcher went to great lengths to demonstrate that she would continue to consult the Service Chiefs by holding regular meetings with each of them. However, she then unleashed a reforming evangelist, Michael Heseltine, as the Conservative Party's Secretary of State into the Ministry of Defence. Heseltine was becoming her chief agent for pursuing government efficiencies and he had a strong personal ambition to succeed her as Prime Minister. For both philosophical and personal advancement, Heseltine began a messianic drive to improve the bureaucracy of the MoD.

Heseltine introduced reforms that benefited efficiency, but undermined the clarity of command and control. He removed many of the budgetary, operational and manpower responsibilities from the Single Service Chiefs and brought them under a central Defence Staff. He created Deputy Chiefs of the Defence Staffs for commitments (or operations), personnel, and future equipment. He also created an Office of Budget and Management to oversee the whole financial programming process, headed by a top civil servant, the Second Permanent Under Secretary. This represented a major shift of power away from the single services (who lost their Vice Chiefs) towards the Civil Service and the centre of the MoD. In doing so, it decoupled power from responsibility, for the Service Chiefs remained constitutionally, morally and obviously responsible for the correct prosecution of armed conflict, but now lacked the tools to discharge it.

In parallel, whilst it strengthened his role amongst his Service Chiefs, the Chief of the Defence Staff was now in a much more exposed position overall. He had to fight off the newly powerful Treasury/MoD Civil Service financial axis, give attention to all the personnel and moral issues of the whole fighting force and forge a close relationship as the single point of contact with the Prime Minister and Defence politicians—and, to cap it all, CDS now had strategic command of all of the UK's combat operations as well.

It might have been useful at this point to recognise the new skills required of the Chief of the Defence Staff and to work out more seriously how a person might be better trained to discharge this role properly. Instead, training as a Service Chief (in their own rather narrower and reduced world) continued to be thought good enough for advancement to the top job, with all the challenges of sharp financial competence, expert programming ability, joint and combined arms war-fighting, statecraft and grand strategy glossed over.

Selection of a Service Chief

The selection of an individual Service Chief is a grand ballet, with variations reflecting the nature of the individual services and all the differences between them examined in the chapter five. For instance, in the Royal Navy, 40 per cent of naval officers are commissioned from the ranks—'the lower deck'— but for practical reasons of age and experience, none of these officers can reach the highest ranks, limiting the source of candidates for the top jobs to the remaining 60 per cent. Additionally, the head of the Navy has always been found from the Seaman Branch, reducing the pool for selection very much further. Nor have any officers from the Royal Marines been selected for the top naval appointments (partly because they form a relatively small percentage of the officers in the Royal Navy). Yet two of the most capable officers in the MoD Main Building in the last decade were Royal Marines: Lieutenant General Sir Robert Fulton and Lieutenant General Sir Rob Fry. Both found a ceiling at the three-star rank and were not considered for the top positions in the Navy's gift, although both officers comprehensively demonstrated their skills at the Whitehall game and their particular effectiveness with tasks at the top of the MoD.[8] So the pool of talent that the Royal Navy puts forward for its highest positions has been very much smaller than their officer strength suggests and invariably selection is from a single sub-branch.

The situation is similar in the RAF. The whole *raison d'être* for the RAF is to support a pilot in an aircraft and it is understandable that the aircrew speciality remains firmly atop the tree of influence within that service. It is not surprising that aircrew fill most of the senior appointments held by RAF officers in the MoD and provide all of the Chiefs of the Air Staff.

So, like the Royal Navy, the group of RAF officers considered for senior appointments in the MoD is much smaller than it seems, given the headline strength of the service. Moreover, these are people with very similar experience, who have succeeded in a specialist selection process and then spent half a lifetime concentrating on one activity. The experience of flying aircraft and operating large, complex but static air bases conditions senior RAF officers to see things in a rational and logical way, to fight in an ordered and efficient manner, to have a functional approach and be practical not sentimental about group morale, to believe in the power of technology, to make an unbreakable link between success and equipment quality and numbers and to have a view about terrain as seen from above.

The Army route to higher rank is different. Advancement requires equal success in both command and as a staff officer—mediocre performance at either would nearly always bring a career to a halt. Second, the numbers from which to choose are many times greater than the other two services, for the Army is numerically several times larger and the net for consideration is drawn much wider across the Army than the other two services.[9] Field Marshal Sir William 'Wully' Robertson served for twelve years as a private soldier in the cavalry and then rose through all the intervening ranks to become Chief of the Imperial General Staff in 1916–18. General Sir Peter Wall served the first half of his career as a field engineer before being appointed as Chief of the General Staff in 2010. Lieutenant General John Stokoe completed his career as Commander of the Field Army in 1997, having joined as an apprentice signalman.

A senior Army officer of recent years will have certain marked characteristics. He will be familiar with physical hardship—hard-lying on operations—and suspicious of those who make judgements about field conditions without having experienced them. His generation will have seen chaos first-hand, most probably during the riots and bloodshed of the Troubles in Northern Ireland but other civil wars as well, and the descent into disorder that follows when nothing is done to correct it. He might have been personally shot at, or even blown up, but most certainly will have experienced the sight of violent death—a formative experience unlikely to be shared in the other two services.

He might well have served in Special Forces. He will identify very strongly with the lot of the common soldier, probably more than the individual needs or deserves, and will retain numerous conscious and unconscious strings back to his regimental parent. He will be angry at the size of the Army's equipment budget in comparison to others, be over-sentimental about his own tribal heritage, and deep down he will believe that the other services are there to support his efforts.

But an officer does not reach the pinnacle of becoming Service Chief without being an all-round ace—hugely capable, professional, driven and effective within it. Given the size of the officer pool, the career streaming, grooming and peer competition, the chance of a dud appearing at the top of any of the military tribes is very slim. Crucially, they become settled, mature and formed individuals long before they get near to the job they are now required to undertake in the centre of the MoD. That experience makes them sufficiently different, one from another, for the Chiefs to take a unified position about matters of defence and national policy in Whitehall.

Thus the three services produce three distinctly different types of people. The sharpest difference is probably between the logical, analytical approach of the Royal Air Force and the more emotive, sentimental attitude of the Army, meaning that these will never be close bedfellows. Standing between them, but slightly apart, is the somewhat patrician style of the Royal Navy officer, forged from the lonely years of warship command. The act of will required for all of them to be collegiate and cooperative is hardly recognised, given that they are, in reality, standing on ever-separating tectonic plates.

Military Chiefs in a Political World

Not only are they all very different people, but they have limited schooling about a Whitehall mastered by politicians and directed by the elite of the Civil Service, for their field experience in uniform is in sharp contrast to what they find themselves doing in a suit in London. As General Sir Mike Jackson observed: 'I did not find the MoD a comfortable place; its values were not mine.'[10]

These worlds collide when there is a debate about commitment to battle. Such a decision is a deeply serious matter for the Chiefs, emotionally connected to those who might die and for whom defeat is utterly unthinkable, but it could be a more casual question to others. In the wider Whitehall there is a readiness to 'try it out a bit' to see what might happen, with withdrawal if it didn't work, for the political world is the province of ambiguity, and deliberately so. As President Abraham Lincoln once replied in answer to a military request for guidance, 'my policy is to have no policy'.[11] There is also a difference in the time horizons of the two groups: the politicians are focused on the five-year life of a parliament and the demands of getting re-elected; whereas the military are determined on victory however long it takes (but suffering a lack of continuity because of the military posting in and out cycle every two to three years). As H. H. McMaster explains in *Dereliction of Duty*, his damning exposé of the American High Command in the 1960s, this is not new, for President Lyndon Johnson was continually distracted from the task of managing the Vietnam War by his desire to introduce the 'Great Society' social reforms in the United States—and the need to get re-elected to be able to carry them through.[12]

The Chiefs, by contrast, trade in absolutes or in fine judgements of risk, forged from the binary 'win or lose' of the battlefield, and it is counter-intuitive for them to 'fly blind' or engage in a 'suck it and see' approach. They are not comfortable with loose discussions peppered with compromises, or the balancing between competing priorities which is the reality of discussions in Whitehall. They like certainty and decisiveness, not deliberately weaving a web of ambiguity and spinning things out as the political classes inevitably find they have to do. Prime Minister John Major was chided about the lack of clarity in his intentions over the UN/NATO intervention in Bosnia in 1994. As the Dayton Talks approached he was sharply reminded that a military force was a great and cumbersome machine that needed time to wind up if it was not to stumble. He replied: '… aha … but I live in a world of ambiguity … and I like to keep things ambiguous for just as long as possible.'[13] Douglas Hurd, his Foreign Secretary, summed up the problem during a lecture to military officers in 2011 in a similar vein:

'British generals are always pressing for precision from politicians. But politicians live in a confused world; politicians will do their best to provide precision but must fail somewhat. Hence the military must share some of the burden of that confusion and be asked to make the best of a confused situation or a bad job. But the military are not trained to work with such a lack of precision.'[14]

As has been very fully explored already, all of the Service Chiefs are under continuous and severe financial pressure throughout their senior careers and they come to budgetary issues from very different and strongly entrenched positions. So important is it to succeed in the budget area for the future health of their particular service that it easily becomes the principal objective of their time as Service Chief. So when any issue appears at the Chiefs of Staff Committee or on the Defence Management Board's agenda, the conscious and subconscious reaction of a Service Chief would be to be preoccupied by the consequences for his own service budget allocation.

You have already seen how the nature of the chiefly position in the structure had become anomalous. They continued to be the professional heads of their own services whilst also serving as cabinet members of the grand decision-making councils in the MoD, yet much authority had drained away from them to the MoD centre. As General Sir Mike Jackson said:

'The Chiefs of Staff … are seen by the public, by those serving in the Forces themselves, and by the media, as responsible for all matters pertaining to their respective Service—but this is simply not a reality. As CGS I did not hold the budget for the Army … neither logistics … nor procurement … this has diminished the ability of the Chiefs of Staff to take personal charge of the running of their Service.'[15]

Despite all that diminution, they retained the vital role of a 'clan chieftain' to their individual service, with very clear and identifiable responsibilities. When they moved amongst their subordinates, they were seen by them as having ultimate responsibility for solving problems and to be the last resort in distress. They had to make finely balanced adjustments to the internal workings of their clans, requiring considered thought and a deft touch, and they were the representational figures at the head of them. At the same time they were required to drop all that and become even-handed members of the top-level cabinets that ruled the MoD, taking unbiased and clear-sighted positions for the overall good of UK Defence.

Any human would feel more or less schizophrenic in that situation and these twin competing roles came into direct, frequent, unavoidable and destructive collision. Rob Olver, as Chairman of BP Exploration Plc, once said that the heads of operating divisions should never be allowed on the main board of the company, because they would suffer an irreconcilable conflict of interest.[16]

The structure also gave the Service Chiefs a huge workload, for in truth they were called to do two full jobs, either of which would have consumed a capable individual's complete resources, and these twin roles contained nasty contradictions. Could it ever be that anything was more important than properly and reflectively reading ahead for a Chiefs of Staff Committee meeting or a Defence Management Board, and attending either in a contemplative manner with a clear mind? For this is where the nation's enduring military strategies are crafted. But could that really be more important to a Service Chief than, say, being in full uniform at a repatriation service for fallen comrades, accompanying the Sovereign when new colours were presented, reviewing the coming generation of officer cadets at their ceremonial commissioning, or travelling the world on exhausting military–diplomatic excursions? None of the latter activities had anything like the strategic consequences for the defence of the country, or for getting the decisions of the top MoD boards right, but they exerted an irresistible emotional obligation to be present. By valiantly trying to do both at the same time, as all the chiefs do, too often they leave themselves exhausted, shy of originality and drained of compromise.

Selection of the Chief of the Defence Staff

The person selected to be Chief of the Defence Staff—the top position—is de facto found from within an extremely small pool of about four candidates: the existing Heads of Service and the Vice Chief. Compare this with, for example, Permanent Under Secretaries, who could be drawn from several dozens, or ministers who could be found from hundreds, and commercial chief executives for whom the pool ran to thousands. Circumstances would narrow this base even further, leaving politicians with rarely more than two real choices and often only one.

Service Chiefs could write themselves out of the running for the top job by political stumbling or because they were seen to defend their own corner too adamantly. One clear candidate for Chief of the Defence Staff, Admiral Sir Jock Slater, as First Sea Lord publicly criticised the ruling government's plans in 1997 to privatise service married quarters. He did this for the wider benefit of Defence, not his single service. Another, General Sir Richard Dannatt, pressured the government into meeting the 'Military Covenant' through the media. Admiral Sir Jonathon Band's chances to become CDS did not improve when a small naval crew were taken hostage by the Iranians in 2007. Others were excluded so as to spread the post as equally as possible across the three services; General Sir Mike Jackson could have followed General Sir Michael Walker, but two Army candidates in succession would not have been attractive if there was a qualified alternative, which existed in Air Chief Marshal Sir Jock Stirrup. General Jackson's public discomfort with the Civil Service would not have helped his chances either.

Likewise, the officer who best understood the workings of the CDS role, the Vice Chief (VCDS), often took on the mantle of a civil servant manqué and thereby limited his chances in military eyes, even though he was doing exactly what the post demanded of him. There has been the occasional exception, for Field Marshal Sir Richard Vincent became CDS in 1991 after a tour as VCDS and then went on to be a successful Chairman of the NATO Military Committee. In 2013, General Sir Nicholas Houghton, a former VCDS who had not been one of the Service Chiefs, was indeed selected to be the next CDS, prompting one of his predecessors to remark that they 'had clearly run out of suitable candidates amongst the Service Chiefs'. In fact General Houghton may yet surprise his critics, because his time as VCDS has given him the opportunity to assimilate the essential skills of strategy and managing the Whitehall machine, often lacking in the normal route to the top military post.

The potential Chief of the Defence Staff would need two other vital attributes. He would need to have shown that he could work closely with his political masters and, largely, do their bidding. He would also have to have shown that he could work collegiately with his ministers, his other chiefs and be a good chairman of the Chiefs of Staff Committee. His ability as a strategist, if it was scored at all, would come below that. This bears a little more examination later.

The Chief of the Defence Staff

'Command is a mountaintop. The air breathed there … and the perspectives seen … are different.'

Bertrand de Jouvenel, 'On Power'

First amongst the Chiefs, the role of the Chief of the Defence Staff is formally stated by the MoD as being the professional head of the armed forces and principal military adviser to the Secretary of State for Defence and the government. He is responsible for setting the strategy for defence and the future development of the armed forces, and 'subject to ministers' direction' and 'together with PUS' for the conduct of current operations as strategic commander.[17] It is a very big job, requiring exceptional skills of leadership in both combat operations and in Whitehall.

There were four Chiefs of the Defence Staff in the decade 2000–10. General Sir Charles Guthrie (1997–2001), Admiral Sir Michael Boyce (2001–3), General Sir Michael Walker (2003–6) and Air Chief Marshal Sir Jock Stirrup (2006–10). Each was very different.

General Sir Charles Guthrie combined command and soldierly skills—he had served as a leader from a troop commander in special forces through to the Commander of 1st British Corps in Germany—with a legendary deftness in working the Whitehall machine. He was single-minded and focused, he put a high premium on instinct when coming to decisions and he did not agonise over the consequences of decisions once made. This made him a decisive leader, if a more remote colleague. He was an expert contestant in the MoD game and for instance, as CGS, adroitly kept the Attack Helicopter firmly in the programme even though the budget allocated was insufficient to fund the full capability—a financial programming device known as 'entry-ism'—whilst also successfully fending off repeated RAF initiatives for them to fly the machine when the RAF argued it was a 'complex airframe'. He tended to focus on where he wanted to be and worried less about the maelstrom of detail swirling around the MoD, leaving that to trusted subordinates.[18] As Chief of the Defence Staff he often hid the cards in his hand, but consulted widely. His approach was political, in the widest sense, and he was well liked and trusted by the political classes. As a result, he did an extended time as Chief of the Defence Staff and covered the period from the arrival of Tony Blair as Prime Minister, through the ground-breaking Strategic Defence Review of 1998, into the run-up to the invasion of Iraq. Indeed, he remained as an adviser to Prime Minister Blair long after his successor as Chief of the Defence Staff was in post, with influence remaining even after that.

Admiral Sir Michael Boyce was different. He was reserved by nature, very logical in approach, and a man of strong principle, poise and courtesy. Alistair Campbell observed that 'he was very unlike Guthrie as Chief of the Defence

Staff, who had always been pretty can-do. Boyce was quite soft-spoken, very polite.'[19] He had been an outstanding submarine commander, with a reputation for coolness and nerve when tailing Soviet submarines by only yards in the Atlantic. He was an impressive figure: 'intellectually above his peers, tough, demanding, straight as a die and something of a loner'. Another commentator added that Boyce had 'an austere, remote, praetorian presence in a group, although that changed completely when he smiled … and people then relaxed'.[20] As a more junior officer he had held key posts in the MoD system and so was well-versed in head office politics, but he had a disinclination to work the system to the extent that others did. There was always a distance between Boyce as CDS and Sir Kevin Tebbit as PUS, with the result that much of the necessary work between them was conducted by their deputies.[21] Admiral Boyce was often irritated by the PUS's manner, thinking him too much a slave to politics rather than defending the military imperative. Admiral Boyce showed an excellent instinct about operational issues: he quickly understood the ambiguities of a military situation, rapidly recognised the pressure points and willingly sought specialist advice. It was during his time that the UK decided to join the coalition to invade Iraq in 2003, and he did the right thing in demanding a clear undertaking from the government that such armed intervention was legal. But, like many others, he seems to have been less tuned to the challenges posed by nation-building after the invasion, or robust enough with the US about driving home what needed to be done. Admiral Boyce was workmanlike rather than political and did not have as close a relationship with his Secretary of State, Geoff Hoon, as his predecessor had achieved; he lacked the inclination (or the patience) to match the politicians at their own game. Very unusually, he served in the top post for just over two years.

General Sir Michael Walker was another extremely polite, calm and patently honourable officer. He was a large bear of a man, instinctively ordered he seemed to breathe all the tradition, steadiness and unflappability of the British infantry. Courteous, kind, ever-patient and forgiving, he rarely showed pressure or frustration—he was remarkably cool whatever the demands. He was a private man and, although even-tempered and attentive when dealing with all comers regardless of rank, he had an instinct for hierarchy that sometimes kept his subordinates on a short leash. He successfully led the NATO

Allied Rapid Reaction Corps into Bosnia in 1995 after the Dayton, Ohio, Accord was signed and showed skill in managing a complex alliance organisation. He found himself at the eye of the storm during his tenure as CDS and had some tough compromises to make. For instance, he did not allow the UK's Air Assault Brigade to go north to help the Americans in Baghdad in 2003, but did release the UK's 'Black Watch' Battlegroup to deploy as a cordon around Fallujah for the second battle there in 2004, despite media demands not to. He also resisted pressure to embed the British Army as mentors with the new Iraq Army and coped with all the myriad cross-currents in the run-up to the decision to deploy to Helmand in 2006.

If pushed, General Walker would show significant inner steel; Jonathan Powell reported that 'Mike Walker demanded to see Tony in 2004 so that he could tell him that he was going to resign unless there was more money for the military', but he seemed to prefer consensus and even 'wait and see' to more precipitate action.[22] He was unlikely to commit to a decision until due process had been completed, and because of this he was viewed as more of a deft coordinator than decisive leader; indeed one of his close contemporaries observed that he was 'cautious'. He got on well with Prime Minster Blair, although Alistair Campbell noted that 'General Walker was much less friendly than Guthrie'—probably because he, like Admiral Boyce, always played a straight bat to the frustration of the political lobbyist.[23] He established a good working relationship with his key civil servants and he was a notably capable chairman of committees, with the result that MoD Main Building business progressed much more smoothly than it had done under his predecessor.[24] The Secretary of State asked him to extend his tour of duty, but General Walker felt that is was time for a new pair of hands.

Air Chief Marshal Sir Jock Stirrup was the most intellectually capable chief for a decade. He was noted for his systematic, analytical approach to problems and as being 'straight down the line—not one to be challenged'.[25] He had a very sharp mind, was always on top of the facts, was never fazed by issues, did not suffer fools and had a somewhat forbidding manner, showing all the strengths of a gifted senior executive rather than an inspirational military leader. He kept his inner thoughts to a tightly-held group and even some of his command circle felt uncomfortable in discussion with him, perhaps explained by a rather remote, serious manner and his desire for rationality, which could be interpreted as coldness and make him appear secretive.[26] He came from the ordered world of Air Force operations (one of his contemporaries described him 'as the arch-example of the RAF logical, 'linear' brain') but he was also inquisitive of the wider world and, as one civil servant admiringly put it, 'gifted with an excellent brain, he could certainly think outside the box'. He was politically astute, known to be 'canny, someone who understood the political imperatives extremely well' and more than once he would be the steadying influence when nasty events on the battlefield wobbled political heads. As Chief of the Air Staff he demonstrated that he was prepared to be a 'joint' officer, even when that went against his own service.[27]

Air Chief Marshal Sir Jock Stirrup had developed a considerable understanding of counter-insurgency operations, both from conscientious study and from his operational experience (flying Strikemasters) during the insurgency war in Oman in 1974, which he described as very formative. In his Chief of the Defence Staff Annual RUSI Christmas lecture of 2007, he gave a nuanced, clear and arguably better treatise on counter-insurgency operations than many senior Army officers would or could have attempted.[28] By contrast, his explanation for the retreat of British forces from Basra at his annual RUSI lecture in 2008 (where he assured his listeners that it was part of a carefully crafted strategy that had proceeded to plan) brought disbelief from the audience and it appeared that he had been either deluded about the reality of events or adept at deploying camouflage to hide the collapse of political will to remain in Basra.[29] After retirement, he made a forthright defence of the actions leading up to the deployment to Helmand before the House of Commons Defence Committee, with, you may judge, little reflective leavening.[30] He was trusted by his political masters and, like General Guthrie, was extended in office for a year.

Preparation for the Top Job

Unusually for people at the top of public life in the United Kingdom, none of the four Chiefs of the Defence Staff of the decade (nor any of their predecessors, bar one) had attended a university, for three years at university would have meant the loss of the same number of years of in-house military experience. This was not as odd as it might seem at first because, at the time they joined, the services looked inwards to train their young officers and there were far fewer graduates in society at large; it would be inconceivable now, under the impact of the greatly expanded tertiary education in the UK. However, the result was that all the Chiefs of Defence in the decade 2000–10 had escaped the formal intellectual training and broadening experience that a university offers—particularly a grounding in conceptual skills— yet they were dealing with their peers in Whitehall almost all of whom *had* been to university (and the top ones at that), setting them apart in subliminal if not overt ways.

As they progressed up through their services, only two of the four CDSs of the decade, Admiral Sir Michael Boyce and Air Chief Marshal Sir Jock Stirrup, had attended the Royal College of Defence Studies at Seaford House in London, whose specific purpose as funded by the MoD was to train senior officers and officials for high responsibilities:

'To prepare senior officers and officials of the United Kingdom and other countries and future leaders from the private and public sectors for high responsibilities in their respective organizations, by developing their analytical powers, knowledge of defence and international security, and strategic vision.'

Likewise, only one of them (Stirrup) was young enough to have attended the Higher Command and Staff Course (set up in 1988 by the Army at Camberley and becoming 'joint' in 1997) where students received a good education in handling armed forces at the Operational level.[31]

It would be fair to conclude that none of them had sufficient formal education for the job of leading the UK defence forces and certainly none of them had formal training in strategy or statecraft. Sometimes that was substituted for in other ways; Guthrie and Stirrup were both widely read and inquisitive, in particular. Just occasionally a potential candidate had been released into the Whitehall environment to gain wider experience; for instance Admiral Sir James Burnell-Nugent had been an undergraduate at Cambridge University and in his mid forties was seconded to the Treasury for two years, giving him matchless experience in the centre of Whitehall, but his career ended as Commander-in-Chief Fleet. This lack of intellectual development is in stark contrast to the senior echelons of the US military, where a PhD is common, as is attendance at one or all of the War Colleges. The Chairman of the US

Joint Chiefs of Staff in 2013, General Martin Dempsey, joined one of the 'teeth' combat arms as a cavalry officer, but had a first degree in the sciences followed by three master's degrees, the last being in strategic studies.

The Chiefs of the Defence Staff in Action

In any Whitehall meeting or discussion the CDS was inevitably viewed as an elder statesman, not surprisingly so given that he was ten or so years older than the bulk of the political classes and from a respect for the military arsenal that he commanded—what a psychologist would refer to as the 'halo effect'. With that as ammunition, the UK Chiefs of the Defence Staff were generally very deft at managing politicians. Indeed, a Prime Minister taxed and buffeted by party squabbles and events would be seeking such a refuge: the calm, logical, loyal approach of the older military dignitary. This was reciprocated and all CDSs made a point of saying how they had enjoyed excellent relationships with their Prime Ministers. But there were dangers here also and Lieutenant General Sir John Kiszley, one-time Deputy Commanding General of Multi-National Force Iraq and a noted military historian, thought that this closeness and instinct to support would lead the CDS into the trap of seeing it as his job to defend government policy. He observed that 'it has been increasingly frequent for the CDS of the day, resplendent in uniform, to be put up as the MoD spokesman and required to peddle the MoD line—thus compromising his independence'.[32] Kizsley's observation might also go some way to explaining why these highly capable people continually tolerated the MoD system, rather than setting out to reform it.

The effectiveness of a Chief of the Defence Staff depended greatly on his relationship with the Prime Minister and the key defence ministers. In his diaries, Alistair Campbell comments repeatedly on the closeness of the relationship of General Sir Charles Guthrie as Chief of the Defence Staff with Prime Minister Blair and on Guthrie's can-do attitude, in comparison with the CDSs who followed.[33] Guthrie openly declared that this had been his intention, and that 'I made a huge effort to get on with Tony Blair, because that was my job.'[34] He remembered how the incoming Labour government had been initially very suspicious about the military hierarchy, fearing that they were more sympathetic to a right of centre administration; Guthrie said,

THE CHIEFS

'I had to demonstrate that we were loyal to them as the elected government and very soon we were seen as such. Otherwise, I could not have been effective in giving advice.'[35] His successor, Admiral Sir Michael Boyce, was never completely in tune with the Blair vision of liberal interventionism and he seemed to the politicians to be asking awkward questions. Alistair Campbell asked Admiral Boyce why he could not see the 'glass as more half full rather than always as half empty' to which Boyce replied 'my job is to tell you the facts; what you do with them is your decision'.[36] General Sir Michael Walker tried his hardest simply to execute the political intention and he achieved an easier relationship; he said that he was invariably the follower in discussions with the Prime Minister, in support of his Secretaries of State Hoon and Reid.[37] Air Chief Marshal Sir Jock Stirrup started well but Prime Minister Blair had already begun to lose interest in the Iraq war. The initial meeting with Blair's successor Gordon Brown also went well and Air Chief Marshal Sir Jock Stirrup remembers Prime Minster Gordon Brown as 'polite, listening, [a person who] allowed vigorous argument and was receptive to new ideas' in one-to-one conversations, in complete contrast to the hunched, brooding, dogmatic figure more usually portrayed in the popular press.[38] But it never developed into a close relationship, not least because Air Chief Marshal Stirrup had to contend with one of his subordinate chiefs, General Sir Richard Dannatt, repeatedly pressuring the government through the media in order to obtain advantage for the Army.

That said, if they needed to be, the CDSs could be assertive and stand up to politicians—after all, it was their last military job and they had the ultimate totemic sanction of resignation. In practice, they were certainly ready to use this lever over defence funding, but not often enough to challenge the feasibility of state policy, for on the latter their instinct as an elder statesman was to be supportive. Some were more than a little innocent about the trades and wiles of the machinery of government, and none but Guthrie seemed to able to get the wheels of Whitehall to turn fast enough to deliver what had been decided, with Walker frustrated that there seemed to be a layer of 'mattress mice' in Whitehall below him and the Prime Minster who would subvert policy decisions.[39]

The character of the Chiefs of the Defence Staff had a sharp bearing on the way the top of the MoD operated. Some of the Chiefs of the Defence Staff

203

consulted their Service Chiefs deeply before coming to a decision; some consulted them early in their tenure as Chief of the Defence Staff but then short-circuited discussion as they got into their stride; others told them what would happen after it had been decided. To be fair, circumstances often drove them to the latter. Half the CDSs achieved a close working relationship with their PUSs, whilst others were distant or even hostile. General Walker worked closely with Sir Kevin Tebbit (PUS 1998–2005), whilst Admiral Boyce had a much more remote relationship with him, and Air Chief Marshal Stirrup hardly ever discussed operational matters with his opposite number Sir Bill Jeffrey (PUS 2005–10).

One important task of the CDS (indeed all the Chiefs) was to reduce complex military situations to their essentials so that they could be understood in Whitehall and by the informed public. This was a vital task in order that the correct pan-government policies would be forged and so that citizens could understand the reasons for the wars they were being asked to support. The Chiefs were never very good at this, both in public statements (e.g. General Sir Richard Dannatt as CGS used the riddle that 'we are more of the problem than the solution' in Basra, without also explaining the consequences of precipitate withdrawal) and in front of Parliamentary committees, where senior MoD witnesses eternally appeared evasive.

The operational line of command for the two wars went directly from the Chief of the Defence Staff to the Chief of Joint Operations at PJHQ, bypassing the Single Service Chiefs. This presented two problems. First, Central Staffs supporting the Chief of the Defence Staff did not have the same staff horsepower as the individual service possessed. Second, CDS was directing assets 'owned' by the other Service Chiefs. Unless the Chief of the Defence Staff was careful, this could bruise the individual Service Chiefs and it did: General Sir Richard Dannatt was mortified to find out about the deal made in Basra to trade with the Jaish al-Mahdi militia through an informal source and not from the Chief of the Defence Staff himself.[40]

Finally, the Chief of the Defence Staff could find himself making judgements about a fighting environment of which he had little first-hand experience compared with those around him. General Dannatt recalls:

'Sir Jock Stirrup was a fast jet pilot who, although he was brilliant at what he did, could not have been expected to understand the sights, sounds and smells of the battlefield. You don't have to pick up body parts and decide on who lives and who dies when you are in a cockpit flying at the speed of sound.'[41]

Behind this statement lay a belief within the Army that the CDS did not really understand what the Army was trying to do.[42] Added to which there was a suspicion that he did not support the Army view that it needed more helicopters because road deployment had become too dangerous. True or false, it is easy to see how what might have been a sincerely held judgement by Sir Jock Stirrup could make mischief in the emotive area of casualties between people with different military perspectives.

The Chief of the Defence Staff as the War Commander

'Nine-tenths … are certain, and taught in books: but the irrational tenth is like the kingfisher flashing across the pool, and that is the test of generals. It can only be ensured by instinct, sharpened by thought practising the stroke so often that at the crisis it is as natural as a reflex.'

T. E. Lawrence, 'The Evolution of a Revolt'

Each of the Chiefs of the Defence Staff scored significant achievements during their time in office, illustrating that each of them understood the political-military nexus of their position well enough. General Guthrie's handling of the crisis in Sierra Leone meant that the right decisions were taken early and that the whole of Whitehall was behind the operation, leading to a consummate military and political success. Admiral Boyce's leadership of the UK contribution to the invasion of Iraq in 2003 resulted in that complex operation running remarkably smoothly. General Walker got NATO fully behind the new ISAF mission in Afghanistan and ensured that it had the right support from all member nations. Air Chief Marshal Sir Jock Stirrup displayed a remarkably steady nerve when things became very bumpy indeed for the military in Iraq and Afghanistan, sometimes carrying the load for the whole of Whitehall.

These skills are needed because the Chief of the Defence Staff now occupies a unique position in the UK; all the arguments made so far, and all the consequences described, eventually landed on his desk. By contrast, in the United States, the President is the nation's Commander-in-Chief (with a National Security Coordinator and a National Security Adviser) and command passes from the President directly to the uniformed regional four-star Combatant Commanders, bypassing the nation's senior military officer, the Chairman of the Joint Chiefs of Staff.

In the UK, the CDS alone is the militarily 'responsible person'. There is no one in the military chain above him, it is by him that orders are crafted and it is through him that orders are passed down the chain of command. If the Prime Minister or the Secretary of State lacks the right military advice, the CDS is the person who should have given him better. If the orders given to the troops in the wars in Afghanistan and Iraq contained impossible inconsistencies, it was the CDS who was responsible for resolving them before they left London. Everyone else in the story so far had somewhere to hide, but not the CDS.

The CDS has several individuals to whom he could turn for advice. Close at hand is the operational committee of Service Chiefs, especially for representing the interests and advice of their own services.

However, on many occasions only outline or general issues were discussed in the Chiefs of Staff Committee. A dissenting voice would be politely heard, but that might be all. General Sir Richard Dannatt, as CGS and a member of the Chiefs of Staff Committee, lamented the fact that a deeper debate about the problems in Iraq just could not be triggered, comparing it with the greater length of time and detail that had been spent on the design of the service widows' medal, the Elizabeth Cross.[43] Air Chief Marshal Sir Jock Stirrup challenged that view and, reflecting on his time as CDS, said that his Chiefs of Staff were fully consulted on all the key issues: '... the change of approach in Basra and all key Afghan issues were fully debated and agreed by the COS before being put to Ministers for final agreement'.[44] Yet, it is very illuminating that on his appointment as CDS, Air Chief Marshal Sir Jock Stirrup seemed to have little detailed knowledge of the operations for which he was suddenly responsible. In evidence to the House of Commons Defence Committee, he said that he did not know why the UK had gone to Helmand instead of Kandahar, and that he had protested in vain about the lack of intelligence regarding the Taliban before the deployment was ordered. This illustrated just how detached from operational planning Sir Jock Stirrup had been whilst in the subordinate role of Chief of the Air Staff, even though he was still a member of the top MoD committees. These remarks surprised General Sir

Michael Walker, who felt it was inconceivable that such discussions had not included all the Chiefs: 'I would never have taken a decision of that magnitude without going through the Chiefs' Committee.'[45]

I was particularly struck by the answers given to a question that I had posed to both Admiral Sir Michael Boyce and General Sir Michael Walker about events that happened immediately after they handed over as CDS. Both looked straight back at me and simply replied, 'That happened after my time.' The same reply is visible in Admiral Boyce's testimony to the Chilcot Inquiry, whilst General Walker added to me that 'one rapidly became out of date within a matter of days'.[46] This may, of course, be because they were reluctant to pass judgement on any of the actions of their successor. But it left me feeling that the MoD 'system' arranges for them to occupy the highest office for their period of time and requires them to be energetic in solving the problems of the day, like a shift leader, but it does not incentivise them to seek out the long-term solutions to those seriously difficult issues that extend into the future after their watch. How could they profess unawareness of events that took place only days after they had been in full command? You will have to judge whether they wrestled down short-termism with the zeal that the particular malaise deserved, but the issues of the deployment to Helmand and withdrawal from Basra City stand out as questions that were crying out for a long term, strategic approach. This is all supposition, but if the statement by Air Chief Marshal Sir Jock Stirrup—that he was unsighted beforehand on the background to the momentous decision he was required to take regarding Helmand—is added, it seems to show that a discontinuity occurs as the CDSs hand over. By contrast, there is also a folk myth to this day in the Royal Navy that General Sir Charles Guthrie never gave his successor, Admiral Sir Michael Boyce, a proper run at the job of CDS because Guthrie stayed too close a confidant to Prime Minister Blair; but it did show at least how General Guthrie retained a sharp interest in how things developed even after he had left the MoD.

Sometime in the first part of the decade 2000–10 the Chiefs of Staff seemed to drift away from being a close consultative body to which the CDS would refer almost daily. In his book *The Chiefs*, Field Marshal Bramall describes the Chiefs of Staff as a body of senior officers who were close in thought and united in decision;[47] likewise, General Guthrie described consulting his

Service Chiefs daily, believing that he could not move without them.[48] But the relationship became ever more distant. For half a century, civil servants had been pushing politicians to withdraw the Service Chiefs' authority into the Central Staffs, where the mandarins believed that a more 'joint' approach would emerge. And, probably, where they would be able to control matters better themselves. The CDSs themselves found it frustrating to have to carry the broader group of officers with them and it was much simpler to get things done by restricting the debate to an inner circle. After a year in post in 2007, Air Chief Marshal Sir Jock Stirrup as CDS attempted to get administrative business moving better by creating what became known as the 'gang of four' of himself, the PUS and the two Central Staff chief operating officers: the Vice Chief of the Defence Staff and the Second Permanent Under Secretary. Whilst this might have been more businesslike, it did nothing for the inclusivity of the other Chiefs and it caused Sir Sherard Cowper-Coles to observe that he had watched Air Chief Marshal Sir Jock Stirrup 'dominate and marginalise the other Chiefs, who were cut off from discussion, and work around ministers and civil servants [so as] to handle Gordon Brown alone, trying to bully a weak Prime Minster into sending more troops'.[49]

It is no coincidence that these changes took place as the recently-formed PJHQ was finding its feet. What seems to have happened is that the dialogue that once took place between the CDS and his Chiefs was replaced by a more focused discussion between the CDS and his leading experts at PJHQ and on the Central Staff, not least because they were subordinate in rank, hence leaving the position of the CDS unthreatened. The leaders of those two organisations (the Chief of Joint Operations at PJHQ and the Deputy Chief of the Defence Staff, Commitments in the MoD) remained at three-star rank, although there was a clear case that at least the Chief of Joint Operations at PJHQ should be a four-star officer, so that he could interact with greater authority in the US-led coalitions. Leaving it as it was made things easier for the CDS to hold taut and close discussions in the short term, but it allowed other key figures in the MoD system to become too detached or feel left out. General Sir Michael Walker was renowned for saying 'let the system work it through' or 'let the boys [i.e. the Staff] do the work' before coming to a decision, but this gave others the impression that 'the laboratory rats had taken over the experiment' with key subordinates such as the highly capable and articulate Lieutenant General Rob Fry as the MoD Director of Operations and the trenchant, gifted Yorkshireman, Lieutenant General Nicholas Houghton, as Chief of Joint Operations down at PJHQ, holding sway. It won't have helped, either, that General Sir Richard Dannatt, whilst CGS, broke cover and used the popular press to exert pressure in favour of Army needs; he was distinctly cold-shouldered by his brother chiefs at Chiefs of Staff Committee meetings after that.

The Chief of the Defence Staff could also have expected to have wise counsel from his institutional equal and senior civil servant in the MoD, the Permanent Under Secretary. However, such were the accounting problems in the MOD during the decade that both PUSs seem to have been consumed with trying to sort them out. Being the holder of the purse strings was never a popular position to occupy when facing those who wished to spend the cash. So this troubled time for Ministry of Defence finances made relationships complex, regardless of anything else. As it was, relations between the holders of the two top posts were often only lukewarm at best. It didn't need to be like that. As a long-time MoD hand, General Sir Charles Guthrie, like Admiral Mountbatten before him, had set out to have good relationships with the civil servants, deliberately spending time whilst CDS in their offices on their home turf. Guthrie found working the desks and chatting to the middle layer to be very effective in getting people on side, and he made the time to do it. General Sir Michael Walker did much the same.

So, for a number of reasons, it was the CDS who emerged as very powerfully placed at the centre of prosecuting the wars of the decade, and he was militarily responsible. The man at the top of the UK's national command chain needed three essential characteristics: imagination, experience and a questioning mind, for the actual mechanics of fighting and sustaining wars were what the armed forces were trained to do. The chain of command would perform very well if clear, decisive orders were fed into it from the top and it was optimised for that purpose.

To produce effective orders (i.e. ones that could be carried out by the tactical commander with a sporting chance of success) required that they be crafted by someone with the imagination and experience to comprehend the challenges facing the tactical commanders charged with delivering the results. Yet it is clear that conditions on the ground were often not understood in

London. If they had been, the UK would have better anticipated the post-conflict operations needed after the invasion of Iraq, as just one instance of many. Likewise, Major General Richard Shirreff would not have been allowed to initiate Operation Sinbad, an idea so grossly under-resourced that it inevitably had to stop far short of success, and Major General Jonathan Shaw would not have been allowed to fall into the strategic trap of negotiating with the Jaish al-Mahdi militia.

Furthermore, it is clear that the orders handed down were riven with internal contradictions (drawn together in the previous Chapter 11 under 'Emerging Criticism and Flawed Strategies'). You are to appeal to 'hearts and minds', but you are also to eradicate drug production, thereby putting the Helmand farmers out of work. You are to defeat the insurgency ('the people are the prize'), but you have been given so few troops to do it with that defence is only possible by using your heavy weapons, killing civilians you had been sent to save. You are to get out of Basra, but the Iraqi population in the city is nevertheless to be protected, etc., etc.

The person signing off the orders had, of course, to make decisions based on the best information available at the time amidst a sea of political considerations—not always an easy thing to do. But that person also had to make sure that the right strategic question was being addressed and to be very curious about the assumptions underpinning an offered staff plan, probing them hard. In answer to a formal question by Dr John Reid, the Secretary of State in 2005, General Sir Michael Walker as CDS stated that the UK would be able to conduct simultaneous operations in Iraq and Afghanistan without difficulty and that he had a note from the staff to prove it. As events turned out, it was very soon clear that the UK wasn't able to commit sufficient forces to do both.

Likewise, it fell to the CDS to probe the intelligence behind the plan to deploy to Helmand Province in Afghanistan, given that it is clear that intelligence about the possibility of meeting a hornets' nest of Taliban fighters on arrival had existed somewhere in the system. Even if the answer had been 'we just don't know', then it was the responsibility of the person at the top to ensure that sufficient troops were earmarked and ready to cover the part that they 'didn't know'. But that did not happen.

Finally, however much Brigadier Butler was blamed for expanding his task into north Helmand without the resources to do so, Air Chief Marshal Sir Jock Stirrup as the CDS at the time had just visited Brigadier Butler and was aware of the pressures he was under from Governor Daoud (as was the Deputy Chief of Joint Operations, Major General Peter Wall, who had been visiting in theatre, *and* as were the Service Chiefs, who discussed the matter in committee on 26 May 2006). All these officers would have known the likely response by a UK tactical military commander with the mission he had been given.[50] As Secretary of State Des Browne remarked later 'It was within the range of decisions that it was legitimate for him [Ed Butler] to make'. Not being in the room where and when the decision was taken cannot be an excuse. The really important question, of course, is not whether it was right or wrong to deploy northwards outside the security lozenge, but why the UK was caught so much unawares by the fact *that it might have to do it*, which demonstrated a lack of strategic curiosity at the very least.

Conclusion

It is self-evident that officers of high ability achieved the top military post of UK Chief of the Defence Staff in this period. As already shown, they were able, dedicated, committed and independently-minded. But a question arises as to whether that was sufficient, for they were charged with managing a very large and complex bureaucracy, whilst at the same time finding the time for reflection in order to forge enduring strategies about profoundly complex situations. They were officers who were undoubtedly extremely practised in their own service's script, but were less sure-footed about the other services' and 'joint' activities. Each of them had missed the early intellectual development at university invariably found in all the other key people in Whitehall, yet they undertook a job right at the top of the machinery of government without any specific training for it. Some seemed to have been caught out by situations that might have been averted by greater imagination and curiosity beforehand; meanwhile, they found themselves much more singularly responsible for the prosecution of military operations than had been so for their predecessors.

All this took place within a political environment rife with short-termism and in a government department eternally short of money. Of key importance was the fact that the job of CDS was not just another, more important, step up a promotion ladder; instead, it was markedly different from anything the individual would have done before.

As a result of which, success for them was sometimes elusive.

PART 3

WHAT NEXT?

14

THE AFTERMATH

Why Did it Go Wrong?

'Things did not always go right because, amongst other things, we asked our armed services to do far too much.'[1]

Des Browne, Secretary of State for Defence 2006–8

Governance of a nation is complex and there are myriad issues to deal with. Some require quick reaction to put out an immediate political fire, whilst others need wise consideration to deliver a long-term outcome. The issues crowd in upon each other, disrupting one another, and the drama of an immediate crisis easily smothers more poisonous problems of the longer term, denying the latter the attention that they should deserve.

Furthermore, the levers of power in a democracy are diffuse. Presidents and Prime Ministers have to work through their appointed ministers and maintain the broad approval of their elected chambers. Squaring away the different constituencies to get things done is an enduring effort. As Donald Rumsfeld observed of democracy in the United States: '… in our system, leadership is by consent not command. To lead, a President must persuade.' Complex problems rarely have simple short-term solutions, with a clock inexorably counting down to the moment when a government must seek re-election. This squeezes some challenges into an impossibly short timeframe for them to be properly solved.

So, as often before in history, Britain slipped rather unwittingly into wars in Afghanistan and Iraq, on each occasion not understanding that they would be so long, cost so much in lives and treasure or deliver such imperfect solutions.

There were numerous reasons why this happened and there were many contributors. Attitudes in the decade were conditioned by the events of the immediate years before, when the military instrument had seemed to have stabilised Bosnia, Kosovo, Macedonia, East Timor and Sierra Leone. Politicians keenly felt the pressure to act in support of 'just wars'—the New Labour government under Prime Minster Blair being eager to use the UK military as a 'force for good'—not factoring that to be considered 'just', wars had to have a high chance of a positive outcome.[2]

The epic shock of the 9/11 atrocities demanded a hard-headed, frontline military response, even when opportunities for any practical action were limited. The UK found herself as the principal partner in the coalition that was formed by the US and was determined to support its leader in pursuit of the historic 'special relationship'. The psyche in Whitehall even today retains imprints of Great Power status—membership of the nuclear powers on the UN Security Council, for instance—which continue to define the UK's approach to problems. So it was with the military, who always insisted on taking the leading subordinate position for any deployed operations within coalition chains of command. Indeed, retaining command of the NATO Allied Rapid Reaction Corps was given priority over other elements of the UK's armed forces after the end of the Cold War. But this resulted in a muddle, where the UK was playing strong hands without the resources or will to deliver them. When, for instance, the US trusted Britain to bring security to the south of Iraq, including securing the vital coalition line of supply from Kuwait northwards, she was rightly furious when the British effort just seemed to dissolve as things got difficult. Likewise, Britain actively lobbied to take on the security of Helmand Province in Afghanistan, partly to badger what the UK dismissively regarded as the more timid members of NATO, but then allowed the situation to blow up in her face when she was not prepared to meet the scale of the challenge presented by the Taliban. America had to bail out the UK once again, committing US Marines in force to Helmand. As someone commented, the UK 'was playing high stakes poker, with too few good cards in her hand', which by the law of averages meant she would be dismissed from the card table given enough time.[3] To get a sense of the UK's truly global ambition, it is worth reading the campaign objectives for *Operation Veritas*, the UK's response to the 9/11 outrages written in 2001 and given in full at the endnote, where the tone set gives the impression that the UK is thinking like a superpower.[4]

There was a lack of proper governmental process and formal Cabinet consultation in the way that the Prime Minister Tony Blair ran his administration—sofa government, with no properly constituted permanent War Cabinet—meaning that the institutional checks of which Whitehall was perfectly capable were often not triggered. It seemed that by the time the machinery started to analyse the risks and prospects of proposed actions, many decisions had already been taken. General Sir Mike Jackson recalled saying at a meeting at which ministers were present, 'We need a Minister for Iraq!', but was dismayed when it did not occur because it was seen to run the risk of draining authority and resources away from existing ministries and fiefdoms.[5]

Finally, the complex counter-insurgency phases of the wars in Iraq and Afghanistan cried out for a whole-of-government approach, where the military would establish local security for the other government departments—justice, education, economic development, etc.—to exploit. This simply never happened. Boyce, Walker and Stirrup all agreed as Chiefs of the Defence Staff that a matter might be settled with Prime Minister Tony Blair, and subsequently Gordon Brown, but they would then find that neither Prime Minister would exert the will or exercise the authority to make sure that it was carried through. In Blair's case, he would say 'I agree—fix it with Gordon' (who was then the Chancellor of the Exchequer), only to find that Gordon Brown stonewalled the approach and would not release the funds to achieve the task.[6]

But there were also special problems that rested with the military alone.

First, the British High Command gave its support to wars without ensuring that the wider Whitehall elite had a clear understanding of what was involved or the risks presented, and that sufficient political will existed to see the expeditions through in the longer term. The bleat in Whitehall afterwards was that the 'generals never told us it would be so difficult'. As a result, once the invasion of Iraq had been successfully achieved, there were *never* sufficient troops to deal properly with the military tasks that emerged in both Iraq and Afghanistan. An adequate reserve was never prepared—so as to recover things swiftly when the situation deteriorated—thereby breaking one of the first rules of warfare. As Brigadier Justin Maciejewski bitterly observed after serving in Iraq: 'scant regard was given to what was needed in Basra; force levels were set and then applied to the tactical problem, rather than the tactical problem defining the level of force required'.[7] The result was that an arbitrary cap was always put on the number of servicemen who would be sent to the combat theatres.

The military also failed to anchor the political will strongly enough to the consequences of what might develop; recall how huge pressure from the British tactical commander in Iraq to reinforce his winning strategy of Operation Sinbad in Basra fell on deaf ears in London, or how the UK was completely unprepared for the sudden expansion of violence in Helmand soon after the British deployed there.

Second, a number of decisions were taken without a proper underpinning analysis to support the proposals being made. On occasions an 'executive of two' of the Prime Minister and the Chief of the Defence Staff would agree a course of action and only after that would the Ministry of Defence get involved. The MoD was left deciding how to carry it out—repeating the mistakes of the deployment of the UK Airmobile Brigade to Bosnia a decade before—not analysing beforehand whether the decision was feasible or if the risks involved were properly understood. Sometimes it was unclear how and from what level the decision had arrived, with a consensus forming across Whitehall led by one or other department that 'it might be a good idea to …'. Lieutenant General Sir Rob Fry as the MoD Director of Operations (DCDS Commitments) recalls how he was bemused to hear the senior representative of the Foreign and Commonwealth Office at one Chiefs of Staff Committee meeting proposing that the MoD should undertake a particular operational task, only for the same individual to disavow that advice completely when the mood in Whitehall had changed two weeks later.[8] Furthermore, the underpinning analysis for many strategic decisions, if it had existed at all, was not available to an incumbent's successors. Recall how General Sir Richard Dannatt had trawled the minutes of the Chiefs of Staff Committee to discover how the decision to reinforce in Afghanistan had been taken, without success, and how both General Sir Mike Jackson and Air Chief Marshal Sir Jock Stirrup were unclear on the reasons behind the decision to go to Helmand Province, even though they were members of the Chiefs of Staff Committee at the time it was taken. The result of all of this was that the MoD became absorbed with making plans *work*, instead of pausing sufficiently to probe whether the plans themselves were *workable*.

Third, the UK military command structure was not designed to function efficiently within a coalition. Instead, it was optimised for the UK fighting alone, or when forces were transferred wholly under NATO command as happened in the Cold War. In contrast to the commanders of the US-led coalitions, who were located 'forward' in theatre in both Iraq and Afghanistan, Operational command was held back in the UK and the senior British commander on the spot was invariably only a two-star (major general) divisional commander, a tactical commander. The crucial level of Operational command (where the commander should be closely in touch with the battles and the local politics, but not embroiled directly in them) was vested in PJHQ in a London suburb, an hour's journey from Whitehall; PJHQ was neither close enough to the battles, nor the local political picture, nor the in-theatre coalition commanders. Nor was it intimately in touch with the UK military nerve centre at the MoD. The staff of PJHQ got many things right—mounting and sustaining the deployed forces and increasingly providing very valuable institutional continuity as the campaigns developed—but they could never provide effective Operational-level command. This was tragically illustrated when Major General Shirreff, as the in-theatre commander, had a head-on collision over several long months with PJHQ about the resources needed to progressively re-take Basra from the militias, and he lost. The Chief of Joint Operations at PJHQ, Lieutenant General Nicholas Houghton, bluntly told Major General Shirreff that he did not wish to see 'any unnecessary displays of military testosterone' on the streets of Basra.[9] The gap was further illustrated by the way that London tended to deal directly with the deployed UK Brigade commanders on the key strategy issues, bypassing all the other links in the chain of command. General Sir David Richards recalls that even when he was Commander ISAF in Afghanistan—the top NATO commander with operational control of all the fighting troops in theatre—Air Chief Marshal Sir Jock Stirrup as the UK CDS hardly ever consulted him and always went directly to the local British Brigade commander instead.[10] Too late in the decade was this corrected by establishing a proper three-star (lieutenant general equivalent) UK National Contingent Commander on the spot in Kabul,[11] with the rank and authority to be effective within a coalition and, most crucially, wresting part of the Operational level of command forward into theatre and away from PJHQ.

Fourth, the coordination between the British tactical commanders and their coalition commanders, and with the deployed representatives of the other government departments (the Foreign Office, the Intelligence Services, the Department for International Development, etc.), was often grossly inadequate in both theatres. The individuals themselves invariably bonded well, but the physical separation between the parties and the difficulties of travel meant that close contact, with all its benefits of common purpose, was often absent. The UK commanders in Basra frequently complained about the miles along dangerous roads between themselves and the UK's political representatives. To read the detached and mocking tone of the UK Ambassador in Afghanistan when describing the British military in his memoirs is to realise that something was seriously wrong in UK political/diplomatic/military relations.[12]

Fifth, the structures, processes and working practices of the Ministry of Defence did not foster clarity of purpose. For instance, the length of time it repeatedly took to get the correct military equipment fielded into a theatre was, at times, disgraceful. The MoD was proving to be a cumbersome organisation, where responsibility and authority were not always aligned; it was difficult to make winning the wars the priority it should have been. There was sometimes mischief at work, for as the campaigns dragged on the Royal Navy and RAF became increasingly concerned with their domestic issues, leaving the Army to feel it was carrying a disproportionate burden. The top operational committee, the Chiefs of Staff Committee, was isolated from important decisions made by its Chairman, the Chief of the Defence Staff, who instead frequently made key judgements in collaboration with his staff subordinates. The Chiefs of Staff Committee was also institutionally dysfunctional: it was not a proper decision-making body where the key concerns were always raised and debated, and its members were required to be loyal to both Defence as a whole and yet strongly champion their individual services, which was an impossible conflict of interest. If the services had fractured relationships one with another, there was also insufficient common purpose between them and the institutional sheet anchor of the MoD, the Civil Service. Politicians appointed as defence ministers lacked the will and expertise, and often the longevity in post, to bring these diverse factions together. The MoD was also a huge organisation, where issues sometimes simply got lost. However much we might otherwise admire the top military commanders of the time, they tolerated the unreformed arrangements in the Ministry of Defence, which allowed these things to happen.

Sixth, as the decade progressed, the Chief of the Defence Staff increasingly became a single focus for the conduct of military operations. This certainly delivered focus, but it cut out wider influences which might crucially have questioned assumptions and conclusions. It became a high-wire act for the last CDS of the decade, Air Chief Marshal Sir Jock Stirrup, as he tried to wrestle down extremely complex politico-military challenges almost single-handedly; often he informed, but did not consult, either his Chiefs or his Permanent Under Secretary. Moreover, by chance, the CDSs of the decade were scantily prepared for the increased responsibilities that had accrued to them following their enhanced position under the Nott-Lewin reforms of 1982. This required them to have new skills of strategic direction, political interfacing, management of the Whitehall caucus and balancing resources Defence-wide. They had neither formal education in statecraft, experience in other government departments, nor the widening experience of a university tertiary education. Moreover, whilst not their fault at all, they were crafting orders for Operational-level commanders to carry out in complex, messy, coalition, counter-insurgency wars with insufficient Operational-level command experience themselves. For Admiral Boyce and Air Chief Marshal Stirrup there was the added challenge of capturing the detail of land combat and producing wise judgements in this alien (to them) tactical environment.

Seventh, there was a lack of clarity back in London about the real situation—the 'ground truth'—and there were even differing pictures held by the military and their political masters. This is understandable given the distances between the deployed troops and the UK and complexity of the circumstances, but it was deeply destructive. The politicians thought that they were delivering what the military were asking from them, whilst the military were always downgrading their requests to what they thought would be politically acceptable. Too often the military in the MoD meekly accepted their lot and tried their best, rather than demanding what was necessary for success and acting on what those in the front line were telling them was needed with the greatest clarity.

Eighth, once they had ordered military deployments, politicians became detached surprisingly quickly from their wars—perhaps even gave up on them—concentrating on more pressing domestic issues, notably re-election. Prime Minister Tony Blair wrote only half a page in his long memoirs about the decision to deploy to Helmand, even though he was the principal architect of it, and he becomes very remote from military issues for the eighteen months while he was seeking re-election and when his battles with Gordon Brown over succession were at their height. For their part, the military High Command did not prevent this neglect from happening.

How Things Could Improve

How could all of this be done better in the future? Many of these problems are understood well enough and only require the institutional courage and reforming zeal of the top individuals to sort them out. Whatever the soothing words used to disguise it, the British public have not seen the success that they would have expected in Iraq and Afghanistan, given the costs in resources and casualties that they have been called to bear. It is sobering to consider that the British contribution to the wars in Iraq and Afghanistan have cost the nation between £30–40 billion, whereas an estimate of the money required to rebuild all of the UK's currently broken road surfaces would be 'only' £12 billion.

Reform must start at the top with the Prime Minster directing much more closely the wars that he chooses the UK to fight. A proper War Cabinet must be established and due process followed. A rigorous strategic analysis must be undertaken when military operations are first proposed; this can be done in a couple of days, if hearts are set to it and the right top minds energised.

The Service Chiefs should not be put in the position, nor allow themselves to be, of having to 'make do' with fewer forces than they know is required, either for success of the operations or to reduce the risk to soldiers' lives. Of greatest importance, sufficient reserves must be earmarked and readied beforehand to meet the unexpected. If these elements are not in place, the military High Command must say so unambiguously—and highlight the consequences for the success of the proposed operation without fear or favour.

Armed conflicts require such a profound commitment from the nation that it should be much clearer who is making the proposals for the deployment of armed forces, where the orders have come from, what arguments were made and what conclusions were reached—all retained for the public record ('Restricted' if necessary until they can be released, but still recorded and available).

The command arrangements must be so ordered that the UK can fit better into a coalition structure, if it is fighting within one. General Sir Rupert Smith describes this as the 'bifurcation' (or division) of command, where orders flow not only from London, but from NATO, UN, coalition headquarters and from organisations in theatre, such as the government of President Karzai in the case of Afghanistan.[13] One of the most pernicious effects of this for the UK was for each side of the 'bifurcation', be it in London, Baghdad or Kabul, to expect the other side to sort out difficult problems when they occurred, so sometimes nobody did. Whatever scheme is adopted, an Operational-level military authority must always be deployed into theatre. Likewise, the political/military interface must be reformed so that the principal leaders are always physically co-located in theatre—it must never be entertained that they could be separated, with the ideal being an empowered, vice-regal duopoly of military and political persons.[14] To improve senior military commanders' part in this, education in strategy must be mandatory for all top board members and commanders well before appointment, so that such analysis comes naturally to them.

Some of these concerns have already been addressed. Following pressure from several sources and with a change of government, the creation of a new body—the UK National Security Council (NSC)—has formalised decision-making on security issues at the top of government.[15] This Council is chaired routinely by the Prime Minister, with other key ministers inevitably required to be present. The uniformed services are represented by the Chief of the Defence Staff, both in his own right and supporting his Secretary of State for Defence. Business is conducted based on previously circulated papers and full minutes are recorded.

These new arrangements are very similar to the British Committee of Imperial Defence, created more than a century ago (as described in Chapter 13). In this respect, the British talent for getting things wrong then adjusting to correct them in an evolutionary not revolutionary manner has won through again. But the NSC is no great departure; rather hard-won experience that had slipped through hands over time and, if history is any guide, the challenge will be to keep it alive.

There have been other changes in the MoD itself. Surprisingly, these reforms were not prompted by any deep audit of the performance of the British High Command in the wars in Iraq and Afghanistan (which has yet to occur), but because the MoD had effectively become bankrupt. As the management of the Defence budget deteriorated—driven by the peripheral costs of the wars in Iraq and Afghanistan and following under-provision in the 1998 Defence Review—the demands to wean departmental authority away from the 'mismanagement' of the uniformed element in the Main Building only strengthened. To correct this, a financier with previous experience as a chief of defence procurement, Lord Levene, was appointed by the new coalition government in 2010 to suggest how the MoD could be made more accountable for the money it spent, and to propose a new organisational structure to achieve this.

Initially, the changes that Lord Levene proposed seemed to give greater power to civil servants in the MoD at the expense of the Service Chiefs; indeed a highly qualified career accountant was appointed as the MoD's Permanent Under Secretary for the first time. The Single Service Chiefs were excluded from the top MoD Defence Board, where the Chief of the Defence Staff remained as the sole representative of the uniformed services. Furthermore, the two top posts in each service (e.g. in the Navy, the Chief of the Naval Staff and Commander-in-Chief of the active fleet) were merged into one and relegated with their budgets to their field headquarters in Portsmouth, Andover and High Wycombe.

In one respect there has been another return to the *status quo ante*. Presented with these proposals, the incoming CDS (General Sir David Richards) managed to convince ministers that distancing the Single Service Chiefs in this way was unworkable, disrupting the essential linkage of authority, responsibility and accountability. Instead, he got agreement to create a subordinate monthly Armed Forces Committee in 2011. This committee is chaired by the CDS, with the Permanent Under Secretary and the uniformed Service Chiefs as full members. It is here that most defence issues are thrashed out before submitting recommendations to the Defence Board for final approval. In many respects this has put the CDS in a powerful position compared to his Civil Service colleagues; not surprisingly the move was resisted by some of them. General Richards re-established the habit of the CDS consulting his Service Chiefs fully at the weekly Chiefs of Staff Committee meetings before making any move or giving political advice, imitating how things operated a decade before.[16] He believed that these arrangements and his position on the National Security Council allowed sound military advice to be put to the government in an acceptable way, commenting that 'at the military–strategic level, Libya worked (whatever its long-term outcome may yet be) and we are not in Syria, despite much pressure on me to concede that we should become involved'.[17]

This has not solved all the problems. Under the Nott-Lewin reforms, the CDS was granted singular authority for the strategic direction of operations—which is good—but on all other issues the Single Service Chiefs still deal directly with their political masters, which given his many other responsibilities risks marginalising the CDS on key issues. When asked why he did not get to grips with the feuding Single Service Chiefs in his time, Air Chief Marshal Sir Jock Stirrup replied, 'But I didn't command them; if I had given them orders they could have refused.'[18]

Likewise, when asked how the new policy for substituting reserves for one fifth of the regular servicemen in the Army happened (whilst he was CDS)—a deeply controversial decision—General Sir David Richards replied: 'I didn't agree with it, the Prime Minister and I had set the bar in 2010 at 94,000, well above the reduction that came out, but I had little to do with the decision-making that produced the cut. It was proposed at the National Security Council and we were sort of told that it was going to happen'.[19] Even the head of the Army, the Chief of the General Staff, was caught unawares by the size of this cut to his manpower strength when it was published, having little warning of the results of the 'Three-Month Review' that formalised a reduction of 20,000 regular soldiers.[20]

This is intriguing and informative. It is, of course, the exception that proves a rule. If the Chief of the Defence Staff was not directly involved in the decision-making for the Reserves Study and the Chief of the General Staff was surprised by the result of the Three-Month Review that implemented it, where was the decision taken? What still seems to happen is that ministers raise concerns and develop new ideas with their civil servants and special advisers, who help to investigate the issues involved and shepherd progress through the MoD system. The Single Service Chiefs are only consulted when required and the CDS is largely absent from those discussions. Whilst the CDS clearly controls combat operations, the idea of the CDS as a strong hand for *all* issues of defence that affect the uniformed services is false. The result is that whilst a coordinated single service discussion might take place, or a joint voice can emerge in the Armed Forces Committee, the actual line of decision on critical issues still bypasses all of this. With that remaining a possibility, there is no incentive for the individual services to commit completely to a collegiate view and, in the fevered bartering for resource allocation in the MoD, there is no discouragement to the hugely distorting and self-interested lobbying of individual interests. This state of affairs will continue until the services, chaired by the CDS, discuss all resource allocation for the long term, 'pan-defence', and come up with coherent, truly joint advice to ministers, undistorted by other channels of influence.

A good example of the dialogue that should exist between the generalist politician and his expert military officers occurred when President Obama was asked by the Pentagon to approve a surge of 40,000 extra troops to Afghanistan, very soon after taking office in 2009. To the military the answer to the question was obvious: sign up to a surge of further troops into Afghanistan in order to match the deteriorating situation there. But Colin Powell, a former chairman of the Joint Chiefs, said to President Obama: 'You don't have to put up with this. These guys work for you. Because they're unanimous in their advice doesn't make it right.'[21]

Obama walked around that direct request by asking the Pentagon what they thought the aim of their efforts in Afghanistan was. This confused the military staffs, for they had an aim that addressed the threat that the *military* faced in Afghanistan—defeat the Taliban—not what was in the *wider* interest of the USA. After several months of discussion, with Obama holding his own thoughts unseen, a better aim emerged that addressed the wider issues: that was, to provide security for the Afghan people to allow them to develop their broken state, in order that the Taliban would be rejected.

Even at this stage, Obama did not agree to a troop surge, although neither did he rule it out. He started to drill down into what the extra troops would be used for if he authorised them, without commenting whether the uses were right or wrong. This triggered an important further debate about whether the way to achieve the now-agreed aim would be through counter-terrorism or counter-insurgency, and if the latter, whether enough troops could be surged into Afghanistan to face down such an insurgency.

Under this latest questioning the military consensus started to fracture and strong positions were taken. Obama continued to support his chairman of the Joint Chiefs of Staff throughout, but he also called for views from his National Security Adviser, General Jim Jones, and the Service Chiefs individually. He got different answers from all of them, with his own Vice President Joe Biden an articulate supporter of a more limited counter-terrorism strategy.

By this time all concerned realised that a trivial answer would just not be accepted—nor to their credit did they want to give one, once they had woken up to the challenge—and a vigorous debate reaching down into the middle ranks of the military staff took place. Finally a completely different package was eventually submitted to the President—one that contained several genuine options.

The result was that the US presence in Afghanistan was more purposeful with the field commanders having a much better idea of the outcome they were trying to achieve. It led to General Stanley McChrystal, the coalition commander in Kabul, turning the existing approach on its head and eschewing violence in preference to 'courageous restraint'. It alerted the Pentagon to difficulties that were going to arise downstream and they were no longer travelling blindfolded. All of this was achieved by a President who had no military experience but with the ability to ask the right questions, supported by an expert military staff capable of debate. Earlier, President Bush had been in a similar position when he had to decide whether to withdraw from Iraq, or to surge in more troops to Baghdad. He could choose between the outcome of the bipartisan Iraq Study Group set up by Congress in 2006 chaired by James Baker, or contrasting ideas submitted by Kagan and Keane from the American Enterprise Institute, allowing Bush to consider alternatives before making a choice.

It could be argued that President Obama stopped probing his policy options at too low a level; perhaps he should have continued the process to seek out wider options between the military 'kinetic' route and the diplomatic one of brokering an accommodation between the Taliban and the Kabul government, for instance. But nothing like this approach occurred in the UK when it was deciding to leave Basra or to deploy to Helmand. If it had, both the mortal danger that the Baswari citizens were placed in by the UK's disengagement, and the absolute inevitability of Britain being called to venture outside its selected security lozenge into the northern Helmand valley, might have been anticipated.

Who is to be in Charge and How should Decisions be Taken?

You will have picked up long ago that there are two themes in this book that are in conflict one with another. On the one hand the fact that the Service Chiefs were excluded from operational decision-making is lamented; on the other hand it is suggested that much mischief was caused because the Service Chiefs were powerful lobbies within the MoD. Likewise, the Civil Service could say 'yes' or 'no' to things through their role in financial and policy supervision, even though they were outside the chain of command, sometimes without even leaving a trace of their fingerprints.

To sort this out, the first imperative must be to decide whether the Service Chiefs and senior civil servants are going to be in or out of the decision process. If the Service Chiefs are to be in, they should be fully in, not partially so as at present; if they are to be out, their roles should be narrowed to generating combat forces and they should no longer be held morally or institutionally responsible for strategic decisions that are taken. If senior civil servants are to continue to be formally outside the chain of command, the power they have accrued by controlling the budget process should be tamed and civil servants should be restricted to the constitutional and financial supervisory role as auditors intended by Parliament, with finance being controlled instead by a cadre of professional accountants and policy made by trained strategists.

The second imperative is that all major decisions should be taken by a single constituted authority, such as the Armed Forces Committee, not bartered about between powerful parallel groups in the MoD or through back-channels to politicians.

The third imperative is that there should be complete transparency at the time a decision is taken—and records kept forever after—as to who had taken it and why; this exposure would discipline all those involved to their responsibilities.

The fourth imperative is that senior posts should change from being filled by generalists to experts, who would remain in post long enough to be inside the lifecycle of the decisions being taken; usually this would mean at least five years. A qualified cadre needs to be established in the areas of strategic planning, risk assessment and intelligence formed from people who are beyond doubt expert in their disciplines. It is truly amazing that the post of the MoD's Chief of Defence Intelligence invariably goes to an officer with no prior specialisation in intelligence.

Lord Levene in his report in 2011 made many of these points in attempting to align responsibility and authority, but he dodged the biggest issue. Ultimately, the only way to achieve this would be for the CDS to have full command of the single services, as is the case now in every advanced nation other than the USA. When General Richards proposed this idea during the Levene process, it was resisted by both the Single Services and the Civil Service, who feared that it would reduce their influence and place too much authority in the hands of the CDS. Here are echoes of Lord Mountbatten's previous attempt to gain authority for operational decisions, now possessed by the CDS. This only happened later under the Nott-Lewin reforms, following shortcomings exposed during war in the Falklands. Much as the Single Service Chiefs would hate to find themselves reduced in status, it would solve the terrible bind that they find themselves in—as the quotations earlier by General Sir Mike Jackson and others had demonstrated and the cruel events of the previous decade had exposed.

Turning to straight operational matters, the awful decision to commit to war still has the danger of being taken too freely. Too often in recent years the reasons for going to war either have not been clear, or have changed repeatedly, and the costs always exceeded. Going to war should be highly disciplined, with an auditable trail right from the top down to the formal orders given to the field commanders. Likewise with the fighting that follows. The risks must be listed and the means to extract physically and politically from the military deployment worked out beforehand. The sort of events that might trigger this should be thought through. Of course things will change, but this work should be formally signed off and retained so as to record the starting point, the aims sought and to ensure that all government agencies are coordinated and committed. At present it is done in a piecemeal way, if at all.

None of this need be an elaborate or lengthy process. As previously suggested, it should be a day's work provided the top team are fully engaged, not spun out over weeks—and, however imperfect, it is infinitely better than not doing it, or it being done *for* the top team but not *by* it. General Stanley McChrystal, former commander of ISAF in Afghanistan, observed:

'the process of planning for campaigns… is not about getting smart people together and writing a brilliant paper that produces a strategy. [It is about] bringing the right people together… and *they will devise a strategy in an afternoon* (author's italics)'.[22]

The presence of the key decision-makers is critical, as was seen in the process that allowed flaws to go un-trapped in the decision to deploy to Helmand in 2006. Here, an exhaustive analysis carried out beforehand by the middle-ranking staff produced a document which not only failed to highlight the essential hazards but hid them in the detail, where they remained unseen by the top team. Contrast this with how governments come to important agreements amongst themselves (at the EU or the G8, for instance), where the final decisions are taken at prolonged sessions by assembled national leaders, going on through the night if required, not by the experts who have prepared the facts for them beforehand.

Little improvement is visible so far over this. As an example, the loose way in which the UK reacted to the alleged use of chemical weapons by the Assad regime in Syria (September 2013) showed that the heart still holds sway over cold logic. Prime Minster Cameron was enthusiastic about a punishment strike on Damascus without apparently calculating where that would lead the West if the Syrian Assad regime simply ignored it. Exceptionally, the situation was rescued on this occasion by the UK Parliament vetoing the proposed military venture, largely on the basis of the government being unable to answer the questions why, how, what, for how long, and with what results—as well as what to do if the other side did not comply.

The Chiefs will always feel pressured not to challenge political orders to go to war too vigorously, either through loyalty to the democratic process or from institutional conformity. To get out of this corner, it should be made a *constitutional* duty for the Chiefs to satisfy themselves that the correct or essential planning prerequisites are in place, at least in outline. In the United States there is much more readiness to put legislative and constitutional constraints on the Commander-in-Chief and senior commanders, and the US military has little difficulty in working within them.

Once the policy requirements from the National Security Council are received by the MoD and the strategy decided is passed (along with the CDS's guidance) to military staffs to create the operational plan, the Chief of Joint Operations should be required to reply formally and for the official record, stating his view on the feasibility, risk and likelihood of success in a signed reply. A similar process should be followed if there are significant changes to the circumstances. In parallel to the periodic Force Reviews that are already conducted by PJHQ, there should be a top-level *strategy* review, revisiting the circumstances with the arguments and results recorded. In all of this the aim is simple: to ensure that the military strategy evolves to serve the policy objective, with clarity established about who said what to whom, and who recommended what solutions in response to which circumstances. In parallel, because the Permanent Joint Headquarters at Norwood has not proved fit for purpose as the UK's Operational level Headquarters as was once hoped, it should be brought into the MoD Main Building as a coherent unit restricted to mounting and sustaining operations—perhaps occupying a single floor— for there is little further purpose in the imposed separation.

To achieve a step change in relations between the military and civilian parts of an armed intervention, the command arrangements should recognise beforehand that a change of primacy from military to civilian occurs naturally once the first intense 'kinetic' phase is completed. This could be realised by appointing a civilian as the principal deputy to the overall military commander *before* deployment. Once initial security has been gained, the positions would be reversed, with the military commander now becoming the military subordinate of the civilian lead. People might forget that Field Marshal Templer took charge of the Emergency in Malaya in 1952 not as a military officer, but as a civilian British High Commissioner, underlining the need for the lead in theatre to be political. This change would have dramatic advantages: the military commander's war plans would be constantly reviewed in the light of what had to follow them; the essential habitual relationship between the political and military chiefs in theatre would be formed very early on; political ascendancy in military decision making would be emphasised from the start.

Finally, the military can only be one part of a wider effort. Everybody has bemoaned the lack of a whole-of-government approach in the last decades of interventions (which the military describes as the 'Comprehensive Approach') and arrangements must finally be formalised to make this mandatory. If the other government departments in Whitehall will not sign up with clear undertakings to contribute their parts to a proposed armed operation, the MoD should flatly say that the conditions do not exist for a successful military intervention.

Choosing and Training the Chief

Considering the top post, the Chief of the Defence Staff might even occasionally be chosen from a wider group than his immediate subordinate chiefs, which is a very small and precious pool. After all, Wellington, Napoleon and Alexander the Great all demonstrated that great responsibility can be placed on different shoulders as long as the individuals are exceptional in their field.

The caucus of British senior officers needs to become much more at ease with strategic notions and tenets. Few senior officers today really understand the strengths and weaknesses of such concepts as the Schlieffen Plan, or what it was that really gave Britain victory against the communists in Malaya, or could explain why the Russians allowed themselves to be drawn in and fail in Afghanistan. Professor Sir Hew Strachan sets the challenge thus:

'... if operational thinking is core business for senior officers, are they also not required to address the strategic implications of their advice? If they do not, are they in danger of guaranteeing the incoherence of strategy from the outset? Must they not confront unrealistic political ambitions with professional realism, given that this is how strategy ought to be made?'[23]

At the moment officers are promoted to high rank because they are good operators, not especially because they are good or original thinkers or accomplished strategists. Whilst being good at operations remains essential, senior officers need better conceptual frameworks on which to hang their hard-won experience and instincts, and they should more instinctively view military circumstances in strategic terms. The cry should not be for more *strategists*, but for the military elite to *think more strategically*. Too often today the immediate reaction is to sort out the challenges as they appear.

In discussion with the most recently retired CDS, General Sir David Richards, I talked through the characteristics required of a successful Chief of the Defence Staff, especially one in a time of great change and contraction in the UK's armed forces. He was firmly of the view that operational experience and previous high field command were the essential virtues for a CDS, so as to be able to deal with an immediate crisis sure-footedly and almost instinctively. This was echoed in a discussion with one of his predecessors, Admiral Lord Boyce, who put command experience at the top of the prerequisites for a successful CDS. I widened the question to General Richards: that a task of equal importance was to ensure the enduring effectiveness and good health of the UK armed services—getting right the long-term structures and the balance of resource spending in a time of severe contraction? Whilst it was true that the absolute daily priority of the CDS was to ensure that today goes well, especially when his soldiers are deployed in harm's way, surely the demands of the long term must be made to hold equal sway? Not shifting from his view about the pre-eminence of strategic command, General Richards gave a list of the challenges that he had faced as CDS whilst the armed forces were being restructured in 2011, showing just how special that individual has to be to succeed both as the master of the day-to-day and the architect of the future.

Education can help enormously here, and the priority it once had in officers' careers must be restored. One way to build strategy as a core instinct in officers would be to have specific education in the subject. It should become a rite of passage for all senior officers to complete a Defence Fellowship in some aspect of higher-level political/military strategy, for it is the only time that they would be truly detached from the order and certainty of their military life and required to think from first principles. A scheme for this already exists, but it is infrequently used by those on the fast route and there is no obligation to do so. Instead, when selected for promotion to senior/general rank, individuals should be required to choose a subject for a period of study of six to twelve months at a university. This would also allow aptitudes to be developed and intellectual mettle exposed. It would encourage individuals to think about aspects of strategy for a number of years in preparation, giving strategy a profile in the military world that simply does not exist at the moment. The individual would also gain a period of invaluable decompression from daily tasks: allowing reflection (leading to creativity), and providing thinking time about their future roles. It would promote curiosity. If required of everyone across the board on promotion to senior rank, those who select the future military elite would have a much better idea of what they were getting intellectually; and they could then promote accordingly.

15

FIT FOR THE FUTURE?

'With two thousand years of examples behind us, we have no excuses when fighting for not fighting well.'

T. E. Lawrence, 1888–1935

Has the story of how Britain's High Command performed in Afghanistan and Iraq become just so much history? Can that chapter be closed, reflecting ruefully on how things might have gone better, but sympathising with the contradictions the leaders faced and their struggles to resolve them? Do the blandishments of the latest team in the UK High Command ring true: that things are now much better, that mistakes could not be repeated, that lessons have been learnt?

It does not appear so. The deficiencies that made the Ministry of Defence 'system' incapable of solving the problems of Iraq and Afghanistan logically and coherently still exist; the way resources are allocated continues to embed rivalry between individual services; the tussle between the 'military headquarters' (uniformed officer) and the 'department of state' (civil servant) factions is unresolved; the critical linkage between authority, responsibility and accountability remains out of alignment. Where these things remain unreformed it is a failure by the people at the top to correct them, however otherwise gifted and well-intentioned.

Yet the leadership of the UK armed forces faces daunting near-in challenges. This book is about recording history, not future-gazing, but it is worth

235

flying a few kites at the very end about some of the things that that will test the High Command's strategic ability and vision as never before. About the future you will come to your own conclusions, but here are some ideas.

First, the UK's military leadership has lost much of the inherent trust and goodwill that it once enjoyed and people, with some justification, question its competence. Whilst widespread affection remains for the military body, faith in its top officers has been severely wounded following the events of Iraq and Afghanistan and there is a common perception of too much inter-service squabbling. The deployed forces and individuals themselves without question performed superbly, but too often they seemed to be sent in the wrong direction strategically, or even up a dead-end. Citizens want more success for their taxes; they want reassurance that the lives of their young men and women are not risked casually or to little avail, and that Britain's military heritage will be safeguarded. Credibility and trust in these aspects have to be restored.

Second, the puzzle of how to allocate scant resources is as acute as ever, if not worse. It is a judgement of the probability of something happening against the risk of the consequences of not providing for it. At one end of the spectrum, countering piracy and insurgency still require the same high density of armed servicemen that they always did—'boots on the ground', battlefield helicopters, fleets of low-tech ships. These are invariably wars of choice but remain by far the most common forms of warfare—representing 80 per cent of the conflicts of the last hundred years—so they are very likely to recur. Yet, at the other end of the spectrum, the much less frequent open warfare between sophisticated states is only won by having the best technology and the most robust economy. So the UK High Command has to choose how much to spend on numbers of men and women for optional wars, and how much to reserve for spending on the advanced technology indispensable to winning a much less frequent war of vital national interest.

This calculation is made more difficult because the UK's armed forces have finally, undeniably, sunk below the level where they could ever fight alone again in major combat operations; and yet there is no guiding strategic theme about what the UK wants its armed forces to do. For the current security policy from the UK Foreign Office remains—and here I shall abbreviate—for the armed forces to be prepared to do almost everything, everywhere, guided by the current UK National Security Strategy that emphasises that there is to be no reduction in the UK's global influence.[1] In the absence of better direction and with insufficient funds, this inevitably forces the interpretation of what to provide for (and the balance between the different combat capabilities) onto the military operators in the Ministry of Defence. For instance, with insufficient resources provided for maritime defence, they are asked to decide between concentrating on the defence of the British Isles and associated European waters, or, on retaining the ability for the UK to project carrier Maritime Strike across the globe thus intercepting problems 'upstream'?[2] So far the latter has won, with the UK continuing to build its largest warship ever.[3] Meanwhile, the number of coastal patrol vessels and frigates in UK waters in 2012 declined so low that the dedicated university naval training fleet was used instead. For there is one certainty in all of this: if the equation linking the military aims set is out of kilter with underpinning military resources provided, catastrophe or stalemate are more likely than success, exactly as we have just experienced.

Urgently, the UK needs to look unemotionally at the threats that confront it and decide what part it will play in facing them. To take just one example: if the Iranian leadership acquired a deployable nuclear weapon in the coming years, as they have threatened to do, would the UK retaliate to an Iranian nuclear attack on itself or its allies by launching an ICBM from one of its Trident submarines on Tehran, killing its hostage population in the process? Of course not. Or would the UK send its solitary aircraft carrier near the Persian Gulf to launch air strikes against Iran, a country equipped with capable Russian-supplied air defence weapons and missile-carrying fast naval corvettes? Or try to gain a bridgehead and land an armoured brigade on the Iranian mainland, given that the Iranian Army has a total strength of 700,000 soldiers? Such responses by the UK as a medium-sized power are extremely unlikely, to the point of vanishing altogether, even as part of a coalition. But what if the UK stationed one or two of its silent, 'Astute' hunter-killer submarines seaward of the entrance to the Straits of Hormuz and started sinking Iranian oil tankers one a day (or even just threatened to do so), would not the UK be capable even by itself of bringing Iran to its knees economically in weeks?

So the challenge lies in imagining the military problems the UK actually needs to address and the armed forces that will be required to solve them. Although without question they must remain followers politically, it is inescapable that the UK military caucus must lead their politicians to script such a new strategic doctrine, placing the UK ambition firmly where it can be afforded. Until recently the UK has set out to be a sort of 'United States Lite', possessing armed capabilities across the whole piece, but she has never allocated nearly enough resources to do it properly. So in many respects she became Mao's paper tiger, dangerously picking fights above her weight. Other nations, by comparison, have taken a different route, consistently fielding very professional, very modern, very well-equipped niche forces as contributions to all the recent coalition campaigns, keeping alive their military competence without attempting to provide the full spectrum of armed forces. For instance, the armoured squadrons supporting the British in the Helmand campaign were always from Denmark, equipped with the latest Leopard 2 main battle tanks. At the same time, these nations made sure they retained modern, robust forces for their homeland defence. Is now the time for the UK to shape itself towards being something along these lines, realising that it can no longer do everything? Instead, identifying where its true priorities lie and properly resourcing them? I don't argue here for either route, only that the calculation should be honestly made and to stop giving out silly instructions such as that the UK's military ambition is undiminished at the time when the forces available to achieve it are being cut by up to a third.

Third, a dramatic step-change is taking place in the way wars are fought by the richer nations. The 'horse or tank moment' has been replaced by a 'tank or sensor moment'.[4] Munitions are now delivered reliably from distant launch systems and brought onto target by units that can remain hidden (they no longer need to give away their positions by shooting the weapons themselves or by excessive movement). The other side of that penny is that, under the 'persistent stare' of high-grade sensors detecting all movement using Doppler radar, a combat unit that moves will inevitably reveal itself and be obliterated. One that has to stay still in order to protect itself will not be able to adjust its position to battle advantage, so will be of little use. Ergo, the current formations of main battle tanks, fleets of ships and fighter aircraft and anything else (armoured infantry battalions, artillery, etc.) that currently intend to manoeuvre around the battle fracture zone against a comparable enemy will place themselves at mortal risk. Similar changes have taken place in naval warfare and aerial combat requiring similar adjustments. For all their might, do carrier battle fleets steaming at 30 knots into a distant war zone have much utility when their enemy has space systems that will inevitably detect their mass, and has designed ballistic missiles systems that can sink them whilst still thousands of miles away, as have the Chinese?

This will compel unprecedented modernisation on navies, armies and air forces when facing matched opponents in major combat operations. At present, they show little sign of recognising this. For the British Army, it means the demise of infantry battalions, tank regiments and armoured brigades as they are currently structured for major combat operations, hitherto used to manoeuvre as formations so as to bring a crushing overmatch of combat power onto an opposing enemy. Instead, they will be need to replaced by small, mobile, self-sufficient and very well protected observer units, cueing the munitions of weapon systems further away on air, sea and land platforms. Once the enemy begins to collapse and the threat of precision attack diminishes, they will need to re-combine to occupy the battlefield that has been gained, and be flexible enough to be used as larger units in counter-insurgency operations.

Where is the evidence for this? As far back as 1991 the movement of tank squadrons by Saddam Hussein's Iraqi Republican Guard units were systematically tracked by prototype USA J-STARS aircraft, stealing any element of surprise from the former.[5] Twelve years later in 2003, the same Iraqi divisions were tracked as they manoeuvred into positions to block the US Army's advance towards Baghdad, allowing them to be written down in air attacks and by depth weapons before the advancing US armoured formations mopped them up. The movement of tanks from Gaddafi's Thirty Second 'Khamis' Brigade towards Benghazi in 2011 was easily detected by surveillance aircraft and they were destroyed at leisure by NATO aircraft. In the Libyan capital, Tripoli, the location of Gaddafi's sniper positions was entered hourly on to Google Maps as red pins by Libyan opposition observers; the French air command centre downloaded these locations into their Air Tasking Table, once they realised what they represented, and many of the sniper positions were destroyed. Yet the British Army has taken no moves to reshape itself away from fielding combat tank squadrons and infantry companies towards creating well-protected forward observer units to cue stand-off weapon systems. The Royal Navy persists in funding an aircraft carrier (with all its singularity and vulnerability) at the expense of a more balanced fleet with plentiful drones flying from more numerous, less complex platforms.[6] The Royal Air Force spends far more on a few exotic manned airframes than it does on unmanned aerial vehicles, or unmanned aerial combat aircraft, or battlefield helicopters, or the missile systems to go on its airframes.[7]

Finally, the armed forces urgently need to be organised within a more effective command structure at the top, capable of analysing challenges with proper reflection and coming up with realistic options, not following sheep-like any political whim or media pressure. A habit of correctly framing the military strategy at the beginning is needed, preventing the armed forces from finding themselves overwhelmed, impotent or defeated in a theatre of operations later. Otherwise, don't go there. To achieve this, there must be much greater unity in the Ministry of Defence, deploying well-constructed arguments of military judgement which prevent politicians from committing the UK to un-winnable or disproportionately expensive adventures for the gains achieved. The Operational level of command must be placed where it should be, invariably in-theatre. Whatever arrangements are chosen, they must unite the military and political leaders in theatre together. The military should never again be sent as the only instrument of power, without properly binding in all the other contributing Whitehall departments. The question is how.

To tackle these challenges the MoD and Whitehall will have to perform much better than they have done in the last decade and much better than the current reforms have so far delivered. The people at the top must both master their system and reform it, behaving more objectively and in a more collegial way, and gain the education and instinct to act more strategically. The cost in blood and treasure of going to war demands no less.

Prime Minister Tony Blair assured President George Bush on 17th July 2002 that *'Our job is to be there with you. You are not alone.'*

America and Britain marching in step militarily as well. UK Secretary of State for Defence Geoff Hoon welcomes US Secretary of Defense Donald Rumsfeld for talks with military chiefs in London.

General Tommy Franks (left), Commander of US Central Command, briefed the UK Chief of the Defence Staff Admiral Sir Michael Boyce on 5 June 2002. Whatever was discussed, Admiral Sir Michael Boyce was unable to tell his Chiefs of the US plans until the end of 2002, some six months later.

Sir Kevin Tebbit, as Permanent Under Secretary he was the top civil servant in the MoD 1998–2005. His years as the head of GCHQ, the UK's surveillance agency, should have given him all the tools needed to prevent the mis-assessment of the Taliban strength in Helmand Province in 2005-2006 taking hold in the MoD.

Sir Bill Jeffrey followed Sir Kevin Tebbit as Permanent Under Secretary in the Ministry of Defence 2005–2010. He had an astute mind and had played a major part in implementing the Good Friday agreement that brought peace to Northern Ireland, but little other previous experience with military matters.

The best Permanent Under Secretary the MoD never had. Sir David Omand served most of his career in defence and intelligence and had risen to be a very successful three-star MoD Policy Director before becoming Head of the UK listening agency GCHQ. However, he was chosen to be the top civil servant in the Home Office instead of the MoD. If anyone could have bridged the gap between the different tribes in the MoD, it would have been Omand.

Admiral Sir Alan West inspects an Iraqi naval honour guard in Um Quasr, Basra in 2003 as the UK First Sea Lord. West was to complain bitterly that he was not included in the core operational planning in the MoD for the operations in Iraq and Afghanistan. With strong views and plenty of energy left on retirement, he became a minister in the Labour Government.

General Sir Michael Walker took over as Chief of the Defence Staff on 2 May 2003, immediately after the invasion of Iraq was complete. As the strategic commander of UK Armed Forces until just before the Helmand operation began in 2006, he had the most testing of times, but he remained calm, unflappable and courteous throughout.

General Sir Michael Jackson, a warrior Chief of the General Staff (head of the Army), was always on the front foot and widely respected. He became very frustrated at the UK's strategy for Iraq. He handed over to General Sir Richard Dannatt in 2006.

Admiral Sir Jonathon Band took over from Admiral West as head of the Royal Navy in 2006. He was appointed a month before the decision was taken to move into Helmand, so had to cope with the consequences of a plan moulded by others even though his Royal Marines were to play a crucial part in the fighting there. Like Navy Chiefs before him, he felt keenly the responsibility to keep the UK's new aircraft carrier programme on track.

The leaders of the military clans, representing their servicemen and women at the Cenotaph in Whitehall in 2005, lead by HRH The Prince of Wales. They found themselves in a very difficult position because much of their authority had leaked away into the central MoD staffs over the preceding decades and they were often excluded from key strategy decisions, yet their servicemen, the press and the public still held them responsible for events. Left to right: Air Chief Marshal Stirrup, HRH, General Jackson, an ADC, Admiral West.

Prime Minister Tony Blair mixing with his troops. Here they are operating in Basra without wearing body armour.

Things didn't stay calm for long and by 2004 the relatively unprotected Snatch patrol vehicles had become an easy target for road side bombs. It left the UK with a dilemma of whether to continue to patrol in light vehicles so as to normalise things, or to provide large armoured vehicles giving better protection but alienating the population.

The British Army surrounded the notorious Jumait Iraqi police station where two UK special forces soldiers were being held captive on 19 September 2005. A crowd gathered and an armoured infantry fighting vehicle was set on fire by a petrol bomb. The crew escaped and the hostages were later recovered from a house, bound, almost naked and ready for execution. This picture of a soldier in flames began to convince the outside world of how bad things had become in Basra.

US Secretary of Defense Robert Gates with Lieutenant General Sir David Richards, NATO's Commander of ISAF in Kabul in 2006. Richards was astute and nobody's fool, just as much at ease with private soldiers as with top political leaders. Before deploying to Kabul with the Headquarters of the NATO Allied Rapid Reaction Corps he had demanded that the UK provide him with a theatre reserve, but none was forthcoming leaving him with too little flexibility when problems arose. He was the last non-American to command the coalition force in Afghanistan and four years later in 2010 he became the UK's Chief of the Defence Staff.

Air Chief Marshal Sir Jock Stirrup was Chief of the Defence Staff and UK strategic commander from 2006–2010. He held things together during the worst period for the UK in both Iraq and Afghanistan. Stirrup was very much his own man and the most intellectually capable Chief of the decade.

General Sir Richard Dannatt speaks to the press outside the Ministry of Defence on 13 October 2006. Largely excluded from the operational chain of command, Dannatt was to use the media to pressure the MoD and the government on issues he felt were important for the Army.

Dr John Reid, escorted here in Camp Bastion by Lieutenant Colonel Henry Worsley, was a dedicated career politician who had prepared himself beforehand, over ten years or more, for the role as Secretary of State for Defence 2005–2006. As the political architect of the UK's deployment to Helmand, he certainly had expected that that it would be a tough operation, but he expressed the hope in public that it could be achieved without a shot being fired. This was to rebound savagely on him as the situation deteriorated rapidly. He confessed himself astounded that the UK forces had expanded northwards up the Helmand Valley only weeks after he had handed over to Des Browne.

Brigadier Ed Butler led part of 16 Air Assault Brigade into Helmand in 2006. Under intense pressure from Governor Daoud, he ordered his forces to leave the 'Security Lozenge' and to defend government outposts in the towns northwards up the Helmand valley. 'He would be damned by some if he did, and lynched by others if he didn't'.

Major General Richard Shirreff decided that the militias in Basra were not going to force the British Army out of the city in 2006. He was an energetic, tough-minded, Oxford-educated officer who initiated Operation Salamanca/Sinbad so as to take back the city, police district by police district, but the initiative faded away after an initial success through lack of resources. To his great frustration.

UK Secretary of State Bob Aisworth, notably balanced and caring, being briefed a year after the withdrawal from Basra by Major General Jonathan Shaw, another tough-minded, Oxford-educated, thinking soldier who followed Shirreff. Shaw had decided that the problem in Basra was more to do with criminality than insurgency; he declared that Basra 'was Palermo, not Beirut' and made the deal with the Jaish Al Mahdi that prepared the way for the British to withdraw from Basra.

Tony Blair handed over to Gordon Brown as Prime Minister in 2007, just as the situation in Basra was unravelling, and Air Chief marshal Sir Jock Stirrup as CDS had to dissuade Brown from a precipitious withdrawal from Iraq. He was mistrusted by the military after long years of parsimony as Chancellor of the Exchequer, but Jock Stirrup found him 'polite, listening, [a person who] allowed vigorous argument and was receptive to new ideas'.

ANNEX 1

EVENTS AND PRINCIPAL UK DEFENCE PERSONALITIES

Events

11 September 2001	'9/11'. The attacks on the Twin Towers and the Pentagon in the USA.
October–December 2001	The invasion of Afghanistan and defeat of the Taliban.
January 2002	ISAF formed in Kabul.
March 2003	The invasion of Iraq.
April–May 2006	UK deployment to Helmand.
January 2007	UK Operation Sinbad begins in Basra.
July 2007	'The Deal' with the Jaish al Mahdi in Basra.
December 2007	Provincial Iraqi Control is declared in Basra.
March 2008	The Iraqi controlled operation 'Charge of the Knights' retakes Basra.
March 2009	UK withdraws from Iraq.

Personalities

Prime Minster of the United Kingdom

Rt Hon. Tony Blair MP   May 1997–June 2007

Rt Hon. Dr Gordon Brown MP   June 2007–May 2010
Rt Hon. David Cameron MP   May 2010–

Secretary of State for Defence

Rt Hon. Geoff Hoon MP   Oct. 1999–Nov. 2005
Rt Hon. Dr John Reid MP   Nov. 2005–May 2006
Rt Hon. Des Browne MP   May 2006–Oct. 2008
Rt Hon. John Hutton MP   Oct. 2008–June 2009
Rt Hon. Bob Ainsworth MP   June 2009–July 2010
Rt Hon. Liam Fox MP   July 2010–Oct. 2011

Permanent Under Secretary of the Ministry of Defence

Sir Kevin Tebbit   1998–Nov. 2005
Sir Bill Jeffrey   Nov. 2005–Oct. 2010

Chief of the United Kingdom Defence Staff

General Sir Charles Guthrie   April 1997–Feb. 2001
Admiral Sir Michael Boyce   Feb. 2001–May 2003
General Sir Michael Walker   May 2003–April 2006
Air Chief Marshal Sir Jock Stirrup April 2006–Oct. 2010
General Sir David Richards   Oct. 2010–July 2013

First Sea Lord (Head of the Royal Navy)

Admiral Sir Michael Boyce   July 1998–Jan. 2001
Admiral Sir Nigel Essenhigh   Jan. 2001–Sept. 2002
Admiral Sir Alan West   Sept. 2002–Feb. 2006
Admiral Sir Jonathon Band   Feb. 2006–July 2009
Admiral Sir Mark Stanhope   July 2009–April 2013

Chief of the General Staff (Head of the British Army)

General Sir Roger Wheeler   Feb. 1997–April 2000
General Sir Michael Walker   April 2000–May 2003

General Sir Mike Jackson	May 2003–Aug. 2006
General Sir Richard Dannatt	Aug. 2006–Aug. 2009
General Sir David Richards	Aug. 2009–Sept. 2010
General Sir Peter Wall	Sept. 2010–

Chief of the Air Staff (Head of the Royal Air Force)

Air Chief Marshal Sir Richard Johns	April 1997–April 2000
Air Chief Marshal Sir Peter Squire	April 2000–Aug. 2003
Air Chief Marshal Sir Jock Stirrup	Aug. 2003–April 2006
Air Chief Marshal Sir Glenn Torpy	April 2006–July 2009
Air Chief Marshal Sir Stephan Dalton	July 2009–July 2013

Deputy Chief of the Defence Staff, Commitments (MoD Director of Operations)

Lieutenant General Sir Anthony Pigott	March 2000–July 2003
Lieutenant General Rob Fry	July 2003–Dec. 2005
Vice Admiral Charles Styles	Jan. 2006–Aug. 2007
Lieutenant General Peter Wall	Aug. 2007–July 2009
Lieutenant General Simon Mayall	July 2009–Nov. 2011

Chief of Joint Operations, Permanent Joint Headquarters (the Operational Commander)

Vice Admiral Sir Ian Garnett	Aug. 1998–Aug 2001
Lieutenant General Sir John Reith	Aug. 2001–Oct. 2004
Air Marshal Glenn Torpy	Oct. 2004–March 2006
Lieutenant General Sir Nicholas Houghton	March 2006–March 2009
Air Marshal Sir Stuart Peach	March 2009–Dec. 2011

ANNEX 2

PRINCIPAL UK FIELD COMMANDERS

1. Iraq:

Operation Iraqi Freedom/Operation Telic 1 Jan. 2003–11 July 2003

1ˢᵗ (UK) Armoured Division

Major General Robin Brims	23 Feb.–13 May 2003
Major General Peter Wall	12 May–12 July 2003

3ʳᵈ (UK) Division

Major General Graeme Lamb	11 July–23 Dec. 2003

7ᵗʰ Armoured Brigade

Brigadier Graham Binns	15 Feb.–1 May 2003

16ᵗʰ Air Assault Brigade

Brigadier Jacko Page	3 March–25 May 2003

3ʳᵈ Commando Brigade

Brigadier Jim Dutton RM	7 Feb.–1 May 2003

HIGH COMMAND

Senior British Military Representative and Deputy Commanding General, Multi-National Force, Iraq

Major General Freddie Viggers	May–Sept. 2003
Major General Andrew Figgures	Sept. 2003–March 2004
Lieutenant General John McColl	March 2004–Oct. 2004
Lieutenant General Sir John Kiszely	Oct. 2004–April 2005
Lieutenant General Robin Brims	April 2005–Oct. 2005
Lieutenant General Nicholas Houghton	Oct. 2005–March 2006
Lieutenant General Sir Rob Fry*	March 2006–Sept. 2006
Lieutenant General Graeme Lamb	Sept. 2006–July 2007
Lieutenant General William Rollo	July 2007–March 2008
Lieutenant General John Cooper	March 2008–March 2009
Lieutenant General Chris Brown	March 2009–July 2009

Deputy Commanding General, Multi-National Corps, Iraq

Major General Andrew Graham	March 2004–Sept. 2004
Major General Andrew Farquhar	Sept. 2004–Feb. 2005
Major General Mark Mans	Feb. 2005–Aug. 2005
Major General Nick Parker	Aug. 2005–Feb. 2006
Major General Peter Everson	Feb. 2006–Sept. 2006
Major General Simon Mayall	Sept. 2006–Jan. 2007
Major General Gerry Berragan	Jan. 2007–Oct. 2007
Major General Bruce Brealey	Oct. 2007–July 2008
Major General Richard Barrons	July 2008–March 2009
Major General William Moore	March 2009–2010

General Officer Commanding, Multi-National Division (South-East), Iraq

Major General Andrew Stewart	Dec. 2003–July 2004
Major General William Rollo	July 2004–Nov. 2004
Major General Jonathon Riley	Dec. 2004–June 2005
Major General James Dutton*	June 2005–Dec. 2005
Major General John Cooper	Dec. 2005–July 2006
Major General Richard Shirreff	July 2006–Jan. 2007

ANNEX 2

Major General the Hon. Jonathan Shaw	Jan. 2007–Aug. 2007	
Major General Graham Binns	Aug. 2007–Feb. 2008	
Major General Barney White-Spunner	Feb. 2008–Aug. 2008	
Major General Andrew Salmon	Aug. 2008–March 2009	

Brigade Commanders, Basra

Brig. William Moore	19th Infantry Brigade	June 03–Nov. 03
Brigs. David Rutherford Jones/Nick Carter	20th Armoured Brigade	Nov. 03–April 04
Brig. Andrew Kennett	1st Mechanised Brigade	April 04–Nov. 04
Brig. Paul Gibson/Chris Deverall	4th Armoured Brigade	Nov. 04–April 05
Brig. Chris Hughes/John Lorimer	12th Mechanised Brigade	April 05–Nov. 05
Brig. Patrick Marriott	7th Armoured Brigade	Nov. 05–April 06
Brig. James Everard	20th Armoured Brigade	April 06–Nov. 06
Brig. Timothy Evans	19th Infantry Brigade	Nov. 06–April 07
Brig. James Bashall	1st Mechanised Brigade	April 07–Nov. 07
Brig. Adrian Free	4th Mechanised Brigade	Nov. 07–April 08
Brig. Alex Storrie	7th Armoured Brigade	April 08–Nov. 08
Brig. Thomas Beckett	20th Armoured Brigade	Nov. 08–May 09

2. Afghanistan

Commander or Deputy Commander, Combined Force Command, Afghanistan

Major General John Cooper	May–Dec. 2004
Major General Peter Gilchrist	Dec. 2004–2005
Major General Christopher Wilson	Jan.–Dec. 2006
General Sir David Richards (COMISAF)	May 2006–Nov. 2007
Lieutenant General Jonathon Riley	Nov. 2007–Oct. 2008
Lieutenant General James Dutton*	Oct. 2008–Nov. 2009
Lieutenant General Sir Nicholas Parker	Nov. 2009–Sept. 2010
Lieutenant General James Bucknall	Sept. 2010–Nov. 2011

HIGH COMMAND

Brigade Commanders—Helmand Task Force

Brig. Ed Butler	16th Air Assault Brigade	May 06–Nov. 06
Brig. Jeremy Thomas	3rd Commando Brigade*	Nov. 06–April 07
Brig. John Lorimer	12th Mechanised Brigade	April 07–Nov. 07
Brig. Andrew Mackay	52nd Infantry Brigade	Nov. 07–April 08
Brig. Mark Carlton-Smith	16th Air Assault Brigade	April 08–Nov. 08
Brig. Gordon Messenger	3rd Commando Brigade*	Nov. 08–April 09
Brig. Tim Radford	19th Light Brigade	April 09–Nov. 09
Brig. James Cowan	11th Light Brigade	Nov. 09–April 10

* denotes Royal Marine unit

ANNEX 3

SUMMARY OF EIGHT CONTRADICTIONS IN UK STRATEGY

The issues raised in Chapter 11 (the analysis of the contradictions in the strategy pursued by the Ministry of Defence in prosecuting the wars in Iraq and Afghanistan) are grouped into eight broad areas:

1. Why did the UK agree to take part in the invasion of Iraq without also planning ahead for the post-conflict operations in sufficient detail, which its MoD knew was critical for success from its recent experience and published doctrine?
2. Why did the UK accept military tasks without being prepared to provide the resources that its MoD knew were required to carry out those tasks? Why were the earmarked reserves insufficient?
3. Why did the UK MoD accept the task of providing security for Basra and then abandon the population to the hands of the militias?
4. Why did the UK MoD send a military force to Helmand with orders to protect the Afghan people and then cause so many civilian casualties amongst them because the combat forces were insufficient in numbers to conduct counter-insurgency?
5. Why did the UK send armed forces to foreign countries so poorly prepared in language and culture that they were unable to interact with the local population in a meaningful way, a prerequisite its MoD knew to be vital in counter-insurgency operations?

6. Why was the UK's intelligence on local circumstances so consistently poor, when the MoD knew that good intelligence was vital to success in stabilisation and counter-insurgency operations?

7. Why did the UK tolerate corrupt police forces in Iraq and Afghanistan when its armed forces had been tasked to establish the rule of law?

8. Why did the UK volunteer to champion a poppy eradication scheme in Afghanistan without also demanding a parallel economic substitution programme? Why did the MoD allow the UK to lead reconstruction and security in exactly the same province as the eradication programme that it was championing?

ANNEX 4

LIST OF TITLES, ACRONYMS AND RANKS

CAS	Chief of the Air Staff—Head of Royal Air Force
CDS	Chief of the Defence Staff, UK
CGS	Chief of the General Staff—Head of the British Army
CJO	Chief of Joint Operations at PJHQ—the UK's Operational-level commander
DCDS(C)	Deputy Chief of the Defence Staff (Commitments)—the UK MoD's Director of Operations
First Sea Lord	Chief of the Naval Staff and Head of the Royal Navy
HCDC	House of Commons Defence Committee
ISAF	International Security Assistance Force—NATO's forces in Afghanistan
MNC Iraq	Multi-National Corps Iraq—the coalition army corps in Iraq
MND SE	Multi-National Division South-East in Iraq led by the UK
MNF Iraq	Multi-National Force Iraq—the military coalition led by the US
MoD	Ministry of Defence, UK
Main Building	The office complex in Whitehall occupied by the Ministry of Defence

Op Enduring Freedom   The title of the US operations in the global 'War on Terror', also known as the 'Long War'

Op Iraqi Freedom   The title of the US operations in Iraq 2003–12

Op Herrick   The title of the UK's operations in Afghanistan post 2002

Op Telic   The title of the UK's operations in Iraq 2003–9

OP Veritas   The title of the UK's operations in Afghanistan in 2001; it embraced Operation Oracle, Operation Fingal (Kabul) and Operation Jacana (Khost)

PJHQ   Permanent Joint Headquarters—the UK's Operational headquarters at Northwood, Middlesex

Policy Director   A three-star-equivalent senior civil servant working opposite to the DCDS(C)

PUS   Permanent Under Secretary (of the Ministry of Defence)—the head civil servant in the MoD

2nd PUS   The Deputy PUS—the second highest civil servant, responsible for running the Main Building and Finance

S of S Def.   Secretary of State for Defence—the senior politician in the Ministry of Defence

VCDS   Vice Chief of the Defence Staff—deputy to the CDS

Military ranks and civilian equivalents (in 2000–2010)

Grade	Royal Navy	Army	Royal Air Force	Civil Service
Four stars (4*)	Admiral	General	Air Chief Marshal	Permanent Under Secretary (PUS)
Three Stars (3*)	Vice Admiral	Lieutenant General	Air Marshal	e.g. Policy Director

Two Stars (2*)	Rear Admiral	Major General	Air Vice Marshal	Director General
One Star (1*)	Commodore	Brigadier	Air Commodore	Director

The use of stars to denote equivalent ranks derives from the stars used on US badges of rank, but is now accepted across NATO. See STANAG 2116: *NATO Codes for Grades of Military Personnel.*

Officers authorised to display the flag of their command are termed 'flag officers', but the term is used more widely to describe 'flag ranks'. It originated as a naval term, but is now used more generally. In the UK system this applies to two-star officers and above of any service.

NOTES

1. PROLOGUE

1. http://www.iraqinquiry.org.uk/
2. Author discussion with Major General Mungo Melvin CB OBE, 27 February 2014.

2. A CASE TO ANSWER?

1. He later became Commander-in-Chief of the British Army of the Rhine and then Chief of the General Staff, being promoted to Field Marshal on retirement.
2. Ministère des Affaires étrangères et européennes.
3. Tim Ripley in his book *Operation Deliberate Force* quotes Field Marshal Sir Peter Inge as saying about the critical Cabinet meeting (p. 116):

   'The advantage of 24 Brigade was that it had more oomph, it had greater flexibility to allow us to get in quicker,' recalled Inge. General Smith was now consulted in Sarajevo to get his opinion. 'When asked, Rupert opted for 24 Brigade,' said Inge, 'although [the overall UN commander in Zagreb] did not express much enthusiasm for either option.'

   Ripley, *Operation deliberate force: the UN and NATO campaign in Bosnia 1995*. Lancaster: CDISS, 1999.
4. Discussion between General Sir Rupert Smith and the author, March 2013.
5. General Mladic held discussions on separate occasions with the UK's CGS General Sir Charles Guthrie and Lieutenant General Rupert Smith, the UN commander in Sarajevo, and agreed with both that he would not hinder the departure of the British battalion. To Mladic this made eminent sense; it left him alone to engage

the ABiH without interference from UN troops. Discussion with General Sir Rupert Smith and author interview with Field Marshal Lord Guthrie, London, 19 April 2013.

6. R. Smith, R., *The utility of force: the art of war in the modern world*. London: Allen Lane, 2005, pp. 311–12.

7. Sir Sherard Cowper-Coles. Lecture at Taylor Institution, Oxford, 29 May 2013.

3. JUMPING TO THE CONCLUSION

1. Lecture to the Oxford University Strategic Studies Group, All Souls College, 'Strategy and the Wars of 9/11', by Lieutenant General Sir Rob Fry, 21 May 2013.

2. An elected parliamentarian not holding any government or opposition ministerial post.

3. J. Boswell, *The life of Samuel Johnson: including a Journal of his tour to the Hebrides*. London: John Murray, 1839, vol. 3 1776–1780, p. 307.

4. Author interview with Desmond Bowen CB CMG as MoD Policy Director 2004–8, London, May 2013.

5. Panel discussion at IISS, London, 17 July 2013.

4. INSIDE THE MINISTRY OF DEFENCE

1. A. Clark, *The donkeys*. London: Pimlico, 1991.

2. Frank Davies and Graham Maddocks, *Bloody red tabs: General Officer casualties of the Great War 1914–1918*, London: Leo Cooper, 1995.

3. http://www.thesundaytimes.co.uk/sto/newsreview/features/article1408846.ece

4. Robin Neillands, *The Great War Generals on the Western Front*. London: Robinson, 1998, p. 514.

5. Dr Jim Storr (based upon his own observations and historical research) makes a convincing argument that successful leaders possess a 'golf-bag' of accumulated ideas that they know will work and reach for without much further consideration. This frees their intellectual and moral resources to focus on the new or unique aspects of an emerging situation. Dr Jim Storr, 'The Commander as Expert'. See: http://www.dodccrp.org/files/Potts_Big_Issue.pdf

6. Author interview with Sir Ian Andrews as 2nd PUS MoD 2002–8, London, July 2013.

7. http://www.archive2.official-documents.co.uk/document/deps/hc/hc898/898.pdf

8. Jack Straw on BBC Radio 4 'Reflections', 9 a.m., Thurs 18 July 2013. See http://www.bbc.co.uk/programmes/b036w394

9. Author discussion with Professor Karen Carr, Shrivenham, November 2012. The MoD itself has been very much alive to this issue and Professor Karen Carr at UK Defence Academy was tasked by the MoD to review the cognitive processes, from a scientific basis, that influence decision-making, particularly at the strategic level. The results of Professor Carr's work are summarised in Joint Doctrine Note 3/11 'Decision Making and Problem Solving; Human Factors and Organisational Factors'.
https://www.gov.uk/government/publications/joint-doctrine-note-3–11-decision-making-and-problem-solving-human-and-organisational-factors

10. Correspondence between the author and Air Chief Marshal Lord Stirrup, February 2014.

5. THE TRIBES AND THE SYSTEM

1. Discussion between author and Lord Browne of Ladyton, London, 23 March 2014.
2. Author interview with Desmond Bowen CB CMG as MoD Policy Director 2004–8, London, May 2013.
3. Ibid.
4. In September 2006, while discussing the forthcoming Labour Party leadership election, Hutton gave an anonymous quote to the BBC journalist Nick Robinson that Gordon Brown would be an absolute 'effing disaster' as Prime Minister. See http://www.bbc.co.uk/blogs/nickrobinson/2009/12/hutton_brown_disaster.html retrieved 14 November 2013.
5. 'Folly in Foreign Policy: An Afghan Case Study'. Lecture by Sir Sherard Cowper-Coles to Oxford Centre for Islamic Studies, Taylor Institution, 29 May 2013.
6. House of Commons Defence Committee, 'Operations in Afghanistan', HC 554 Ev 110. See http://www.publications.parliament.uk/pa/cm201012/cmselect/cmdfence/554/554.pdf
7. Discussion between author and Lord Browne of Ladyton, London, 23 March 2014.
8. Paraphrased by Desmond Bowen CB CMG in discussion with the author, 23 May 2013.
9. http://www.civilservant.org.uk/northcotetrevelyan.pdf
10. Author interview with Admiral Lord Boyce, London, October 2013.
11. A. Sampson, *Who runs this place? The anatomy of Britain in the 21st century*. London: John Murray, 2004, p. 160.

12. Sir M. Jackson, *Soldier: the autobiography of General Sir Mike Jackson*. London: Corgi, 2008, pp. 358–9.

13. Discussion between author and Admiral Lord West, London, 7 June 2013.

14. Author interviews with General Sir Mike Jackson, Great Bedwyn, June–September 2013.

15. Ibid.

16. Evidence to the Chilcot Inquiry. Transcript of oral evidence p. 61.

17. J. Powell, *The new Machiavelli: how to wield power in the modern world*. London: Vintage, 2011, p. 71.

18. Paraphrased by Desmond Bowen, MoD Policy Director 2004–8, in discussion with the author, 21 May 2013.

19. Author interview with Vice Admiral Sir Jeremy Blackham, London, October 2012.

20. Author interview with Desmond Bowen CB CMG as MoD Policy Director 2004–8, London, May 2013.

21. Author interviews with General Sir Mike Jackson, Great Bedwyn, June–September 2013.

22. Essay by Desmond Bowen CB CMG, 17 February 2010, 'The Political–Military Relationship on Operations', quoted in *British Generals in Blair's wars*. Farnham, Surrey; Burlington, VT: Ashgate, 2013, ch. 23.

23. These titles originate from when the Secretary was a Sovereign's appointment and gradually became a political one. To distinguish their apolitical role, the senior civil servant became the *Under* Secretary.

24. Although, following Civil Service precedent, neither he, nor the Second Permanent Under Secretary, nor the MoD Finance Director of the time had professional training as an accountant.

25. Interview with a senior civil servant, 3 May 2013.

26. James Boswell, *The life of Samuel Johnson: including a Journal of his tour to the Hebrides*. London: John Murray, 1839, vol. 2, p. 52.

27. Sir M. Jackson, *Soldier: the autobiography of General Sir Mike Jackson*. London: Corgi, 2008, p. 382.

28. C. von Clausewitz, *On war*. Princeton: Princeton University Press, 1976, p. 51.

29. Author interviews with General Sir Mike Jackson, Great Bedwyn, June–September 2013.

30. Author interview with General Lord Walker, London, November 2013.

31. R. K. Massie, *Dreadnought: Britain, Germany and the coming of the Great War*. London: Pimlico, 1993.

32. http://www.telegraph.co.uk/culture/tvandradio/tv-and-radio-reviews/10497820/
The-Silent-War-BBC-Two-review.html and interview with Commander Bill
Nimmo-Scott, one of these officers.

33. J. C. Wylie, *Military strategy: a general theory of power control.* New Brunswick,
NJ: Rutgers University Press, 1967.

34. J. R. Hill, *Arms control at sea*, Routledge, 1989, p. 35 cites Marder, *From the
Dreadnoughts to Scapa Flow*, Barnsley: Pen and Sword Books, p. 332.

35. BBC 2 programme, *The Silent War*, shown on Sunday 29 December 2013: http://
www.bbc.co.uk/programmes/b03lb1vc

36. Lord West of Spithead finished his naval career as First Sea Lord, having suffered
the loss of his ship and sixteen of his crew when attacked by Argentinean aircraft
in Falkland Sound in 1982.

37. Powell, The new Machiavelli, p. 273.

38. Mitch Williamson, *British Naval Supremacy: Some Factors Newly Considered.*
http://home.europa.com/~bessel/Naval/MW2.html

39. Ibid.

40. So strong is this affiliation, or the perceived need for it, that most senior officers
continue to display tribal accoutrements on their uniforms long after they have
progressed to higher command or the General Staff.

41. Quoted in Bishop, P.J., *Wings: one hundred years of British aerial warfare.* London:
Atlantic, 2012. p 157

42. The Battle of Britain was largely fought during daylight and from home airfields.
It was surely a unique experience in the history of warfare for the combatants to
have been engaged in intense and mortal combat all day and then return to their
homes, wives, children and firesides in the evening. You have to ask 'Well, why
not?' for there was no practical reason not to do so, and it endures in the continued practice of air force pilots living in relatively comfortable accommodation when supporting combat troops in war zones, despite the derision directed
by others existing in far harsher circumstances while fighting on the ground.

43. Bishop, P.J., *Wings: one hundred years of British aerial warfare.* London: Atlantic,
2012. p178

44. Air Chief Marshal Sir Peter Squire, Chief of the Air Staff 2000–3, led a Harrier
squadron in the Falklands conflict. His aircraft was hit by ground fire but sur-
vived and, on a separate sortie, he ejected from his aircraft after it suffered engine
failure. Four out of the ten aircraft in the squadron he commanded were lost to
ground fire (3) or engine failure (1).

45. Cecil Lewis, quoted in Bishop, P.J., *Wings: one hundred years of British aerial warfare*. London: Atlantic, 2012. p 111.

46. Discussion between the author and Air Marshal Sir Brian Burridge, London, 15 April 2013.

47. *British Generals in Blair's wars*. Farnham, Surrey; Burlington, VT: Ashgate, 2013.

48. F. Ledwidge, *Losing small wars: British military failure in Iraq and Afghanistan*. New Haven, CT; London: Yale University Press, 2012, p. 117.

49. Ibid.

50. T. E. Ricks, *The generals: American military command from World War II to today*. New York: Penguin Press, 2012.

51. N. F. Dixon, *On the psychology of military incompetence*. London: Pimlico, 1994.

52. Discussion between the author and Nicholas Heaven, October 2012.

53. Discussion between Colonel (retd) Christopher Davies MBE and the author, March 2013.

54. Author interview with Vice Admiral Sir Jeremy Blackham, London, October 2012.

55. Correspondence between the author and Matt Kavanagh, Special Adviser to the Defence Secretary 2006–7 and Special Adviser to the Prime Minister 2007–10, March 2014.

56. Discussion with the author 19 February 2014. Amyas Morse has been the UK Comptroller General Auditor General of the National Audit Office since leaving the Ministry of Defence in June 2009.

57. Three options were proposed by the staffs, with only the third package containing substantial numbers of ground troops.

58. See the yearly reports of the House of Commons Defence Committee and the UK Parliament's National Audit Office; also 'Review of Defence Acquisition— An independent report by Bernard Gray Executive Summary', where an argument is made that the UK MoD lost £6 billion a year through 'friction' in the system. See http://webarchive.nationalarchives.gov.uk/20120913104443/http://www.mod.uk/NR/rdonlyres/78821960–14A0–429E-A90A-FA2A8C292 C84/0/ReviewAcquisitionGrayreport.pdf

6. SETTING THE CONDITIONS FOR SUCCESS AND FAILURE

1. 'The Uses of Military Power'. Weinberger's Six Principles:

• The United States should not commit forces to combat unless *the vital national interests* of the United States or its allies are involved.

- US troops should only be committed wholeheartedly and with the clear intention of winning. Otherwise, troops *should not be committed.*
- US combat troops should be committed only with clearly defined political and military objectives and with the capacity to accomplish those objectives.
- The relationship between the objectives and the size and composition of the forces committed should be continually reassessed and adjusted if necessary.
- US troops should not be committed to battle without a 'reasonable assurance' of the support of US public opinion and Congress.
- The commitment of US troops should be considered only as a last resort.

2. '… forces trained for high intensity combat can adapt to peace support operations but the reverse is not the case.' Peter Inge. 'The Roles and Challenges of the British Armed Forces'. *RUSI* Journal, vol. 141, no. 1, February/March 1996.

3. James de Waal; *'Depending Upon the Right people: British politico-military relations 2001–10'.* Chatham House, London.

4. '*The Military-Industrial Complex; The Farewell Address of President Eisenhower'.* Basements publications 2006.

5. 5 RUSI Journal April/May 2014 vol. 159 no 2. p. 65.

6. The Powell Doctrine:

   - Is a vital national security interest threatened?
   - Do we have a clear attainable objective?
   - Have the risks and costs been fully and frankly analyzed?
   - Have all other non-violent policy means been fully exhausted?
   - Is there a plausible exit strategy to avoid endless entanglement?
   - Have the consequences of our action been fully considered?
   - Is the action supported by the American people?
   - Do we have genuine broad international support?

7. Hew Strachan, *The direction of war: contemporary strategy in historical perspective.* Cambridge: Cambridge University Press, 2013, p. 19.

8. Indeed he had a photograph of a bombed ambulance on his wall with the words underneath it 'Nice one NATO', following a strike by NATO aircraft on a Bosnian Serb decoy.

9. Professor Freedman was later to be horrified that his jottings had been used to frame such a new world policy. See *British Generals in Blair's wars.* Farnham, Surrey; Burlington, VT: Ashgate, 2013, ch. 1.

10. A key aspect of Prime Minster Blair's speech was five major considerations for intervening. He said: 'So how do we decide when and whether to intervene? I think we need to bear in mind five major considerations:

- First, are we sure of our case? War is an imperfect instrument for righting humanitarian distress; but armed force is sometimes the only means of dealing with dictators.
- Second, have we exhausted all diplomatic options? We should always give peace every chance, as we have in the case of Kosovo.
- Third, on the basis of a practical assessment of the situation, are there military operations we can sensibly and prudently undertake?
- Fourth, are we prepared for the long term? In the past we talked too much of exit strategies. But having made a commitment we cannot simply walk away once the fight is over; better to stay with moderate numbers of troops than return for repeat performances with large numbers.
- And finally, do we have national interests involved?'

See: http://www.pbs.org/newshour/bb/international/jan-june99/blair_doctrine4–23.html

11. http://news.bbc.co.uk/1/hi/uk_politics/1743985.stm

12. W. G. F. Jackson, *The chiefs: the story of the United Kingdom chiefs of staff.* London: Brassey's, 1992.

13. See http://webarchive.nationalarchives.gov.uk/20121026065214/www.mod.uk/NR/rdonlyres/65F3D7AC-4340–4119–93A2–20825848E50E/0/sdr1998_complete.pdf

    Later, as CGS, General Sir Richard Dannatt reflected that 'Go First, Go Fast, Go Home had a very short shelf life as a policy aspiration.' See http://www.rusi.org/downloads/assets/Dannatspeech2008.pdf

14. Subsequently it has emerged that elements in the Albanian population in Kosovo had set out deliberately to antagonise their Serbian rulers, so as to draw in that NATO force.

15. In 1999, with the situation deteriorating, Brigadier David Richards as a UK Joint Force Commander was deployed to organise the evacuation of foreign nationals. Instead, he decided that his force could be used to stabilise the government of President Kabbah and, with British help, the rebels could be defeated. It turned out he was right. See: http://news.bbc.co.uk/1/hi/programmes/from_our_own_correspondent/8682505.stm

16. D Squadron 22 SAS and A Company 1st Battalion Parachute Regiment. The operation freed 5 soldiers and 25 Sierra Leone civilians; none of the hostages was killed and only one member of the assault force died; but 25 West Side Boys were killed, 18 were captured including their leader, and the remaining 300 rebels surrendered to UN forces within a fortnight. See http://en.wikipedia.org/wiki/Operation_Barras

7. A LONG PEACE IS SHATTERED

1. The US Nasdaq technology index declined from nearly 5,000 in year 2000 to just over 1,000 in year 2003 before a recovery started. The price of Amazon went from $107 to $7 and Cisco declined by 86 per cent, although both have rebounded strongly since.

2. https://archives.nbclearn.com/portal/site/k-12/browse/?cuecard=1419

3. 'We were all swept up by the drama of the moment. Immediately after the attacks, the British wanted to show support for the Americans in every way possible. As the head of one UK Army delegation, I flew to Washington for talks with my opposite number. We were amongst the first to land in the reopened Dulles airport and watched President Bush's speech with our hosts on a huge TV screen. Emotion was running very high and everyone was captivated by what he was saying. At the "you are either with us or against us" moment, a strong cheer of support rippled around the room. I said rather softly, but with all the smug discourtesy of which the British are capable, "… you must now appreciate how we have felt about the funding and support coming to the Provisional IRA for all these years". There was a moment of silence and I wished fervently that I had not said it. Then a four-star general turned around and said, with typical American openness, "I never realised …" and gave a great bear hug. We never felt closer to each other as nations than we did at that moment.'

4. http://georgewbush-whitehouse.archives.gov/news/releases/2001/09/20010920–8. html, quoted in A. Mallinson, *The making of the British Army*. London: Bantam, 2010.

5. T. Blair, *A journey*. London: Hutchinson, 2010, p. 410.

6. http://news.bbc.co.uk/1/hi/uk_politics/3076309.stm

8. WAR COMES TO AFGHANISTAN IN 2001

1. Robert Gates, *Duty: Memoirs of a Secretary at War*. Knopf, 2013.

2. See *Operation Veritas—Summary Report* at: http://webarchive.nationalarchives.gov. uk/+/http://www.operations.mod.uk/veritas/summary_oct-dec01.htm, accessed 15 April 2013.

9. THE WAR ON TERROR OPENS IN IRAQ IN 2003

1. Quoted by Dr Niall Barr in a lecture to the Joint Services Command and Staff Course at the Defence Academy, 16 April 2013.

2. Extract from a memo classified 'Secret and Strictly Personal UK Eyes Only' by Matthew Rycroft, a foreign policy aide at 10 Downing Street, which provided a record of a discussion between Prime Minister Blair and his closest associates. See: http://downingstreetmemo.com/docs/memotext.pdf

3. Chilcot Inquiry. See: http://www.iraqinquiry.org.uk/

4. *British Generals in Blair's wars*. Farnham, Surrey; Burlington, VT: Ashgate, 2013, ch. 13.

5. In a Congressional committee on 25 Feb. 2003 General Shinseki said (in response to a question from Democrat Carl Levin about how many troops would be required): '… something in the order of several hundred thousand soldiers are probably, you know, a figure that would be required. We're talking about post-hostilities control over a piece of geography that's fairly significant, with the kinds of ethnic tensions that could lead to other problems. And so it takes significant ground force presence to maintain safe and secure environment to ensure that the people are fed, that water is distributed, all the normal responsibilities that go along with administering a situation like this.'

Later Deputy Secretary of Defense Paul Wolfowitz condemned this estimate with 'some of the higher-end predictions that we have been hearing recently, such as the notion that it will take several hundred thousand US troops to provide stability in post-Saddam Iraq, are wildly off the mark'.

Quoted in: http://www.theatlantic.com/technology/archive/2008/12/karmic-justice-generic-shinseki/9162/

6. Extract from a memo classified 'Secret and Strictly Personal UK Eyes Only' by Matthew Rycroft, see note 2, this page.

7. Cross is eloquent and direct about this in his evidence to the Chilcot Inquiry. See: http://www.iraqinquiry.org.uk/transcripts/oralevidence-bydate/091207.aspx#pm

8. T. E. Ricks, *The generals: American military command from World War II to today*. New York: Penguin Press, 2012.

9. Ibid.

10. *British Generals in Blair's wars*. Farnham, Surrey; Burlington, VT: Ashgate, 2013. Justin Maciejewski, ch. 13.

11. Discussion with Lieutenant General Robin Brims, July 2013. Also see Jack Fairweather, *A war of choice: the British in Iraq 2003–9*. London: Jonathan Cape, 2011.

12. The toll on commanders was immense, with the British Chief of the Defence Staff, General Sir Michael Walker, describing seeing General Casey at the end of his tour as 'a broken man, really'. Evidence of General Lord Walker to the Chilcot

Inquiry. See: http://www.iraqinquiry.org.uk/media/45534/100201-walker-final. pdf, p 59.

13. Speech given under the Changing Character of War Programme at All Souls College, Oxford, reported by Professor Sir Hew Strachan.

14. Author interviews with General Sir Mike Jackson, Great Bedwyn, June–September 2013.

15. Commentary at http://www.guardian.co.uk/world/2006/jan/12/topstories3.iraq. Full text is at: http://www.army.mil/professionalWriting/volumes/volume4/february_2006/2_06_1_pf.html

   Despite the media comments, the text was largely fair, balanced and helpful and US Major General Petraeus was one of those who suggested that it should be written.

16. Evidence to the Chilcot Inquiry. Evidence by General The Lord Walker, pp. 32–3. See: http://www.iraqinquiry.org.uk/media/45534/100201-walker-final.pdf

17. On 1 May 2004 Private Beharry was driving a Warrior tracked armoured vehicle that had been called to the assistance of a foot patrol caught in a series of ambushes. The Warrior was hit by multiple rocket-propelled grenades, causing damage and resulting in the loss of radio communications. The platoon commander, the vehicle's gunner and a number of other soldiers in the vehicle were injured. Due to damage to his periscope optics, Pte Beharry was forced to open his hatch to steer his vehicle, exposing his face and head to withering small arms fire. Beharry drove the crippled Warrior through the ambush, taking his own crew and leading five other Warriors to safety. He then extracted his wounded comrades from the vehicle, all the time exposed to further enemy fire. He was cited on this occasion for 'valour of the highest order'.
   While back on duty on 11 June 2004, Beharry was again driving the lead Warrior of his platoon through Al Amarah when his vehicle was ambushed. A rocket-propelled grenade hit the vehicle six inches from Beharry's head, and he received serious shrapnel injuries to his face and brain. Other rockets then hit the vehicle, incapacitating his commander and injuring several of the crew. Despite his life-threatening injuries, Beharry retained control of his vehicle and drove it out of the ambush area before losing consciousness. *London Gazette* (Supplement), no. 57587, pp. 3369–70, 18 March 2005.

18. Muhammad al-Wa'ili was eventually assassinated on 28 September 2012. See: http://www.shiitenews.com/index.php/iraq/5162-former-shia-governor-of-basra-mohammed-misbah-waili-assassinated

19. The Explosively Formed Projectile was a method of making a device that could

penetrate most armour. In Basra, a shallow, dish-shaped piece of steel was united with an explosive charge on its back face and then detonated from the opposite side to the plate. The shock wave set up struck the steel dish and 'explosively formed' it into a high-speed slug of metal. It would then penetrate most things in its path. The forming of the shallow steel dish needed metal-working skills and a metal press; it was probably done in Iran. See: http://en.wikipedia.org/wiki/Explosively_formed_penetrator

20. See Chilcot Inquiry. Evidence by General The Lord Walker, pp. 32–3: http://www.iraqinquiry.org.uk/media/45534/100201-walker-final.pdf

21. F. R. Dannatt, *Leading from the front: the autobiography*. London: Bantam, 2010, p. 224.

22. http://www.dailymail.co.uk/news/article-355251/Options-future-UK-force-posture-Iraq.html#ixzz2PDorwBhb

23. This paragraph is an extract from the diary of a senior serving UK officer interviewed by the author in October 2013.

24. Author interview with Air Chief Marshal Lord Stirrup, London, October 2013.

25. In his final speech to the officer cadets before their commissioning at Sandhurst, Major General Patrick Marriott as Commandant offered the following advice in today's world of shifting and ambiguous behaviour. He said: 'don't do what you *want* to do … consider first what you *ought* to do'.

26. Extract from the unpublished diary of Major General Patrick Marriott CB CBE, revealed in correspondence with the author in January 2014.

27. *British Generals in Blair's wars*. Farnham, Surrey; Burlington, VT: Ashgate, 2013. Justin Maciejewski, ch. 13.

28. Author interview with Air Chief Marshal Lord Stirrup, London, October 2013.

29. The sentence is from the diary of a senior serving British Army officer, interviewed October 2013.

30. T. E. Ricks, *The gamble: General David Petraeus and the untold story of the American surge in Iraq, 2006–2008*. London: Allen Lane, 2009.

31. *British Generals in Blair's wars*. Farnham, Surrey; Burlington, VT: Ashgate, 2013, ch. 13.

32. Lieutenant General Richard Shirreff said in his statement to the UK Iraq Inquiry: 'It was clear to me that there could be no transition to Iraqi control without security.' See: http://www.iraqinquiry.org.uk/media/44178/20100111am-shirreff-final.pdf p. 5.

33. Operation Salamanca became Operation Sinbad following a directive from Prime Minister Maliki not to target the Basra Shia militias directly. Author interview with Air Chief Marshal Lord Stirrup, London, October 2013.

34. Statement by Lieutenant General Richard Shirreff to UK Iraq Inquiry, p. 14. http://www.iraqinquiry.org.uk/media/44178/20100111am-shirreff-final.pdf

35. *British Generals in Blair's wars.* Farnham, Surrey; Burlington, VT: Ashgate, 2013, ch. 13.

36. James de Waal, review of *Britain's Generals in Blair's Wars, International Affairs* 89: 6, 2013. London: Royal Institute of International Affairs.

37. Correspondence between author and Air Chief Marshal Lord Stirrup, February 2014.

38. See: http://news.bbc.co.uk/1/hi/6046332.stm

39. For Prime Minster Blair's reaction see T. Blair, 1953–, *A journey*. London: Hutchinson, 2010. Blair said: '… in October 2006 … the new CGS General Sir Richard Dannatt gave an interview in the *Daily Mail* … saying that we had reached the end in Iraq, we were as much a risk to the security as keeping it and we should transfer our attention to Afghanistan, where in effect we had a better chance of success … As you can imagine, I wasn't best pleased.'

40. http://www.thesundaytimes.co.uk/sto/news/Features/Focus/article158734.ece

41. T. Blair, *A journey*. London: Hutchinson, 2010, p. 470.

42. Discussion with Major General James Cowan, who as a colonel had been Chief of Staff to Major General Shirreff. Oxford, March 2013.

43. Correspondence between the author and Air Chief Marshal Lord Stirrup KG, January 2014.

44. Quoted in Michael Knights and Ed Williams, 'The Calm before the Storm: The British Experience in Southern Iraq', Washington Institute for Near East Policy, Policy Focus #66, February 2007, p. 33: 'In essence, the deep south has become a "kleptocracy" where well-armed political–criminal mafiosi have locked both the central government and the people out of power.'
As journalist Steve Negus wrote in August 2006: 'The region's political parties have done almost nothing for the common good. Those with street credibility and a militia now have the power … A year ago, people were clamouring for greater autonomy from Baghdad. Some people in this anarchic port city are now calling for the central government to save them from their elected leaders.'
See: http://www.washingtoninstitute.org/uploads/Documents/pubs/PolicyFocus66.pdf

45. Jack Fairweather, *A war of choice: the British in Iraq 2003–9*. London: Jonathan Cape, 2011, p. 305.

46. Extract from the unpublished diary of Major General Patrick Marriott CB CBE, revealed in correspondence with the author in January 2014.

47. Statement to Chilcot Inquiry by Major General Jonathan Shaw. See: http://www.iraqinquiry.org.uk/transcripts/oralevidence-bydate/100111.aspx#pm

48. Jack Fairweather, *A war of choice: the British in Iraq 2003–9*. London: Jonathan Cape, 2011, p. 328.

49. See http://www.iraqbodycount.org/

50. Statement by Lieutenant General Rollo to the Chilcot Inquiry: '… after the CPA was wound down … the coalition forces still had overall responsibility for maintaining security'. See: http://www.iraqinquiry.org.uk/media/41891/20091215 pmrollo-cooper-final.pdf p. 3.

51. See CSIS, 'Transferring Provinces to Iraqi Control', 2 September 2008; csis.org/files/media/csis/pubs/080902_iraq-anbar_and_provinces.pdf

52. Author interview with Desmond Bowen CB CMG as MoD Policy Director 2004–8, London, May 2013.

53. This paragraph is an extract from the diary of a senior serving British Army officer, interviewed October 2013.

54. Blair, T., *A journey*. London: Hutchinson, 2010, p. 472.

55. Discussion between the author and Major General Mungo Melvin CB OBE, Chilmark, 27 February 2014.

56. Speech by General Jack Keane, given at the Royal Military Sandhurst, 5 May 2011.

57. Blair, T., *A journey*. London: Hutchinson, 2010, p. 470.

58. *British Generals in Blair's wars*. Farnham, Surrey; Burlington, VT: Ashgate, 2013, ch. 14.

59. Correspondence between the author and Air Chief Marshal Lord Stirrup, February 2014.

60. Blair, op. cit.

61. Blair, op. cit., p. 470.

62. Blair, op. cit., p. 471.

63. Address to 'Whither Warfare' conference at RMA Sandhurst, 5 May 2011.

64. Extract from the unpublished diary of Major General Patrick Marriott CB CBE, revealed in correspondence with the author in January 2014.

65. Ibid.

66. Extract from the diary of a senior serving British Army officer, interviewed October 2013.

67. Discussion between author and Lord Browne of Ladyton, 24 March 2014.

10. BATTLE RETURNS TO AFGHANISTAN IN 2006

1. The UK established the first PRT in the north-west at Mazar al-Sharif, a role subsequently taken over by Germany.
2. http://www.bbc.co.uk/news/uk-13855804
3. Operation Enduring Freedom was originally called Operation Infinite Justice and was the US operation to prosecute the global 'war on terror'. It had separate operations in Afghanistan, Philippines, Horn of Africa, Pankisi Gorge (Georgia Train and Equip Programme), Trans Sahara, and Caribbean and Central America. Once it was realised that the original name was used by adherents of several religions as an exclusive description of their God, a change of name was quickly required.

   The US attitude to ISAF had been 'Well, if you want to do that [stabilise Afghanistan], fine. Just don't get in our way chasing al-Qaida',[3] although the US did field eight Provincial Reconstruction Teams (PRTs) tasked with supporting reconstruction efforts and guiding local governments to govern their constituents more effectively.
4. The ARRC was commanded by a British Lieutenant General, David Richards (who had previously let the UK intervention into Sierra Leone and was later to become the UK Chief of the Defence Staff). He had a boyish, optimistic persona and got on well with President Karzai, but that hid a resolute character and a calculating, well-honed political instinct, an ideal choice to kick-start the expanded responsibilities of NATO in Afghanistan.
5. General McNeil was followed by Generals David McKiernan (June 2008–9), Stanley McChrystal (June 2009-June 2010), David Petraeus (July 2010–July 2011), and then in the following decade by John Allen (July 2011-February 2013) and Joseph Dunford (February 2013–14). During McChrystal's time the combined ISAF force rose to 130,000 troops, following the surge in US forces authorised by President Obama.
6. The story of how the UK came to take on Helmand Province is well told in *The Afghan papers: committing Britain to war in Helmand, 2005–6*. Abingdon: published on behalf of RUSI (the Royal United Services Institute for Defence and Security Studies) by Routledge Journals, 2011.
7. Parker was replaced by Lieutenant General James Bucknall in November 2010, by Lieutenant General Adrian Bradshaw in November 2011 and Lieutenant General Nick Carter in September 2012.
8. http://www.publications.parliament.uk/pa/cm201012/cmselect/cmdfence/554/55405.htm#a7

9. 29 Commando Regiment Royal Artillery served in the second brigade troop rotation into Helmand. One of its batteries in the previous decade had been 145 (Maiwand) Battery, the designation being a battle honour recalling the event.

10. http://www.bbc.co.uk/news/uk-13855804

11. Ibid.

12. A significant number of challenges were identified in the 'Helmand Plan' (notes below extracted from a copy of the plan released to the BBC):

The current governor, chief of police and director of education are illiterate. 70% of the population is estimated to be illiterate.

The dominance of opium fuels a growing internal addiction problem and pervades public life through the influence it buys. Many prominent public figures are alleged to be involved in the trade, including those charged with suppressing it. The chief of the counter-narcotics police in Helmand has 20 staff and two ageing vehicles to cover a province three times the size of Wales with a population of more than one million.

The police force is widely thought to undermine the safety of the population rather than secure it. Reform of the police, perceived by the population as untrained, uneducated, unprofessional, drug-taking and corrupt … will require years to compete.

Provincial government in Helmand is dominated by patronage networks, tribal affiliation and alleged links to the narcotics trade. Interlocutors in the provincial capital of Lashkar Gah complain about the corruption of key government officials and the sale of government land for private gain.

The security situation is perceived to have deteriorated over the last six months. The insurgency has been targeting government officials and Coalition forces. There is collusion between insurgents and narcotics traders. Illegally armed groups proliferate, particularly in inaccessible regions. Afghanistan's porous borders with Pakistan and Iran enable relatively unhindered transit through Helmand of insurgents and drug traffickers alike.

See http://www.bbc.co.uk/news/uk-13855804

13. Intelligence agencies seemed to have reported that the Taliban's Shura in Quetta had decided to target the British in particular as they arrived in theatre. The Afghan Papers, p. 17.

14. D. Beattie, *An ordinary soldier: Afghanistan—a ferocious enemy, a bloody conflict, one man's impossible mission*. London: Pocket, 2009.

15. Author discussion with Major General Chris Wilson, at the time the senior British officer in Kabul and Deputy Commander ISAF. 24 May 2013.
16. Jack Fairweather, *A war of choice: the British in Iraq 2003–9*. London: Jonathan Cape, 2011, p. 243.
17. Ibid., p. 344.
18. House of Commons Defence Committee, *Operations in Afghanistan Fourth Report of Session 2010–12* HC 544 p. 28.

> 53. General Houghton told us, from his rereading of the Chiefs of Staff Committee minutes, that Brigadier Butler had briefed the Chiefs of Staff on 24 May 2006 on the platoon house concept. He had also noted in the minutes of 3 May that there might be a requirement for an earlier than planned and more significant deployment to the north of Helmand to support the governance of Governor Daoud. The actual moves to the north of Helmand took place in late May—on 26 to 27 May to Sangin and 28 May to Musa Qala and Now Zad—although there had been a presence in these areas and some fighting in the build up period.
>
> See:http://www.publications.parliament.uk/pa/cm201012/cmselect/cmdfence/554/554.pdf

19. See http://webarchive.nationalarchives.gov.uk/20121026065214/http://www.mod.uk/DefenceInternet/DefenceNews/HistoryAndHonour/19LightBrigadeRememberThoseLostInAfghanistan.htm
20. http://www.bbc.co.uk/news/uk-10629358
21. A. King, 'Understanding the Helmand campaign: British military operations in Afghanistan'. *International Affairs*, 86(2), pp. 311–32.
22. Air Chief Marshal Sir Jock Stirrup. House of Commons Defence Committee, *Operations in Afghanistan Fourth Report of Session 2010–12* HC 544 Ev 599 See http://www.publications.parliament.uk/pa/cm201012/cmselect/cmdfence/554/554.pdf
23. General Sir Mike Jackson quoted in conversation by Deborah Haynes. See http://www.thetimes.co.uk/tto/news/uk/defence/article2547216.ece
24. House of Commons Defence Committee, *Operations in Afghanistan Fourth Report of Session 2010–12* HC 544 q 599 http://www.publications.parliament.uk/pa/cm201012/cmselect/cmdfence/554/11050402.htm
25. Statement by Dr Reid to Chilcot Inquiry:

> 'In January 2005, before I became Secretary of State … the Chiefs had … agreed in principle to a proposal that we would refocus our military efforts from the north to the south of Afghanistan.'
>
> http://www.iraqinquiry.org.uk/media/45011/20100203am-reid-final.pdf p. 55.

26. Statement by Dr John Reid to the Chilcot Inquiry, p. 55. See: http://www.iraq-inquiry.org.uk/transcripts/oralevidence-bydate/100203.aspx

27. Statement by Dr John Reid to the Chilcot Inquiry. http://www.iraqinquiry.org.uk/media/45011/20100203am-reid-final.pdf p. 56.

28. Statement by Dr John Reid to the Chilcot Inquiry, p. 58. http://www.iraqinquiry.org.uk/transcripts/oralevidence-bydate/100203.aspx

29. Statement by Dr John Reid to the Chilcot Inquiry, p. 59. http://www.iraqinquiry.org.uk/transcripts/oralevidence-bydate/100203.aspx

30. Author interview with General Lord Walker, London, November 2013.

31. Quoted by Deborah Haynes in *The Times*. See http://www.thetimes.co.uk/tto/news/uk/defence/article2547216.ece

32. See *The Afghan papers: committing Britain to war in Helmand, 2005–6*. Abingdon: published on behalf of the Royal United Services Institute for Defence and Security Studies by Routledge journals, 2011, p. 20.

33. Author interview with General Lord Walker, London, November 2013. General Walker reflected on when he was Commander of the ARRC in the initial deployment to Bosnia. He lacked a protection company and contacted the UK CDS to see if the UK would provide one. Field Marshal Inge, the CDS, replied 'absolutely not, it has got to come from within NATO. I think that was my first lesson in [Alliance operations].'

34. Lieutenant General Richards caused considerable fuss about the inadequacy of the forces he was to be assigned in the months before he became Commander of ISAF in Kabul. He was especially concerned about the smallness of the forces assigned by Britain and Canada to Helmand and Kandahar. He lobbied the UK for a theatre reserve and additional helicopters. He was eventually told to cease and was forbidden from speaking to ministers about his concerns but managed to telegraph some of them to Secretary of State for Defence John Reid in the margins of a routine meeting and was granted a private discussion with him later in Berlin. As a result, artillery and others were added to the UK's order of battle, demonstrating that the full military challenge of the deployment to Helmand was understood by John Reid before he took the decision to order the deployment. Discussions between author and General Sir David Richards, London, July–October 2013.

35. Discussion between author and Major General Mungo Melvin CB OBE, Chilmark, 27 February 2014.

36. Discussion between author and Lord Browne of Ladyton, London, 23 March 2014.

37. http://www.publications.parliament.uk/pa/cm201012/cmselect/cmdfence/ 554/55403.htm

11. EMERGING CRITICISM AND FLAWED STRATEGIES

1. R. North, *The Ministry of Defeat: the British war in Iraq, 2003–2009*. London, New York: Continuum, 2009.
2. S. Grey, *Operation Snakebite*. London: Penguin Books, 2010.
3. J. Fairweather, *A war of choice: the British in Iraq 2003–9*. London: Jonathan Cape, 2011.
4. J. Fergusson, *A million bullets: the real story of the British army in Afghanistan*. London: Bantam, 2008.
5. S. Cowper-Coles, *Cables from Kabul: the inside story of the West's Afghanistan campaign*. London: HarperPress, 2012, p. 177.
6. *The Afghan papers: committing Britain to war in Helmand, 2005–06*. Abingdon: published on behalf of the Royal United Services Institute for Defence and Security Studies by Routledge journals, 2011.
7. 'The Afghan Decisions'. Four articles by Charles Styles, Josh Arnold-Foster, Mat Cavanagh and Mungo Melvin. RUSI Journal, April/May 2012, vol. 157 no. 2 ISSN 0307–1847.
8. F. Ledwidge, *Losing small wars: British military failure in Iraq and Afghanistan*. New Haven, CT; London: Yale University Press, 2012.
9. Anthony King, 'Understanding the Helmand Campaign: British military operations in Afghanistan', *International Affairs* 86, 2 (2010), pp. 311–32.
10. The term coined by Brigadier John Lorimor, at the time that he was Commander 12th Mechanised Brigade.
11. http://www.iraqinquiry.org.uk/
12. *British Generals in Blair's wars*. Farnham, Surrey; Burlington, VT: Ashgate, 2013.
13. Ibid.
14. Strachan, H., *The direction of war: contemporary strategy in historical perspective*. Cambridge: Cambridge University Press, 2013, p. 43.
15. Quoted by Professor Sir Hew Strachan in *The direction of war: contemporary strategy in historical perspective*. Cambridge: Cambridge University Press, 2013, p. 29.
16. J. C. Wylie, *Military strategy: a general theory of power control*. New Brunswick, NJ: Rutgers University Press, 1967.
17. Hew Strachan, *The direction of war: contemporary strategy in historical perspective*. Cambridge: Cambridge University Press, 2013, p. 45.

18. C. S. Gray, *The strategy bridge: theory for practice*. Oxford: Oxford University Press, 2010.

19. Hew Strachan, 'Strategy and the Limitation of War', *Survival: Global Politics and Strategy*, vol. 50, Issue 1, 2008, p. 37.

20. Chief of the Defence Staff Annual Lecture 2009, held at the Royal United Services Institution, London. See http://www.rusi.org/cdslectures/

21. Lieutenant General Sir Rob Fry was Deputy Chief of the Defence Staff (Commitments). Comment made during 'Strategy and the Wars of 9/11', Lecture to the Oxford University Strategic Studies Group, All Souls College, 21 May 2013.

22. Major General Whitely was the Senior British Land Adviser to the Commander of the Coalition Forces Land Component Command (CFLCC) Kuwait and Iraq from November 2002 to May 2003 and Deputy Commanding General CFLCC (with particular responsibility for Post Hostilities) February 2003 to May 2003. His evidence to the Chilcot Inquiry is at http://www.iraqinquiry.org.uk/media/51267/statement-MajGenAlbertWhitley.pdf

    Major General Tim Cross CBE was the UK's Joint Force Logistic Component Commander (JF Log C Comd) of the Joint Force before becoming International Deputy to Lieutenant General Jay Garner in the Coalition's Office for Reconstruction and Humanitarian Assistance for Iraq. See; http://www.iraqinquiry.org.uk/media/39160/timcross-statement.pdf

23. 'Phase 1' is planning and preparation, 'Phase 2' is deployment to theatre, 'Phase 3' is combat operations and 'Phase 4' is post-combat operations.

24. Discussion with Dr Rob Johnson, Oxford, Dec 2013

25. See http://www.rand.org/publications/randreview/issues/summer2003/burden.html and James T. Quinlivan, 'Force Requirements in Stability Operations', *Parameters*, Winter 1995, pp. 59–69.

26. Quoted in E. A. Cohen, *Supreme command: soldiers, statesmen, and leadership in wartime*. London: Free Press, 2003, p. 130.

27. In the 1970s and 80s in Northern Ireland the British military rapidly became adept at recognising a terrorist 'come on', where the terrorists attempted to get the military to over-react, damaging the security forces' relationship with the population. The British were able to do this because they had systematically developed deep links into the local population at all levels.

28. *British Generals in Blair's wars*. Farnham, Surrey; Burlington, VT: Ashgate, 2013.

29. R. Stewart, *Occupational hazards: my time governing in Iraq*. London: Picador, 2007.

30. R. Stewart, *Can intervention work?* New York, London: W. W. Norton & Co., 2011.

31. Ken Guest, 'RAM' Seeger and Lucy Morgan Edwards, 'The Tribal Path—A Better Alternative?' See http://smallwarsjournal.com/jrnl/art/the-tribal-path-a-better-alternative

32. Discussion with Dr Rob Johnson, Oxford, Dec 2014

33. Discussion with Dr Rob Johnson, Oxford, Dec 2014

34. E. Simpson, *War from the ground up: twenty-first-century combat as politics.* London: Hurst & Co., 2012.

35. Secretary of State for Defence Des Browne highlighted the linkage between the two, saying: 'you cannot build a police force without first having a functioning justice system, even though the US spent $6 bn training police officers in Afghanistan they have little success to show for it' Discussion between author and Lord Browne of Ladyton, London, 23 March 2014.

36. This referred to a pan-government operation embracing all the involved government departments.

37. Author interviews with General Sir Mike Jackson, Great Bedwyn, June–September 2013.

38. The website www.iraqbodycount.org records civilian deaths in Basra caused by insurgents as follows: 2007, the year when the British withdrew from Basra—40 deaths; 2008, the year when the militias were in charge—160 deaths; 2009, the year after the Charge of the Knights–10 deaths.

    Also: 'UK has left behind murder and chaos, says Police Chief. Basra is not a better place. We have found women who have been beheaded—and their bodies lying in the street. No one reported that is happening, they are all too frightened to talk.' *Guardian*, 17 December 2007.

    Also: F. Ledwidge, *Losing small wars: British military failure in Iraq and Afghanistan.* New Haven, CT; London: Yale University Press, 2012, p. 51.

39. Discussion between author and Lord Browne of Ladyton, London, 23 March 2014.

40. Discussion between the author and Major General Mungo Melvin CB OBE, Chilmark, 27 February 2014.

41. Testimony by Admiral the Lord Boyce to the Chilcot Inquiry. See http://www.iraqinquiry.org.uk/transcripts/oralevidence-bydate/091203.aspx

42. Author interviews with General Sir David Richards, London, July–October 2013.

43. From an essay by Desmond Bowen CB CMG, 17 February 2010, 'The Political–Military Relationship on Operations', quoted in *British Generals in Blair's wars.* Farnham, Surrey; Burlington, VT: Ashgate, 2013, ch. 23.

12. MAKING MILITARY DECISIONS

1. Author interviews with Lieutenant General Sir Rob Fry as Deputy Chief of the Defence Staff (Operations) 2004–6, London and Sherborne, July–December 2013.
2. Author interview with Admiral Lord West, London, June 2013.
3. Evidence to the Chilcot Inquiry. See http://www.iraqinquiry.org.uk/media/40465/20091203-final.pdf
4. Discussion between the author and Admiral Lord West, London, 7 June 2013.
5. Discussion on 'The Afghan Papers' held at RUSI, Whitehall on 29 February 2012.
6. Author interview with Admiral Lord West, London, June 2013.
7. Author interview with General Lord Walker, London, November 2013.
8. Author interviews with General Sir Mike Jackson, Great Bedwyn, June–September 2013.
9. Author interview with Admiral Lord West, London, June 2013.
10. Ibid.
11. Ibid.
12. Author interview with General Lord Walker, London, November 2013.
13. Author interview with Admiral Lord West, London, June 2013.
14. Author interviews with Lieutenant General Sir Rob Fry as Deputy Chief of the Defence Staff (Operations) 2004–6, London and Sherborne, July–December 2013.
15. House of Commons Defence Committee, 'Operations in Afghanistan', HC 554.
16. *Times* Correspondent Deborah Haynes wrote: 'No one contacted by *The Times* was able to say categorically why, when dividing up the south in early 2005, Britain ended up with Helmand, rather than the more important province of Kandahar. 'Search me, guv,' said General Sir Mike Jackson, then head of the Army; General Jackson was CGS 2003–6. See http://www.thetimes.co.uk/tto/news/uk/defence/article2547216.ece
17. Author interview with General Lord Dannatt, London, December 2012.
18. Author interview with Air Chief Marshal Sir Glenn Torpy, London, December 2012.
19. Author interview with Admiral Sir Jonathon Band, London, January 2013.
20. Discussion between the author and Lord Browne of Ladyton, London, 23 March 2014.
21. Correspondence between the author and General Sir David Richards, February 2014.

22. Discussion between the author and one of the principal staff officers in the UK, 1st Mechanised Brigade, during the deployment to Basra.
23. Author interview with Brigadier Andrew Sharpe and Professor Matt Uttley, Shrivenham, April 2012.
24. Correspondence between the author and General Lord Dannatt, 30 March 2014.
25. Discussion between the author and General Lord Dannatt, 29 March 2014.

13. THE CHIEFS

1. Quoted in J. F. C. Fuller, *Generalship, its diseases and their cure; a study of the personal factor in command.* London: Faber and Faber, 1933.
2. That said, the Royal Navy delivered the Army to the theatre of war without a hitch.
3. Quoted in Nicholas Lambert, 1967en;, *Sir John Fisher's naval revolution.* Columbia, SC: South Carolina University Press, 1999, p. 88.

   Fisher said in a letter to his son, as he was preparing to give evidence to the War Office Reconstruction Committee, chaired by Lord Esher in 1903:

   'I have got a new big scheme hatching next year … my idea is for 23 millions [pounds sterling] only for the Army, 37 millions for the Navy and three penny income tax. The Army will be a Lord Lieutenants' army, each county providing its own military force a la militia and a small expeditionary army for extraneous purposes.'
4. F. A. Johnson, *Defence by committee: The British Committee of Imperial Defence, 1885–1959.* London: Oxford University Press, 1960, p. 35.
5. Ibid., p. 40.
6. Arthur Jacob Marder, *Fear God and Dread Nought, the correspondence of Admiral of the Fleet Lord Fisher of Kilverstone.* London: Cape, 1953, vol. 3, p. 537.
7. W. G. F. Jackson, *The chiefs: the story of the United Kingdom chiefs of staff.* London: Brassey's, 1992.
8. To be fair, it was a bit more involved than that. Fry had impressed the Secretary of State Dr John Reid, and Reid arranged for Fry to be extended in service (doing a study) for an extra nine months, so that he would be present for the competition to become First Sea Lord or Vice Chief of the Defence Staff. In the event, others were chosen.
9. Not always; for instance, there have been long years in the twentieth century when either the cavalry or Rifle Brigade dominated.
10. Sir M. Jackson, *Soldier: the autobiography of General Sir Mike Jackson.* London: Corgi, 2008, p. 360.

11. E. A. Cohen, *Supreme command: soldiers, statesmen, and leadership in wartime.* London: Free Press, 2003, p. 22.

12. H. R. McMaster, *Dereliction of duty: Lyndon Johnson, Robert McNamara, the Joint Chiefs of Staff, and the lies that led to Vietnam.* New York: HarperCollins, 1997.

13. Discussion between the author and Prime Minister John Major, Lancaster House, London, July 1994.

14. Lord Hurd, Foreign Secretary during the government of John Major, speaking at the Joint Services Command and Staff College, 9 June 2012.

15. Sir M. Jackson, *Soldier: the autobiography of General Sir Mike Jackson.* London: Corgi, 2008, p. 382.

16. A. King, 'Understanding the Helmand campaign: British military operations in Afghanistan'. *International Affairs*, 86(2), pp. 311–32.

17. https://www.gov.uk/government/people/david-richards

18. On leaving, he was asked why as CGS he had consistently left no time to change the advice that his staff were proffering prior to the weekly Chiefs of Staff meeting, to which he replied, 'Well, we didn't get much wrong, did we?'

19. A. Campbell, 1957en;, *The Alastair Campbell diaries. Vol. 4, The burden of power: countdown to Iraq.* London: Hutchinson, 2012, p. 16.

20. Interview with three-star senior officer, 2 May 2013. When this remark passed on to him, Admiral Boyce showed his humour by responding, 'Did I smile that many times?'

21. Author interview with Sir Ian Andrews, London, July 2013.

22. J. Powell, *The new Machiavelli: how to wield power in the modern world.* London: Vintage, 2011, p. 115.

23. A. Campbell, *The Alastair Campbell diaries. Vol. 4, The burden of power: countdown to Iraq.* London: Hutchinson, 2012, p. 598.

24. Interview with senior civil servant, 3 May 2013.

25. Discussion with senior RAF officer, April 2013.

26. Sir Sherard Cowper-Coles described him as 'a lonely, solitary individual who dominated the other chiefs and marginalised his ministers'. Author interview with Sir Sherrard Cowper-Coles, London, July 2013.

27. For example, his acceptance of a decision to centralise ground-based air defence away from the RAF and into an Army formation also showed his suitability as a candidate for the top post.

28. CDS Annual RUSI Christmas lecture 2007.

29. CDS Annual RUSI Christmas Speech 2008. CDS said:

'So I want to take this opportunity to lay to rest some of the myths that have emerged. Myths such as: the British had given up in Basra; that they'd done a deal to hand the city over to the militias; and that they failed to support the Iraqis during Charge of the Knights'.

Subsequent events do not support this and show that the UK was urgently drawing down its operation in Basra as the situation elsewhere in Helmand and Afghanistan deteriorated, that the British had indeed done a deal with the Jaish al-Mahdi militia to release their leaders in return for safe passage of British troops out of Basra Palace and that the British military had been caught completely unawares by the Iraqi operation 'Charge of the Knights' to eject the militias from Basra (indeed the senior British commander was away on a skiing holiday when the operation started).

30. House of Commons Defence Committee, 'Operations in Afghanistan', HC 554. Reviewing this observation, one of the peers in the Royal Air Force observed: 'Typical of Teflon Jock (as he was known), who always managed to ensure that bad events never stuck to him!' Interview with senior RAF officer, April 2013.

31. http://www.da.mod.uk/colleges/jscsc/courses/hcsc

32. Correspondence between the author and Lieutenant General Sir John Kiszley, February 2014.

33. A. Campbell, *The Alastair Campbell diaries. Vol. 4, The burden of power: countdown to Iraq*. London: Hutchinson, 2012.

34. Author interview with Field Marshal Lord Guthrie, London, 19 April 2013.

35. Ibid.

36. Author interview with Admiral Lord Boyce, London, October 2013.

37. Author interview with General Lord Walker, London, November 2013.

38. Author interview with Air Chief Marshal Lord Stirrup, London, October 2013.

39. Evidence given by General Lord Walker to Chilcot Inquiry. See http://www.iraq-inquiry.org.uk/transcripts/oralevidence-bydate/100201.aspx#pm

40. Author interview with General Lord Dannatt, London, December 2012.

41. R. Dannatt, *Leading from the front: the autobiography*. London: Bantam, 2010, p. 244.

42. Author interview with Field Marshal Lord Guthrie, London, 19 April 2013.

43. Author interview with General Lord Dannatt, London, December 2012.

44. Correspondence between the author and Air Chief Marshal Lord Stirrup KG, January 2014.

45. Author interview with General Lord Walker, London, November 2013.

46. Chilcot Inquiry: http://www.iraqinquiry.org.uk/transcripts/oralevidence-bydate/091203.aspx

47. W. G. F. Jackson, *The chiefs: the story of the United Kingdom chiefs of staff.* London: Brassey's, 1992.

48. Author interview with Field Marshal Lord Guthrie, London, 19 April 2013.

49. Author interview with Sir Sherrard Cowper-Coles, London, July 2013.

50. Statement by General Sir Nick Houghton to House of Commons Defence Committee 'Operations in Afghanistan', HC 554.

14. THE AFTERMATH

1. Discussion between author and Lord Browne of Ladyton, London, 23 March 2014.

2. Derived from principles laid down by Thomas Aquinas as part of *jus ad bellum* ('the right [to go] to war'). 'Just wars must have a reasonable chance of success. According to the principle of reasonable hope, there must be good grounds for believing that the desired outcome can be achieved.' Don Hubert, Thomas G. Weiss et al., 'The Responsibility to Protect: Supplementary Volume to the Report of the International Commission on Intervention and State Sovereignty'. Canada: International Development Research Centre, 2001.

3. John Ware lists four of the objectives in the MoD/FCO/DFiD 'Helmand Plan' that were impossible to achieve:

   Objective 1.2: Deliver fair and transparent justice: The only existing form of law was summary justice based on Sharia law. Many of those appointed to oversee the new legal processes were corrupt, so people turned their backs on the imposed system, leaving the Taliban to step in and provide their own form of justice.

   Objective 3.2.1: Sustainable development of physical infrastructure: While most of the initial British deployment was non-combat troops, intended to help civilians deliver infrastructure improvements, the security climate meant the civilians had limited ability to operate outside Camp Bastion. Asked what was achieved in the early years, a senior official said 'not very much'.

   Objective 3.4: Education and Skills programmes strengthened and extended: Attempts to recruit and provide a secure teaching environment were undermined by 'night letters'—threats delivered under the doors of anyone that the Taliban believed were working for either the Afghan government or the British reconstruction effort.

   Objective 4: Make drug production a high risk/low benefit endeavour: Where opium crops were destroyed, farmers often had no access to other means of earning a living. Left penniless, some were readily recruited into local militia to fight the British who had removed their livelihood.

See http://www.bbc.co.uk/news/uk-13855804

4. *Operation Veritas* was the codename used for British military operations against the Taliban government of Afghanistan in 2001. British forces played a supporting role to the American Operation Enduring Freedom. It was succeeded by Operation Herrick from 2002 onwards.

The UK's campaign objective for *Operation Veritas 'Defeating International Terrorism'* follows. This is a truly global aspiration for a medium-sized power such as the UK.

1. Our overall objective is to eliminate terrorism as a force in international affairs. There are immediate objectives relating to [Osama bin Laden] UBL, his organisation and Afghanistan and wider objectives relating principally to the campaign against international terrorism more generally.

2. The immediate objectives are:

   (a) to bring UBL and other Al Qa'ida leaders to justice;

   (b) to prevent UBL and the Al Qa'ida network from posing a continuing terrorist threat;

   (c) to this end to ensure that Afghanistan ceases to harbour and sustain international terrorism and enables us to verify that terrorist training has ceased and that the camps where terrorists train have been destroyed;

   (d) assuming that Mullah Omar will not comply with the US ultimatum we require sufficient change in the leadership to ensure that Afghanistan's links to international terrorism are broken.

3. The wider objectives are:

   (a) to do everything possible to eliminate the threat posed by international terrorism;

   (b) to deter states from supporting, harbouring or acting complicity with international terrorist groups;

   (c) reintegration of Afghanistan as a responsible member of the international community and an end to its self-imposed isolation.

4. The immediate objectives will be achieved by all available means, including both political and military:

   (a) Isolating the current Taliban regime from all international support.

   (b) Unless the Taliban regime complies with the US ultimatum, taking direct action against UBL, the Al Qa'ida networks and the terrorist facilities in

Afghanistan, and where necessary taking political and military action to fragment the present Taliban regime, including through support for Pushtoon groups opposed to the regime as well as forces in the Northern Alliance.

(c) Providing economic and political support to Afghanistan's neighbours to help with the burden of this conflict.

(d) Building the widest possible international coalition, with maximum UN support.

(e) Taking immediate steps to deal with the humanitarian crisis confronting Afghanistan and to help neighbouring countries deal with the refugee problem.

5. The wider campaign will be conducted on a broad front:

(a) to make a step change in international efforts to change the climate in which terrorists operate. This will be a complex campaign including strengthening domestic legislation and national capabilities and working through the UN, EU and G8 to cut off the terrorists' funds and make it easier to trace terrorists and bring them to justice;

(b) reconstruction of Afghanistan. Realistically it will be difficult for this to start until there is a secure environment within Afghanistan. But a programme of emergency relief will have to be available early. The cost of reconstructing Bosnia was $5bn and Afghanistan has four times Bosnia's population. Reconstruction of Afghanistan could take 5–10 years to complete. Only sustained international development effort has any chance of ridding Afghanistan of heroin and domination of war lords;

(c) assisting Afghanistan, including through the United Nations, to establish a broadly based Government representative of all groups in the country.

(d) a positive political agenda of engagement with Arab countries and the Islamic world.

(e) a strategy to deal with the wide number of sometimes small groups of terrorists who flourish in states across the world and the linkages between them. This will include sustained pressure on those states that aid and abet terrorism. Where states are powerless to put a stop to terrorism on their territory assistance will have to be made available. Where states are unwilling to take effective action they will face a vigorous response from the wider international community.

(f) renewed efforts to resolve the conflicts which are among the underlying causes of terrorism; and renewed efforts to bear down on WMD proliferation.

6. Any action taken to achieve our objectives will need to be in conformity with international law, including the UN Charter and international humanitarian law.

  See http://webarchive.nationalarchives.gov.uk/+/http://www.operations.mod.uk/veritas/faq/objectives.htm

5. Author interviews with General Sir Mike Jackson, Great Bedwyn, June–September 2013.

6. Author interview with Admiral Lord Boyce, London, October 2013.

7. *British Generals in Blair's wars*. Farnham, Surrey; Burlington, VT: Ashgate, 2013. Justin Maciejewski, ch, 13.

8. Author interviews with Lieutenant General Sir Rob Fry as Deputy Chief of the Defence Staff (Operations) 2004–6, London and Sherborne, July–December 2013.

9. *British Generals in Blair's wars*. Farnham, Surrey; Burlington, VT: Ashgate, 2013. Justin Maciejewski, ch. 13.

10. Author interviews with General Sir David Richards, London, July–October 2013.

11. The first properly empowered UK National Contingent Commander was Lieutenant General Sir Nick Parker who was double-hatted as Deputy Commander ISAF, putting him directly under the Coalition Commander and in close daily contact with him. Parker later returned to become Commander-in-Chief of UK Land Forces.

12. Author interview with Sir Sherrard Cowper-Coles, London, July 2013.

13. Correspondence between the author and General Sir Rupert Smith, February 2014.

14. President Bush achieved this with General David Petraeus and Ambassador Ryan Crocker in Iraq, with exceptionally beneficial results.

15. House of Commons Public Administration Select Committee, 'Who does UK National Strategy?' First Report of Session 2010–11, HC 435. See http://www.publications.parliament.uk/pa/cm201011/cmselect/cmpubadm/435/435.pdf

16. Author interviews with General Sir David Richards, London, July–October 2013.

17. Correspondence between the author and General Sir David Richards, January 2014.

18. Author interview with Air Chief Marshal Lord Stirrup, London, October 2013.

19. Author interviews with General Sir David Richards, London, July–October 2013.

20. The Three-Month Review. A largely secret review of defence expenditure to achieve attempting to close a gap of approximately £25 billion in the MoD's six-year budget. It reported in July 2012. See http://www.theguardian.com/poli-

tics/2011/jul/18/defence-spending-25bn-cameron-osborne and http://www.tele-graph.co.uk/news/uknews/defence/8645851/MoD-sacrifices-manpower-to-pay-for-equipment.html

21. Quoted by Matt Kavanagh in 'Inside the Anglo-Saxon war machine', *Prospect*, 21 October 2010.
22. RUSI Journal April/May 2014, vol. 159 no. 2, p. 42.
23. *British Generals in Blair's wars.* Farnham, Surrey; Burlington, VT: Ashgate, 2013, ch. 26.

15. FIT FOR THE FUTURE?

1. https://www.gov.uk/government/uploads/system/uploads/attachment_data/file/61936/national-security-strategy.pdf
2. The combination of aircraft carriers and their protective screen of destroyers and frigates with embarked aircraft, able to travel to a distant location and launch air power.
3. One senior Labour politician in 2008 described the procurement of the current UK aircraft carrier, which was built in a number of sections in different shipyards around the country, in the following terms: 'I have a new definition of defence procurement: build a large unwanted naval platform in different sections in four separate Labour heartlands … and then assemble it together in the Chancellor's constituency.'
4. 'Indeed in the 1920s … Basil Liddell Hart and "Boney" Fuller struggled to persuade soldiers everywhere that the era of the horse had been replaced by that of the tank and aircraft, even though both had been in service for a number of years.' Quoted from lecture by General Sir David Richards, RUSI, 25 June 2009. See http://www.rusi.org/events/ref:E496B737B57852/info:public/infoID:E4A4253226F582/#.UoORR_xFBSs
5. J-STARS: Joint Target Attack Radar System flown by the US Air Force in E-8 Boeing 707–300 aircraft, designed to provide battle management and command and control by tracking and recording moving targets.
6. The vulnerability for a UK aircraft carrier platform is as a single point of failure; damaged or lost, the whole mission ends. Singular: the French carrier *Charles de Gaulle* limped home in 2000 when her port propeller broke whilst crossing the Atlantic. Vulnerable: even small nations are able to obtain supersonic, sea-skimming anti-ship missiles such as the Indian–Russian BrahMos (200–300 kg warhead travelling at Mach 3 for 500 km, with homing radar/GPS), and China has tested a ballistic anti-carrier missile.

7. UACVs are Unmanned Aerial Combat Vehicles—fighters and bombers without pilots which are instead controlled from the ground. Since even fighter aircraft now launch their missiles at considerable distances from the planes that they are attacking, the need for a pilot to 'dog-fight' in close proximity has ended, thankfully so, given the astronomic cost of modern piloted airframes.

BIBLIOGRAPHY

The Afghan papers: committing Britain to war in Helmand, 2005–6. Abingdon: published on behalf of RUSI (the Royal United Services Institute for Defence and Security Studies) by Routledge Journals, 2011.

Bailey, J., R. Iron and H. Strachan eds. *British Generals in Blair's Wars*. Farnham, Surrey; Burlington, VT: Ashgate, 2013.

Beattie, D., *An ordinary soldier: Afghanistan—a ferocious enemy, a bloody conflict, one man's impossible mission*. London: Pocket, 2009.

Bishop, P.J., *Wings: one hundred years of British aerial warfare*. London: Atlantic.2012.

Blair, T., *A journey*. London: Hutchinson, 2010.

Boswell, J., *The life of Samuel Johnson: including a Journal of his tour to the Hebrides*. London: John Murray, 1839.

Braithwaite, R., *Afgantsy: the Russians in Afghanistan, 1979–89*. London: Profile, 2011.

British Generals in Blair's wars. Farnham, Surrey; Burlington, VT: Ashgate, 2013.

Campbell, A., *The Alastair Campbell diaries. Volume 4, The burden of power: countdown to Iraq*. London: Hutchinson, 2012.

Clark, A., *The donkeys*. London: Pimlico, 1991.

Clausewitz, C. V., *On war*. Princeton: Princeton University Press, 1976; London: Penguin Classicis, 1982.

Cohen, E. A., *Supreme command: soldiers, statesmen, and leadership in wartime*. London: Free Press, 2003.

Cowper-Coles, S., *Cables from Kabul: the inside story of the West's Afghanistan campaign*. London: HarperPress, 2012.

Dannatt, R., *Leading from the front: the autobiography*. London: Bantam, 2010.

Dixon, N. F., *On the psychology of military incompetence*. London: Pimlico, 1994.

BIBLIOGRAPHY

The evolution of military strategy. London: Routledge, Adelphi Papers, 2006.

Fairweather, J., *A war of choice: the British in Iraq 2003–9.* London: Jonathan Cape, 2011.

Fergusson, J., *A million bullets: the real story of the British army in Afghanistan.* London: Bantam, 2008.

Fuller, J. F. C., *Generalship, its diseases and their cure; a study of the personal factor in command.* London: Faber and Faber, 1933.

Gray, C. S., *The strategy bridge: theory for practice.* Oxford: Oxford University Press, 2010.

Grey, S., *Operation Snakebite.* London: Penguin Books, 2010.

The Hutton Inquiry and its impact. London: Politico's Guardian Books, 2004.

Jackson, M., *Soldier: the autobiography of General Sir Mike Jackson.* London: Corgi, 2008.

Jackson, W. G. F., *The chiefs: the story of the United Kingdom chiefs of staff.* London: Brassey's, 1992.

Johnson, F. A., *Defence by committee: The British Committee of Imperial Defence, 1885–1959.* Oxford University Press: London, 1960.

Kampfner, J., *Blair's wars.* London: Free Press, 2004.

Kiley, S., *Desperate glory: at war in Helmand with Britain's Air Assault Brigade.* London: Bloomsbury, 2009.

King, A., 'Understanding the Helmand campaign: British military operations in Afghanistan'. *International Affairs*, 86(2), 2010, pp. 311–32.

Lambert, N. A., *Sir John Fisher's naval revolution.* Columbia, SC: University of South Carolina Press, 1999.

Ledwidge, F., *Losing small wars: British military failure in Iraq and Afghanistan.* New Haven, CT and London: Yale University Press, 2012.

———, *Investment in blood: the real cost of Britain's Afghan War.* New Haven, CT: Yale University Press, 2013.

Maddox, B., 2013. 'The case for an Afghanistan inquiry'. *Prospect.*

Mallinson, A., *The making of the British Army.* London: Bantam, 2010.

Massie, R. K., *Dreadnought: Britain, Germany and the coming of the Great War.* London: Pimlico, 1993.

McMaster, H. R., *Dereliction of duty: Lyndon Johnson, Robert McNamara, the Joint Chiefs of Staff, and the lies that led to Vietnam.* New York: HarperCollins, 1997.

Meyer, C., Sir, *DC confidential: the controversial memoirs of Britain's Ambassador to the US at the time of 9/11 and the Iraq war.* London: Weidenfeld & Nicolson, 2005.

North, R., *The Ministry of Defeat: the British war in Iraq, 2003–2009.* London and New York: Continuum, 2009.

BIBLIOGRAPHY

The Oxford illustrated history of the British Army. Oxford: Oxford University Press, 1994.

Ricks, T. E., *The generals: American military command from World War II to today.* New York: Penguin Press, 2012.

Ricks, T. E., *The gamble: General David Petraeus and the untold story of the American surge in Iraq, 2006–2008.* London: Allen Lane, 2009.

Ripley, T., *Operation Deliberate Force: the UN and NATO Campaign in Bosnia 1995.* Lancaster: CDISS, 1999

Sampson, A., *Who runs this place? The anatomy of Britain in the 21st century.* London: John Murray, 2004.

Simpson, E., *War from the ground up: twenty-first century combat as politics.* London: Hurst & Co., 2012.

Smith, R., *The utility of force: the art of war in the modern world.* London: Allen Lane, 2005.

Stewart, R., *Can intervention work?* New York and London: W. W. Norton & Co., 2011.

Stewart, R., *Occupational hazards: my time governing in Iraq.* London: Picador, 2007.

Strachan, H., *Clausewitz's On war: a biography.* New York: Atlantic Monthly Press, distributed by Publishers Group West, 2007.

———, *The direction of war: contemporary strategy in historical perspective.* Cambridge: Cambridge University Press, 2013

———, *The politics of the British Army.* Oxford: Clarendon Press, 1997.

———, 'Strategy and the Limitation of War', *Survival: Global Politics and Strategy,* 50(1), 2008.

Synnott, H., *Bad days in Basra: my turbulent time as Britain's man in southern Iraq.* London: Tauris, 2008.

Ucko, D. H., 2010. 'Lessons from Basra: The Future of British Counter-insurgency'. *Survival: Global Politics and Strategy,* 52(4), pp. 131–58.

Woodward, B., *Obama's wars.* London: Simon & Schuster, 2010.

Wylie, J. C., *Military strategy: a general theory of power control.* New Brunswick, NJ: Rutgers University Press, 1967.

INDEX

(To avoid confusion, the ranks and appointments shown are those held at time of the entry in the text.)

INDEX

2001	2002	2003	2004	2005	2006	

Operations in Iraq

OP TELIC (land units only shown)

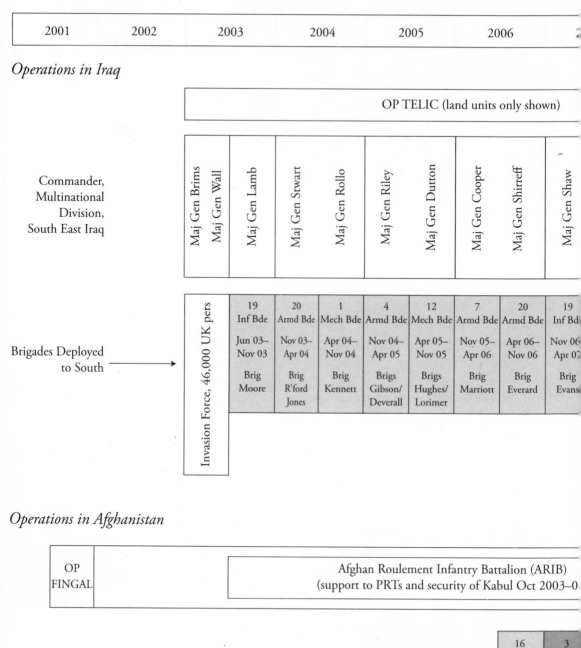

Commander, Multinational Division, South East Iraq	Maj Gen Brims	Maj Gen Wall	Maj Gen Lamb	Maj Gen Stwart	Maj Gen Rollo	Maj Gen Riley	Maj Gen Dutton	Maj Gen Cooper	Maj Gen Shirreff	Maj Gen Shaw

Brigades Deployed to South →	Invasion Force, 46,000 UK pers	19 Inf Bde Jun 03– Nov 03 Brig Moore	20 Armd Bde Nov 03– Apr 04 Brig R'ford Jones	1 Mech Bde Apr 04– Nov 04 Brig Kennett	4 Armd Bde Nov 04– Apr 05 Brigs Gibson/ Deverall	12 Mech Bde Apr 05– Nov 05 Brigs Hughes/ Lorimer	7 Armd Bde Nov 05– Apr 06 Brig Marriott	20 Armd Bde Apr 06– Nov 06 Brig Everard	19 Inf Bd Nov 06 Apr 07 Brig Evans

Operations in Afghanistan

OP FINGAL		Afghan Roulement Infantry Battalion (ARIB) (support to PRTs and security of Kabul Oct 2003–0

UK Force Levels in Afghanistan: 2002   300
2006   3000
2007   4400
2009   9000
2013   7900
ARIB 2003–08   600?

Brigades Deployed to Helmand, → Afghanistan	16 Asslt Bde May 06– Nov 06 Brig Butler	3 Cdo Bd Nov 06 Apr 07 Brig Thoma